RACINE

RACINE

A Theatrical
Reading

DAVID MASKELL

CLARENDON PRESS · OXFORD
1991

Oxford University Press. Walton Street. Oxford OX2 6DP

Oxford New York Toronto
Delhi Bombay Calcutta Madras Karachi
Petaling Jaya Singapore Hong Kong Tokyo
Nairobi Dar es Salaam Cape Town
Melbourne Auckland

and associated companies in
Berlin Ibadan

Oxford is a trade mark of Oxford University Press

Published in the United States
by Oxford University Press, New York

British Library Cataloguing in Publication Data
Data available

Library of Congress Cataloging in Publication Data
Maskell, David.
Racine: a theatrical reading/David Maskell.
p.   cm.
Includes bibliographical references and index.
1. Racine, Jean, 1639–1699—Stage history.   2. Racine, Jean,
1639–1699—Criticism and interpretation.   3. French drama (Tragedy)—
History and criticism.   4. Theater—France—History.   I. Title.
PQ1908.S7M38   1991   842'.4—dc20   90-26066
ISBN 0-19-815161-6

Typeset by Best-set Typesetter Ltd.
Printed in Great Britain by Biddles Ltd,
Guildford and King's Lynn

Acknowledgements

I am indebted to Michael Hawcroft for his comments on drafts of this book.

I thank the Bodleian Library for permission to reproduce plates 24–31 and the Library of the Taylor Institution, Oxford, for permission to reproduce plates 4–23, from books in their collections.

For generous research support I would like to express my gratitude to the Provost and Fellows of Oriel College, Oxford.

D. M.

January 1990

Contents

List of Plates

Note: Plates 4–14 and 18–31 are from the illustrated editions of Racine's theatre listed in the bibliography.

Abbreviations and References

NCR   Raymond Picard (ed.), *Nouveau Corpus Racinianum* (Paris, 1976).

Œuvres   Jean Racine, *Œuvres complètes*, ed. Raymond Picard, 2 vols. (Paris, 1951–2: Bibliothèque de la Pléiade). References to Racine's plays and prefaces are to vol. i of this edition.

SD   Stage direction

RACINE'S PLAYS

Ale.   *Alexandre*

And.   *Andromaque*

Ath.   *Athalie*

Baj.   *Bajazet*

Bér.   *Bérénice*

Bri.   *Britannicus*

Est.   *Esther*

Iph.   *Iphigénie*

Mit.   *Mithridate*

Phè.   *Phèdre*

Pla.   *Les Plaideurs*

Thé.   *La Thébaïde*

References to plays are by act, scene, and line number: e.g. *Bri.* I. ii. 130 means *Britannicus*, Act I, Scene ii, line 130. References by author's name alone refer to the first or only work listed under that author in the bibliography.

Quotations from works in foreign languages, including those of Racine, are given in English translation unless the discussion requires the exact words, metrical form, or punctuation of the original. Square brackets around ellipsis stops indicate abridged quotations and distinguish omissions from Racine's own use of ellipsis stops as a form of stage direction.

Introduction

A cruel emperor hiding behind a curtain to spy on young lovers, a cup of poison dashed from a hand, a frenzied woman struggling to draw her stepson's sword to kill herself, armed men emerging from hiding to ambush a queen—these scenes are not the usual introduction to Racine's eleven tragedies. If we add the spectacle of a litigant falling into a basement and a basketful of uncontrollable puppies in his comedy, *Les Plaideurs*, we may wonder why Racine's drama is so often spoken of as if there were hardly any physical action on stage.

The difference of perception lies in the difference between a literary reading and a theatrical reading. The literary reading tends to focus on tragedy, moral order, catharsis, mythology, imagery, and questions of style. A theatrical reading of Racine reveals a rather different picture. It shows Racine to be very much a man of the theatre.

'Theatrical reading' requires explanation. This book is not about how to stage Racine. It is about reading the text for what it offers to the mind's eye. It is an attempt to redress the balance of those studies of Racine which focus almost exclusively on literary aspects. It endeavours to throw new light on the spectacle offered by his plays, with particular reference to the audiences for whom Racine wrote in seventeenth-century France.

The first step is to use the written text on the page in order to form a mental image of the performance. The next step is to interpret what this performance might signify to the spectators. There are therefore two texts to be interpreted. Firstly the *written text*, which is purely verbal and which is contained in the editions of Racine's works. Secondly, the *performance text*, which is the potential performance of the written text. The performance text embraces a multiplicity of signifiers which are verbal, auditory, and visual. These constitute theatrical language, a language which is latent in the written text and which is actualized in performance when the spectators see the drama on stage.

Various attempts have been made to classify the signifiers of theatrical language. One classification divides them into thirteen categories: words, delivery, facial expression, gesture, movements of actors in dramatic space, make-up, hairstyle, costume, properties, sets, lighting, music, sound effects.[1] All these are relevant to Racine.

The visual aspects of Racinian drama have generally been neglected. Indeed to some people the study of visual effects in Racine might seem as barren a topic as the simplicity of Corneille or the verbosity of La Rochefoucauld. In fact the subject is inexhaustible. Racine's drama was composed to appeal to the spectator in the theatre as well as to the reader in his closet. Consequently, it is possible to analyse the visual effects of Racinian drama in the same way as his words have been so often studied, namely for their dramatic impact and for their power of suggestion.

The concept of a theatrical reading is not new. Racine's contemporaries were familiar with it. Molière talks of reading with theatrical eyes. He warned the readers of *L'Amour médecin* not to read his written text unless they could read with an eye to performance.[2] The same idea is voiced by the abbé D'Aubignac, whose prime concern was with performance on stage, but who did not neglect the reader: 'A dramatic poem [. . .] is composed to be read by people who, without actually seeing anything, have present in their imagination through the force of the verse, the characters and the actions which are introduced into the drama.'[3] There is nothing anachronistic nor incongruous about reading Racine's text for what it offers to a theatrical imagination. But such a reading can benefit from systematic analysis.

The prime source for this study is the text of Racine's plays, which contain stage directions both explicit and implicit. These

---

[1] T. Kowzan, *Littérature et spectacle* (1975), 182–205; this is one way of categorizing the signifiers of drama, but not the only way; M. Esslin, *The Field of Drama* (1987), 53–5, adds the frame; K. Elam, *The Semiotics of Theatre and Drama* (1980), 50–1, mentions technical options such as film and back projection; P. Larthomas, *Le Langage dramatique: Sa nature, ses procédés* (1972) is especially valuable for Racine, because it is based on the French dramatic tradition; A. Ubersfeld, *Lire le théâtre* (1977) and *L'École du spectateur: Lire le théâtre II* (1981) offers strategies for interpreting theatrical language.

[2] Molière, *L'Amour médecin*, 'Au lecteur', p. 95.

[3] D'Aubignac, *La Pratique du théâtre*, ed. H. J. Neuschafer (1971), i. 8, p. 46.

can stimulate the reader to conjure up a performance in the imagination, and may sometimes guide theatrical directors in their productions of Racine. There has been a tendency to underestimate the extent and importance of Racine's stage directions. If critics mention them, it is usually to dismiss them as infrequent and therefore by implication insignificant.[4] Of course the printed page of a Racinian tragedy seems poor in stage directions compared with some later plays. But this is to ignore the conventions of the time, which required that stage directions should be implicit in the speech of the characters rather than italicized additions to the text. Even if it were true that Racine has few stage directions, it would only make more urgent the task of examining the significance of those which the dramatist did take the trouble to include. Racine does specify that characters should speak in certain tones of voice, display certain facial expressions, enter or exit in a particular manner, sit, stand, kneel, embrace, faint, kill themselves, or employ stage properties such as letters or poison. These must be considered as much a part of Racine's theatrical language as the actual words spoken by the characters. A theatrical reading sets out to explore and elucidate this language.

Racine's text also contains guidance on décor. Here again a misconception has distracted attention from the role of stage settings in Racine's plays. It is said that most of his tragedies are set in some vague place, the *palais à volonté*. This is simply not true. The crucial evidence here is the *Mémoire de Mahelot* which gives a list of scenery specifications for Racine's tragedies when they were performed in the main public theatre of Paris. This evidence, together with that contained in the texts themselves, shows that Racine was more concerned with scenery than is usually admitted.

There survives a considerable body of contemporary evidence for the way in which spectators reacted to actual performances of Racine's plays and those of his rivals. The polemical pamphlets attacking or defending Racine and other dramatists show theatre criticism in its embryonic stage. However, these writings are less valuable than they should be. Theatre critics may have axes to grind, or their own cleverness to advertise;

---

[4] e.g. J.-L. Backès, *Racine* (1981), p. 8.

vacuous adulation or mindless denigration often obscure the
realities of the theatrical performance. Cautious detective work
is essential in interpreting this evidence. Racine's prefaces to his
plays also form part of this meta-theatrical material, so Racine
on Racine also needs to be treated with circumspection.

Illustrations to the plays are useful, provided their nature is
understood. The engravings which accompanied the published
texts of French plays hardly ever represent exactly what the
spectators saw on stage. They were conceived as adornments
for books, not material for theatrical history. For some of
Racine's plays, the illustrated editions which he himself super-
vised depict episodes which took place off stage, for example
the death of Britannicus or of Hippolyte. These were designed
to appeal to the imagination of the reader, and they do not relate
directly to the performance of the play. Yet, provided their
limitations are recognized, the illustrations can be very useful.
They can alert the reader to scenes which did take place on stage
and which were considered to have special visual impact. They
can be suggestive of grouping, gesture, and expression. The
series of fifty-seven engravings commissioned by Pierre Didot
in the 1790s provides one illustration for every act of Racine's
theatrical *œuvre*.[5] They are a vigorous aid to a theatrical reading.
A sensitive artist's eye can provide as valuable a commentary on
a theatrical text as the erudition of a literary critic. The illustrations for this book have mainly been chosen for the way in
which they bring out the visual implications of Racine's text.
They have not been used for this purpose before.[6]

Racinian bibliography is much richer in literary studies than
in theatrical ones. This is not to suggest an opposition between
literary and theatrical interpretation. Far from it. Theatrical
language is verbal as well as visual, and the literary approach is
vital. Literary studies of dramatic texts can be too harshly
judged: 'A poetics of the drama which makes no reference to the

[5] I am grateful to Colin Harrison for supplying information on illustrated edns. of
Racine.

[6] Noëlle Guibert's 'L'Iconographie de Racine à la bibliothèque de l'Arsenal' has
some pointers in this direction but the main focus is iconographical not theatrical;
moreover this article makes no mention of the illustrations to *Les Plaideurs*. Siguret's
article on Racine, Le Brun, and Sève is also an iconographical study. C. Osborne's
thesis on Pierre Didot deals with the history of the engravings for his edn. of Racine
(pp. 140–71).

conditions and principles of the performance has little chance of being more than an eccentric annexe of literary semiotics' (Elam, p. 210). Such a judgement would undervalue the achievements of literary criticism relating to Racine. Moreover, the monumental contributions of Raymond Picard to Racinian scholarship, though they are not for the most part focused upon theatricality[7] and though they occasionally provoke dissent, none the less provide an indispensable basis for a theatrical reading.

Certain aspects of Racine's theatricality have received some attention. Maurice Descotes, drawing on memoirs and reviews, has recorded ways in which actors and actresses have interpreted Racine's leading roles.[8] More recently Alberto Capatti has presented Racine refracted through the erratic responses of spectators in the theatre rather than through the normative criteria of the literary critic. His innovative study deliberately accords a large place to evidence from the eighteenth century which has often been despised.[9] Margaret McGowan has explored some connotations of Racinian stage space.[10] Michael Hawcroft has shown how Racinian characters' powers of persuasion keep the attention of the audience.[11] Some general studies concerned with Racine have shown special sensitivity to the theatrical perspective. Georges Le Bidois discusses stage space, décor, and spectacle.[12] In the unlikely setting of a study on politics in Racine, Lucien Dubech offers many insights into Racine's stagecraft and justly takes issue with Le Bidois on a number of points.[13] John Lapp takes dramatic quality as his theme.[14] H. T. Barnwell scrutinizes plot-construction in Corneille and Racine.[15] Of particular importance is the series 'Mise en scène des œuvres du passé' which give full staging

[7] However, his article 'Les Tragédies de Racine: Comique ou tragique' does address the question of theatrical genre from the point of view of performance.

[8] M. Descotes, *Les Grands Rôles du théâtre de Jean Racine* (1957).

[9] A. Capatti, *Teatro e 'imaginaire': Pubblico e attori in Racine* (1975).

[10] M. McGowan, 'Racine's "lieu théâtral"' (1982).

[11] M. Hawcroft, 'Verbal Action and Rhetoric in the Tragedies of Jean Racine' (1988, D.Phil. thesis, Univ. of Oxford).

[12] G. Le Bidois, *De l'action dans la tragédie de Racine* (1900).

[13] L. Dubech, *Jean Racine politique* (1926).

[14] J. Lapp, *Aspects of Racinian Tragedy* (1955).

[15] H. T. Barnwell, *The Tragic Drama of Corneille and Racine: An Old Parallel Revisited* (1982).

directions for *Bajazet* by Xavier de Courville, *Phèdre* by Jean-Louis Barrault, and *Athalie* by Georges Le Roy. A newer series of this nature—'Collection théâtre et mises en scène'—engages less closely with the Racinian text but is abundantly illustrated with photographs and interviews which record the idiosyncrasies of modern directors.[16] The Classiques Garnier edition of Racine's theatre has a series of photographs of the same nature and an appendix on modern productions of Racine.[17] Sound recordings on disc or cassette should not be neglected as a means of access to Racine's theatricality, despite the lack of the visual element.

Because of the preponderance of literary studies on Racine, this theatrical reading will tend to concentrate on visual aspects, but always viewed as an element of a theatrical language which embraces both words and visual effects. Clearly it is a complex task to engage in the double exercise of interpreting the written text as a performance text, and the performance text for its effect on the spectators. All theoreticians are agreed on the difficulty of devising a system of semiotic analysis for the unique combination of the verbal, the auditory, and the visual which constitutes theatrical language. Not only is theatrical language an 'informational polyphony', but the temporal flow of performance means that the duration of a given signal is difficult to determine. Moreover, at any moment in a performance a spectator can focus on any signifier of his choice. Two special problems arise in the analysis of theatrical language, pulling in opposite directions. The first is that the signifiers never work in isolation. The second is that the spectator focuses intently upon the present moment at the expense of the wider context. Theatrical language is continuous in some respects and discontinuous in others. The problem is where to segment it. This *malaise* is evident in any attempt to categorize. Kowzan annotates a performance text to show the signifiers from each category:

Pyramus enters on stage (bodily movement) and approaches the mulberry tree (décor). A bloodstained veil is in the middle of the stage

---

[16] *Phèdre* (1986) has pages on the productions directed by Antoine Vitez (1975) and Jean Gillibert (1981).

[17] Racine, *Théâtre complet*, ed. J. Morel and A. Viala (1980).

(stage property). Pyramus is horrified (gesture + facial expression). 'It is Thisbé's veil, stained with blood. Oh poor wretch, she has been devoured by a lion' (words + tone of voice). Pyramus stabs himself with his sword (gesture + stage property + movement)' (p. 218)

It is obvious that these signifiers demand to be reunited, for the spectator perceives them as a continuum. Another attempt at categorization is made by Elam who employs a tabular approach to analyse the semiotic functions of dramatic dialogue. An eighteen-column table breaks down each segment of the first seventy-nine lines of *Hamlet* and distinguishes each segment of discourse on the basis of a change in deictic orientation and/or illocutionary force (pp. 192–207). Whatever the theoretical advantages of such a system it clearly does not correspond to any theatrical experience. And yet the performance is made up of distinct assaults upon the spectator's attention, each of which has a greater individual impact than the performance does as a whole. Corneille wrote of the 'attachment of the audience to the present action'.[18] Marmontel confirms the idea that 'the theatrical illusion consists in making people forget what they know so that they think only about what they see'. He claimed to know the fifth act of *Rodogune* by heart, but in the theatre, as soon as he saw the poisoned cup approach the hero's lips, he shuddered with fear as if he did not know that the hero would be saved.[19] The spectator is absorbed in a sequence of theatrical moments each giving its peculiar pleasure.

The method adopted here will be to identify the elements of Racine's theatrical language through a close examination of his text. The degree of segmentation will be determined pragmatically according to the recurrent theatrical features in Racine's text. Analysis will also be based on what was judged significant by Racine's contemporaries or on the responses of later spectators, actors, directors, or theatrical readers. Obviously, sensibilities change from century to century, and each performance makes choices which leave other possibilities in the shade; but documented theatrical responses provide a valid starting-point for exploring Racine's text. Such an approach means that initially more attention will be paid to the signifiers and their immediate context than to the significance of the plays as a

---

[18] *Examen* of *Horace*, p. 112.   [19] *Éléments de littérature*, s.v. Action.

whole. But it soon emerges that the visual dimension can often illuminate the whole play.

The first chapter considers the use of scenery and stage space and argues that these are more significant in Racine than has hitherto been recognized. Chapter 2 interprets the visual aspects of entrances and exits. The next two chapters explore various aspects of the interrelation of the verbal and the visual: stage directions embedded in the dialogue, the significance of physical action as a visual language, the ways in which speech can become theatrically active. Chapter 5 on Racine the director shows how the dramatist himself makes words and physical actions work together on stage. Chapter 6 suggests ways in which the visual perspective could lead to a reassessment of Racine's place in the French dramatic tradition and in relation to drama in other languages. Chapter 7 considers how Racine gives visual expression to some key features of the genre of tragedy. It also argues that a theatrical reading of Racine goes beyond the confines of the tragic genre and opens perspectives upon an alternative agenda offered to the spectators.

This study does not claim to lay down how Racine should be performed on stage. It is a theatrical *reading*. But it may provide a means of assessing the extent to which a particular performance accords with the theatrical implications of Racine's text.

I

Setting the Scene

Pour ce combat choisissons quelque lieu
(*La Thébaïde*)

(*a*) Parisian Theatres

It is hard to imagine any venue less suited to the enjoyment of drama than public theatres in seventeenth-century Paris. Any notion that Racine's tragedies were watched in solemn silence by a devout audience, piously attentive to every nuance and subtlety, must be quickly abandoned in the face of contemporary evidence. Audiences were rowdy and turbulent. Most of the spectators would have had great difficulty in seeing the stage at all. The long narrow buildings in which drama was performed were admirably suited for tennis, because that was the function for which they had been constructed, but highly inconvenient as theatres.[1]

It was customary to allow spectators to sit or stand on stage. The highest prices were paid for this privilege and it was an attraction to the aristocracy. These young noblemen had the closest view of the actors and actresses, at least from the side (Pl. 1). Some, however, seem to have stood behind the actors.[2] The next most expensive seats were in the raised *loges* down each side of the wall. These gave an excellent view of the spectators ranged down the opposite wall, but a much less good view of the actors, unless one was fortunate enough to be in the *loge* nearest the stage. People complained that in the *loges* they could only see the stage by peering round sideways.[3] The cheapest tickets gave access to the discomforts of standing room only in

---

[1] See Lough, pp. 58–98. For useful plans and illustrations, see Barlow, 'The Hôtel de Bourgogne according to Sir James Thornhill'.
[2] See illustrations from *La Noce de village* (1666) in Mittman, pp. 43, 56–8.
[3] Sorel, *La Maison des jeux*, i. 406, 463.

the *parterre*. This crush of spectators at least had the advantage of facing in the right direction, and the stage in front of them was conveniently raised about a foot above the head of a spectator of average height. This meant that those standing in the front rows near the stage could, if they stood with their heads angled backwards, obtain a close view of the feet of the actors stamping above their noses; those who stood in the middle ranks could view the actors from a less distorted angle, provided that no tall spectator obstructed their line of vision; whilst those at the back might well have had their view completely obstructed by the seething mass of spectators in front of them packed like sardines (Pl. 2). At the rear of the building behind the *parterre*, the slightly raked *amphithéâtre* provided a raised platform for seats, which would allow a view of the stage over the heads of the standing spectators in the *parterre*. In consequence of this, the *amphithéâtre* spectators perhaps had the best possibility of seeing the stage in proper perspective. Whether every word of the dialogue reached them was another matter.

The play would start with a call for silence. Boursault who was present at the first performance of *Britannicus* in 1669 described how Agrippine, waiting for Néron outside his door, 'imposed silence on all those present to listen to her' (p. 231). During the course of the play, actors might have to combat rowdiness and, according to D'Aubignac, 'actors sometimes have to break off to call for silence' (*Pratique*, i. 7, p. 41). The speeches of lesser characters were 'the time for spectators to talk about what had happened, relax their attention or eat their refreshments'. For the dramatist, the rewards of writing impressive speeches might be loud bursts of applause; but these gratifying acclamations had the unfortunate effect of drowning large parts of the speech (*Dissertation sur Sophonisbe*, pp. 141, 143). Even the seats on stage were no guarantee of hearing or seeing: 'Let's make a show of ourselves there: you can't see anything, it's hard to hear, but it's the most expensive seat.'[4] Clearly the play would be perceived differently in different parts of the auditorium. Indeed, any attempt to reconstruct the impact of the play on the audience must take account of this factor. It would be more accurate to speak of audiences in the

---

[4] *Amusements sérieux et comiques par M Fontenelle* (1704), 59–60; Capatti, p. 48.

plural. Take scenery. One would expect it to be painted in bold impressionistic strokes which made sense at a distance but would seem clumsy close up. Rotrou's *Saint Genest* (1647) contains a discussion on this very point between the leading actor and the scene-painter. Genest complains irritably that the depiction of a temple and park is crude. 'They will appear better from a distance' is the disgruntled scene-painter's reply (Act II, Scene i). The implications of this are that the stage set would look right to those in the auditorium, but to those sitting on stage it could appear crude.

To the spectators on stage, the close proximity of the actors might also interfere with the theatrical illusion, whilst they themselves might break the theatrical illusion for the spectators in the auditorium. Molière was no doubt having fun when he imagined an inconsiderate marquis placing his chair on stage in the line of vision between actors and auditorium, but his jest does evoke the practical problems of spectators on stage: 'Right in the middle of the front of the stage, his broad back insolently turned to the spectators, he hid the actors from three quarters of the *parterre*' (*Les Fâcheux*, I. i. 32).

How many would see the faces of the actors sufficiently clearly to see their expression? Some of the spectators on stage might have had a good view. But the hats worn by the actors and the inadequate lighting by candlelight may have made it difficult for anyone else. Even those in the front ranks of the *parterre* would have a much closer view of the actors' feet than of their faces: 'The feet are more exposed to observation than most of the actors' other members; because the stage is usually elevated to make them more in a line parallel to the eye of the spectator in the foremost row of the pit; the lamps too, serve to render them the more conspicuous.' This complaint dates from the eighteenth century but it fits what we know of the theatrical conditions of Racine's time.[5] An impression of the ideal conditions for viewing may be seen in the engraving which shows Louis XIII as guest of Richelieu in the Palais Cardinal theatre, sitting in well-spaced armchairs at an appropriate distance from the stage with no interventing obstacles (Pl. 3).

---

[5] Roger Pickering, *Reflections upon Theatrical Expression in Tragedy* (London, 1755), 30, quoted in Barnett, 'Postures and Attitudes', p. 12.

It must also be remembered that Racine's plays were not only performed in the public theatres of Paris—mainly the Hôtel de Bourgogne—but they were also put on at court. Doubtless the more exclusive courtly audience did not suffer the grosser inconveniences of the public theatre, but courtiers were not necessarily any more attentive as audiences.

All this is a warning that although it is convenient to speak in general terms of the impact on the audience, and legitimate to read the texts for theatrical cues which evoke performance, the reality of audience perception was undoubtedly subject to many intrinsic difficulties and extraneous hazards. The diversity of the cultural, emotional, and intellectual equipment of the spectators also played its part (see Capatti, pp. 21–85). For the purposes of discussion one has to postulate a hypothetical audience shorn of idiosyncrasies. Corneille deals with the divergence of moral values in the spectator, by supposing that 'our audience is composed neither of very evil men nor of saints, but people of average integrity (*probité commune*)' (*Discours de la tragédie*, p. 30). A theatrical reading presupposes a similar hypothetical spectator.

In spite of all the obstacles to losing oneself in the action of the play, audiences could certainly be transported into the fictional world evoked by the dramatist. One girl, who had never been to the theatre before, was so convinced of the reality of the play *Pyrame et Thisbé*, in which Pyramus mistakenly believes his fiancée has been eaten by a lion, that she urged her mother to go and tell Pyramus that his mistress was not really dead.[6] But, like the cowboy who on his first visit to the theatre drew a gun on the villain on stage, the girl did not understand the codes of theatrical illusion which invite emotional involvement but prohibit personal intervention; that which seems real on stage must be recognized as non-real.[7] The tears that were shed at performances of Racine's tragedies, especially *Iphigénie*, also testify to the emotional involvement of the audience in his plays. For Racine, this was the right response.

(b) Ambiguous Place and Precise Place

One of the obstacles to a theatrical reading of Racine is a misconception concerning Racine's use of stage space and

[6] D'Aubignac, *Pratique*, iv. 6, p. 299.
[7] For the concepts of theatrical illusion and *dénégation*, see Ubersfeld, pp. 46–57.

scenery.[8] There is a tendency to assert that Racine's tragedies were performed in a vague space and that the normal setting was a *palais à volonté* ('a palace at will') or an ante-chamber.[9] But this is not borne out by the evidence. The *palais à volonté* plays a minor role in Racine's drama.

To understand this aspect of Racine's theatrical technique one must grasp certain important distinctions concerning the function of scenery in the later seventeenth century. When Racine began his theatrical career in 1660 two important works had been published on the theory and practice of drama. D'Aubignac's *Pratique du théâtre* was the work of an assiduous theatre-goer in the 1630s and 1640s who had advised Richelieu on theatrical matters and who published the fruits of his meditation on the subject in 1657. D'Aubignac's approach was practical; hence the title of his book emphasizing practice as opposed to theory. Three years later Pierre Corneille, two-thirds of the way through his prodigious career as France's leading dramatist, published his complete theatrical works to date. Each of the three volumes was prefaced by a discourse on an aspect of theatre—on the dramatic poem, on tragedy, on the three unities—and to each play was appended an *examen* or series of observations on the plays by the master himself. On many issues D'Aubignac and Corneille agreed; but there were also disagreements, especially on the matter of stage space.

Both books appeared just at the time Racine was embarking on his theatrical career. He certainly possessed a copy of D'Aubignac and he must surely have read Corneille's discourses and *examens*. Racine as an aspiring dramatist often followed D'Aubignac where he differed from Corneille. It is in the light of Corneille's handling of stage space that Racine's practice can best be appreciated.

By 1660 it was generally accepted that only one single stage set should be used for the whole play. This was a development from an earlier form of stage set called 'multiple décor' where the spectator saw before him all through the play a stage usually divided into five compartments, each with different scenery,

---

[8] The remainder of this chapter is based on Maskell, 'La Précision du lieu' with modifications and additions.

[9] e.g. 'the décor, most often, a *palais à volonté*' (McGowan, p. 172); 'Chacun sait que les tragédies de Racine se déroulent dans une anti-chambre ou un appartement' (Niderst, p. 176); Picard expresses similar views in *Œuvres*, i. 887.

representing different places which remained in full view of the audience all through the play. From around 1640 multiple décor started to go out of fashion and was replaced by a single stage set. But the use of a single stage set did not necessarily mean that it represented a single precisely identifiable place. Because of the difficulty of making plays conform to such a strict requirement, Corneille advocated flexibility in the interpretation of single set décor. Largely to justify his own practice, he elaborated the concept of a fictitious theatrical place, which was a room on to which opened the apartments of different people and in which characters could speak with the same intimacy as if they were in their own private rooms (*Discours des trois unités*, p. 78). Extending flexibility even further, Corneille also argued that the single stage set could actually represent more than one place. This flexibility was particularly important for conspiracy drama, where it was most unlikely that conspirators would plan assassinations in close proximity to their intended victims. This is why Corneille specified two places for the action of *Cinna* (1640), even though there was only one stage set.

The single stage set could therefore represent (i) a single precise place; (ii) Corneille's peculiar concept of the theatrically fictitious place; (iii) two or three different places. Scherer calls the second and third meanings 'composite place' (p. 191). If the single stage set had to represent more than one place, Corneille in practical fashion demanded that the 'places should not require different scenery and that [. . .] none of the places should be named in the course of the play' (*Discours des trois unités*, p. 78). Too much precision of scenery in such cases would invite criticism such as D'Aubignac made of Corneille's *Sertorius* (1662), the action of which takes place in the respective houses of Viriate, Perpenna and Sertorius himself. 'I am not at all convinced, wrote D'Aubignac, that it is plausible that Viriate's rooms, and those of Perpenna and Sertorius should all have the same tapestries, the same pictures, and the same ornaments' (*Dissertation sur Sertorius*, p. 251).

Thus Corneille's handling of stage space and scenery relied on ambiguity. He confessed that only three of his tragedies—*Horace, Polyeucte*, and *Pompée*—satisfied the strict requirement that a single set should represent a single clearly defined place (*Discours des trois unités*, p. 79). The majority of Corneille's non-comic plays are set in an ambiguous place. On the other hand, in all Racine's tragedies except *Esther* the single stage set represents one single precise place. It is as if Racine took up as a challenge the excuses made by Corneille on the subject of unity of place at the end of his third discourse:

It is easy for theoreticians to be rigorous, but if they set out to give audiences ten or twelve poems of this sort [i.e. tragedies], they would perhaps allow even more flexibility in the rules than I have, as soon as they realized in practice how restrictive their rigorousness is, and how many fine things it banishes from our theatres (*Discours des trois unités*, p. 78).

Racine managed to produce exactly ten tragedies which did satisfy the strict rigour of the rule.

The general view that Racine sets all his plays in a *palais à volonté* gives the erroneous impression that, like Corneille, he chose a vague setting for his tragedies. In fact it is in opposition to Corneille and by taking a more rigorous line on scenery and stage space that Racine made his distinctive contribution to the representation of theatrical place.

To understand Racinian scenery we must also ask what exactly is meant by *palais à volonté*. First of all it is not a term used by playwrights but by the scene-painters or stage-managers (*décorateurs*) responsible for constructing the décor. For them the term meant that they could choose, as they wished (*à leur volonté*), a stage set which would be recognizable to the spectators as a palace. This can be seen in the *Mémoire de Mahelot*, which contains lists of the stage sets used at the Hôtel de Bourgogne from about 1640 to the end of the century. In the list by Michel Laurent (1678), the distinction is generally between a *palais à volonté* on its own on the one hand, and, on the other hand, instructions for stage sets where specific items of scenery are mentioned. One must not confuse the *palais à volonté* with stage sets where other elements of scenery are specified. On this basis the striking fact to emerge from the list of stage sets for the nine Racinian tragedies which are in Michel Laurent's list is that only two have a *palais à volonté* in the strict sense of the term—*La Thébaïde* and *Mithridate*. For *Britannicus*, *palais à volonté* is mentioned, but with the important and significant addition of 'two doors and a curtain'. The remaining stage sets are even more varied: tents for *Alexandre* and *Iphigénie*; 'a palace with columns and backdrop with sea and ships' for *Andromaque*; 'a small private room suitable for a king in which there are ciphers [i.e. entwined initials]' for *Bérénice*; 'a saloon in Turkish style' for *Bajazet*; 'a vaulted palace' for *Phèdre*. Of course Racine's last two plays *Esther* (1689) and *Athalie* (1691) do not figure on this list, which dates from 1678, but both have very specific décor. It therefore follows that for Racine's eleven tragedies the *palais à volonté* applies to only two or three of them.

The proportion is quite different among his rivals. For the plays of Pierre Corneille which are in Laurent's list there are twelve *palais à volonté* against one stage set which has the extra specification, 'a room with four doors'. This latter is for *Le Cid* (1637) representing a simplification of the multiple décor for which the play was written. In the case of Thomas Corneille there are four *palais à volonté* against two more specific stage sets which require a sea view and a prison. Nine tragedies are mentioned by authors whose names only figure once or twice in the list. Once again *palais à volonté* predominates over more precise décor, the proportion being six to three. Simply by reading Laurent's list carefully, we can see that Racine uses the *palais à volonté* much less than his rivals, and that in this respect his tragedies differ from others in the repertoire of the Hôtel de Bourgogne in 1678.

(c) Décor and Text

To appreciate the theatrical significance of scenery in Racine's plays we must consider the instructions to the scene-painters in the *Mémoire de Mahelot* just mentioned, and the relationship of these instructions to the text of the plays. The text offers two kinds of evidence: the indication at the beginning of each play of the place where the action unfolds, and the allusions to place and décor written by Racine into the speeches of the characters.

D'Aubignac recommended that the speeches of the characters should contain all the information necessary for the description of scenery and place: 'All the poet's ideas, whether for the stage décor, the movements of the characters, the costume and gestures necessary for the understanding of the subject, must be expressed by the verses which [the dramatist] causes to be recited' (*Pratique*, i. 8, p. 46). Following on from this D'Aubignac stressed the importance of including these instructions in the speech of the characters, and praised the dramatists of ancient Greece and Rome for allowing us to reconstruct the décor, costumes, and gestures out of the speeches of the characters (p. 47). Indeed, the whole of D'Aubignac's chapter 'How the poet must make known the scenery and action necessary in a play' (*Pratique*, i. 8) can serve as a detailed guide to Racine's practice and also to theatrical reading in general.

It was usual for the stage-managers to comb the text for allusions to décor so that appropriate scenery could be built. The same applied to props that might be required. Lancaster's edition of the *Mémoire de Mahelot* shows the close correspondence between the list of scenery and props and the text of the plays. Given this practice one might expect each item of scenery in the list by Michel Laurent for Racine's tragedies to correspond to some mention in Racine's text. This is not the case. It seems puzzling that not all the details of scenery listed for Racine's plays could have been deduced from Racine's text itself. The columns of the palace specified for *Andromaque* are not mentioned in the text. It is not immediately obvious that there should be two doors for *Britannicus*. This may be a significant clue to Racine's dealings with the stage-managers of the Hôtel de Bourgogne, a point which will be discussed later.

Each of Racine's plays has a unique relationship with its scenery and for the most part there are references in the text to the scenery.[10] The importance of décor obviously goes beyond the moment when a character might refer to it. It remains visible to the spectator throughout the play. At any moment the décor may stimulate reflection in the spectator upon the relationship between the décor and the speeches or actions of the characters. The best way to grasp the significance of this aspect of Racine's theatrical aesthetic is to consider briefly each play in turn, from *La Thébaïde* to *Athalie*.

Racine's handling of stage space and scenery can be considered from two angles. 'Scenic place' is the place represented

---

[10] For a different view, see Roy: 'On ne songeait même pas à adapter les décors à la pièce qu'on jouait' ('La Mise en scène des pièces de Racine', p. 19).

by the stage and its immediate environs. 'Geographical place' is the locality where the action is said to unfold. 'Scenic place' corresponds to Issacharoff's concept of 'mimetic space' which he defines as 'that represented by the stage and perceived by the audience'; 'geographical place' corresponds to Issacharoff's 'diegetic space', that is to say space which is 'simply referred to in the speech of the characters and which is limited to verbal existence' (p. 72). In the comments which follow it will emerge that the importance of scenic place in relation to geographical place varies from play to play, and the interaction of these two elements can produce certain specifically theatrical effects in Racinian drama. It will also be seen that there are close links between the speeches and physical movements of the characters in stage space, links which are so frequent that they constitute a characteristic element of Racine's dramatic technique.

(d) The Twelve Plays

La Thébaïde

It was Molière who started Racine on his theatrical career by putting on La Thébaïde at the Palais Royal. So La Thébaïde received its première in the same theatre in which two years earlier the spectator had seen a palais à volonté represent two or three different places in Corneille's Sertorius, an example of a single set being used in an ambiguous manner. But Racine is careful to show that, in his first tragedy, the palais à volonté which Laurent specifies for the scenery represents a single precise place: 'The scene is in Thebes in a room in the royal palace.' In the course of the action, Racine ingeniously contrives that interviews take place in the royal palace, and not outside the city, as was the case in his source, Act II of Rotrou's Antigone, where the great meeting between Polynice and Etéocle takes place under the city ramparts. One might be tempted to smile at Racine's ingenuity, if it were only a clumsily contrived attempt to observe strict unity of place. However, the handling of stage space in La Thébaïde gives the first glimpse of that scenic imagination which was to sustain Racine until the end of his career.

Racine prepares the spectator to appreciate Jocaste's reference to the room represented by the stage. Just before the brothers meet there, Racine makes Etéocle say that 'the obstinate hatred' of the warring brothers was in them even at birth (IV. i. 915). Jocaste rejoices that her sons are now reunited 'in the same palace in which you were born' (IV. iii. 976). All this vividly conveys Jocaste's maternal illusions, as she gestures to the room in which they are assembled and says to her sons: 'Consider these surroundings in which you were born. Does not the sight of them have power over your hearts? It was here that you first saw the day. Everything here speaks to you of peace and love' (IV. iii. 1023). These lines of Jocaste derive their unconscious irony and pathos from the fact that the stage space represents precisely that place which she believes is a place of peace and love, whilst the spectators, thanks to Etéocle's revelations of the life-long hostility between the brothers, know that their place of birth is a place of anger and hatred.

Alexandre

Racine quickly turned from the *palais à volonté* of *La Thébaïde* to a quite different setting for his second tragedy. In *Alexandre* 'the scene is on the banks of the river Hydaspes in Taxile's camp'. Accordingly the stage designer specified that the scenery is 'war tents and pavilions'. Such a backdrop of tents is confirmed by Robinet's account of the first performance (i. 537–8). Louis Racine says that the action is in Taxile's tent (*Remarques*, p. 342). Presumably the downstage area represented the interior of the tent, giving a view of other tents backstage. Taxile's camp is never lost sight of. In Act I Porus reproaches Taxile that the impatient soldiers shut in his camp 'complain that instead of testing their great courage, their idleness in camp dissipates their strength' (I. ii. 131). Intolerant of Taxile's equivocations, Porus urges Axiane to depart with him: 'Let us leave this camp, where Taxile, incense in hand, awaits his sovereign' (I. iii. 263). Once the battle is begun between the Indian kings and the Greek conqueror, Axiane complains: 'Taxile has made his camp my prison' (III. i. 680). Taxile takes advantages of his status to force Axiane's hand, reminding her brutally 'You forget perhaps that if you force me, I can speak as master here' (IV. iii. 1205). Finally, as a prisoner in Taxile's camp, Axiane is in anguish that she cannot leave to join Porus in his fight against Alexandre: 'If only I could leave this place, show myself to him and die before his eyes; but Taxile keeps me imprisoned . . .' (V. ii. 1363). The military aspect of Taxile's camp is powerfully evoked by all the preceding extracts, and additionally in another vein by Axiane's evocation of noises off-stage: 'The cries of the dying almost reach me' (III. i. 700), and 'Shall we hear only shouts of victory?' (IV. i. 957).

The scenery for *Alexandre* is a long way from the banal ante-chamber so often associated with Racinian tragedy. It is precise to the extent that it shows tents and is not a *palais à volonté*. It is also precise to the extent that it represents a specific military camp, that of Taxile. Racine exploits this precision to give a spatial and geographical dimension to the action of *Alexandre*. Not only does the camp serve as a prison for Axiane, but the rivers mentioned in the text—the Euphrates, the Hydaspes, the Indus, the Ganges—mark the steps of Alexander's all-conquering progress. It is on the banks of the Hydaspes that Taxile's camp is pitched. The conqueror has passed the Euphrates; the Indus and the Ganges lie ahead. The spatial elements are thus indispensible for the unfolding of the action and for an understanding of the precise historical moment represented in *Alexandre*.[11]

Andromaque

All through the play characters remind each other that they are in the single precise place indicated at the start of the play: 'The scene is in Buthrotum, a town in Epirus, in a room in Pyrrhus's palace.' Characters are keenly aware of where they are, and that Pyrrhus is master: Oreste, Pyrrhus, Andromaque, and Hermione all speak of it.[12] In particular Pylade warns Oreste: 'These guards, this court, the air around, everything depends upon Pyrrhus' (III. i. 721). Even after the king's death, Pylade reminds his friend of the danger that threatens the Greeks in Pyrrhus's palace (V. v. 1583).

---

[11] This evidence contradicts Lapp's view that 'in *Alexandre* spatial elements are curiously lacking' (p. 66).

[12] *And.* 8, 245, 261, 272, 584.

In the production at the Hôtel de Bourgogne, the stage designer created a set showing 'a palace with columns, and in the background sea and ships'. The backdrop representing sea and ships is an element of scenery closely related to the text. The sea is the path which links Buthrotum to Sparta. The characters allude several times to the sea and especially to Oreste's ships. The depiction of the ships provides a constant visual reminder to the spectator of Oreste's status as visiting ambassador and of the principal theme of the tragedy. The scenic place merges into the geographical place and the mimetic space supports the diegetic space evoked by the words of the characters. Once Oreste has entered Pyrrhus's palace, all his arguments are directed towards the moment when he will set sail again for Greece, taking Hermione with him. In response to his plan for abduction Pylade tells Oreste: 'Our ships are all ready, and the wind beckons us; I know all the secret passages in this palace. You can see that the sea beats against its walls' (III. i. 790). The last line strongly suggests a gesture towards the backdrop which represents sea and ships. Hermione accepts Oreste's offer to kill Pyrrhus, saying: 'Let all your ships be ready for our escape' (IV. iii. 1254). When Oreste claims his reward from Hermione, it is in terms which are linked with the scenery: 'Come to my ships and savour your vengeance' (V. iii. 1494, text of 1668 only). Hermione's unexpected and furious disavowal of her lover derives extra force from the scenic context. No doubt with a contemptuous gesture towards the sea and ships, she addresses her final farewell to the hapless Oreste: 'Farewell. You can leave. I shall remain in Epirus' (V. iii. 1561). At the dénouement, Pylade dutifully tries to guide Oreste: 'That is the direction in which we must go; let us leave in safety' (V. v. 1596). He tries to conduct his demented friend towards the ships which have been waiting since the beginning of the play.

Les Plaideurs

In studies of Racine which equate his theatre with tragedy, his one comedy fits awkwardly into the picture, if at all. It is difficult to reconcile an isolated comedy with the dignity of tragedy, especially if Racine's tragedies are mistakenly believed to be devoid of physical action and visual effects. However, a theatrical reading of Racine embraces *Les Plaideurs* without any problem. The handling of scenery in this comedy shows an exuberant development of the handling of scenery in the first three tragedies.

According to the *Mémoire de Mahelot* (pp. 135–6) the stage set requires two houses—one for each father: Dandin, the obsessive judge, and Chicanneau, the perennial litigant. Up and down the floors of Dandin's house the action races. Dandin sets the ball rolling by jumping from the window above his front door. Thereafter Racine varies the visual impact by having Dandin appear on high at his attic window, then down below in the basement. Apart from using the houses on four levels—attic, first floor, ground floor, and basement—Racine makes great use of the doors to the two houses. The action switches from Dandin's house in Act I, to Chicanneau's house in Act II, Scenes i–vi, and back to Dandin's house for the remainder of Act II. The doors are indispensable to the visual comedy of attempting to gain entry. Chicanneau has Dandin's door slammed in his face by Petit Jean; it reopens long enough for Petit Jean to accept a bribe, but the unfortunate Chicanneau has the door shut on him again (Act I, Scene vi). The door reopens for Petit Jean to complain of the racket made by the quarrelsome Chicanneau and the Comtesse in front of the house: the sudden appearance of Petit Jean in the doorway exacerbates the dispute, and brings it to its climax (Act I, Scene viii). Racine varies the door comedy in Act II where Dandin's secretary disguised as an *huissier* tries to deliver a letter to Isabelle in Chicanneau's house. He struggles to make himself heard through the door, and only by uttering the magic name of Léandre to Isabelle does he succeed. Each line of the dialogue lends itself to a new twist in this doorway comedy (Act II, Scene ii). In Act II, Scene xi, the action has switched back to Dandin's door, which forms part of the extended comedy of the Comtesse and Chicanneau trying to engage the attention of Dandin at the attic window. In a climax of exasperation the two litigants make a combined assault on the door to the Judge's house. Léandre bars their way. The Comtesse's insistence is met by Léandre's intransigent 'No entry!' Only the reappearence of Dandin in the basement diverts the comedy to this lower level.

The third acts sets the mock trial in the space in front of the houses, and the scenery plays no theatrically significant role. But the first two acts of *Les Plaideurs* are hardly intelligible on the page without a mental image of the stage with the doors to two houses. This spatial model is repeated with variations in the next two tragedies, almost as if writing his comedy acted as a catalyst for Racine's exploitation of stage space in tragedy.

Britannicus

The setting of *Britannicus* can only be appreciated by taking Racine's indication of the scenic place, 'The scene is in Rome in a room in Néron's palace', together with Laurent's notes for the décor, 'The stage is a *palais à volonté*; two doors are needed [. . .] and curtains'. Laurent's description of the scenery must be considered attentively, for it contains more than the phrase *palais à volonté*, which on its own might suggest a vague palatial setting. It includes two doors. In *Les Plaideurs* the doors were for theatrical fun. In *Britannicus* this theatrical device is given a serious significance.

The essential feature of the setting of *Britannicus* is that everything happens in front of the door to Néron's apartment. This is made clear in the first lines. Albine is amazed at her mistress's conduct as 'wandering through the palace without suite or escort, the emperor's mother waits alone at his door' (I. i. 3). The door to Néron's apartment is the gateway to power. Agrippine makes to cross the threshold, hoping to regain the influence which is slipping from her grasp; but Burrhus stops her (I. ii. 128), a visual effect which echoes Léandre's 'No entry' barring the Comtesse in *Les Plaideurs*. During Act I, Scene ii, Agrippine has an altercation with Burrhus: 'Do you intend to hide the emperor from me any longer?' (I. ii. 142). Néron is concealed from her—and from the spectator—behind this door. She continues to taunt Burrhus: 'Did I raise you so high in order to erect a barrier between my son and myself?' (I. ii. 144). Her words allude to the physical action by which Burrhus has just barred her way. For Agrippine it is the height of her disgrace 'when Burrhus dares to restrain me at his door' (I. ii. 278). This door, loaded with significance, remains visible throughout the tragedy. Having concealed the emperor in Act I, it opens to let him appear in Act II. In this second act the curtains noted by

Laurent play their part. They conceal Néron as Junie is forced to deceive Britannicus into thinking she has discarded him (Act II, Scene vi). Later Narcisse reminds Britannicus that they are both in front of Néron's door: 'It is not in this place that this mystery can be revealed to you' (III. vi. 929). That Britannicus should choose to remain in that very spot to talk of Junie to Narcisse, and then to kneel before Junie when she appears, is the visual manifestation of that youthful imprudence of his which Agrippine had already remarked upon (I. iii. 287). In the next act Agrippine demands from Néron 'that this same Burrhus who comes to listen to us, should never again dare to stop me at your door' (IV. ii. 1293). And the door dominates the dénouement. For Britannicus it is to open the way to reconciliation with his brother (V. i. 1482); Junie attempts to detain him (V. ii. 1562); Agrippine comes to hasten him through it (V. ii. 1568). To pass through this door means death for Britannicus.

Laurent mentions two doors for the stage set. Undoubtedly Néron's door is the more important. The Sydney production of 1980 placed it the centre of the stage set and made it the focal point of the action. In that production the spatial dynamics 'showed the play to be concerned essentially with the limits of political power, with the moral and emotional forces which are beyond the reach of political power and hold it in check' (McAuley, p. 354). The same view is offered by Dubech: 'One might say that the door is the principal character in *Britannicus* and that the play is a tragedy in front of a door' (p. 64). However, the second door should not be neglected. Junie has been provided with her own apartment, even though she has only just been abducted by Néron (II. ii. 398), and it is likely that the second door leads to Junie's apartment. This would make possible the following theatrical effects. Néron notes the opening of Junie's door and sees her enter (II. ii. 525). She escapes back through it in distress at the end of the spying scene (Act II, Scene vii). Junie's door gives an extra dimension to her anxiety when she chances to meet Britannicus again (Act III, Scene vii). This scene would gain from showing the two lovers between two doors. Junie tries to escape the danger of being seen with Britannicus in front of Néron's door, and her anxiety to leave is given visual emphasis if she is on the verge of re-entering her own apartment. This interpretation of the scenery is supported by Néron's command that the two lovers be arrested: 'Guards, take her back into her apartment, and guard Britannicus in his sister's' (III. viii. 1080). Without Laurent's specification of two doors for *Britannicus* these clues for the theatrical exploitation of the second door might not be apparent solely from Racine's text, though the need for a separate space for Junie was accepted in the 1982 Melbourne production, where 'one exit was reserved exclusively for Junia' (McAuley, p. 356). However, in his next play Racine is more explicit and ensures that both doors are enshrined in the text.

Bérénice

The first eight lines of the play set the scene between two doors: 'Let us stop here,' says Antiochus to Arsace, 'this closet (*ce cabinet*) is where Titus [. . .] sometimes hides himself from his court, when he talks to the queen about his love. His apartment is just beyond this door; the other door leads into the queen's apartment'. Thus the spectator is apprised of the mimetic nature of the stage space. The word 'cabinet' had a precise meaning. Furetière in his *Dictionnaire universel* defined it as 'the most private place in the best apartment in a palace or large house', and adds 'a royal apartment consists of a room, and ante-chamber and a *cabinet*'. That the spectators actually saw a door is attested in an account of the first performance of *Bérénice* at the Hôtel de Bourgogne in 1670: '[Antiochus] enters on stage by a door which he says is that of Titus's closet' (Villars, p. 244). For the reader, Racine heads the published text of his play: 'The scene is in Rome, in a closet (*cabinet*) between the apartments of Titus and Bérénice.'

Not for nothing does Racine spend the first eight lines of *Bérénice* ensuring that the precise setting of the tragedy is known to the spectator and explaining the significance of the two doors. Antiochus immediately sends Arsace into Bérénice's apartment and remains alone before Bérénice's door, in a vacillating posture: 'Let us withdraw; let us depart' (I. ii. 33), but when Arsace returns he asks: 'Arsace, may we enter?' (I. iii. 51). The door is the focus for Antiochus's hesitations (III. ii. 830), and later for Titus's hesitations (IV. iv. 988). When the door finally opens to Titus, Bérénice erupts on stage, tearing herself from the restraining hands of characters off-stage. She will not heed their pleas that she should remain in her room (IV. v. 1040). There is a struggle at the threshold. At the end of Act IV the spectator sees Titus torn between the two doors. Antiochus entreats him to come to the queen to prevent her from committing suicide (IV. viii. 1228). Paulin exhorts him to return to his apartment where the senators await him (IV. viii. 1247). It is a theatrical tableau. Titus's dilemma is represented visually, as Paulin and Antiochus implore him to leave the stage in their respective directions through one or other of the two doors.[13]

The two doors are not Racine's only scenic device in *Bérénice*. Laurent records an essential element of the scenery: the private room is decorated with *chiffres*, that is, ciphers or entwined initials. The Louvre had the entwined initials H and D carved in stone to signify the love of King Henri II of France for his mistress, Diane de Poitiers. Racine's Titus evidently followed this custom. The scenery at the Hôtel de Bourgogne must have displayed T and B entwined for performances of *Bérénice*. It was not mere decoration. In the last act Titus begs his mistress not to leave Rome (Act V, Scene v). But Bérénice justly reproaches him with the decoration of the precise room where the action is taking place:

I see nothing here which does not wound me. All this apartment which you prepared with care; these surroundings, so long a witness to my love, which seemed to assure me for ever of your love for me; these ciphers (*ces chiffres*), where our names, entwined one with the other, offer themselves everywhere to my mournful gaze, they are but imposters which I cannot endure. (V. v. 1320).[14]

Throughout *Bérénice* these ciphers are the visual representation of the liaison between Titus and Bérénice, which all Titus's

---

[13] Voltz accepts this visual symbolism in *Bérénice*: 'une véritable mise en scène de l'espace, et lourdement symbolique' (p. 64). Picard, however, rejects the visual dimension and describes the scenic space in *Bérénice* as 'le lieu abstrait de l'action [. . .] lieu sans couleur [. . .] seulement le point de rencontre des personnages' (in *Œuvres*, i. 1130).

[14] The word 'chiffres' was changed in the 1697 edn. to 'festons' but the essential point remains; a critic of the 1893 Comédie-Française production deplored the 'little TB monograms' without realizing that they are justified by Racine's text; Drésa's set in 1925 had a single TB monogram (Chevalley, pp. 113 n., 116).

speeches aim to break. It is a brilliant invention on Racine's part to emphasize the discrepancy between the emperor's speeches and the décor chosen by him for this private room, situated between the apartments of the two lovers.[15] The rupture between Titus and Bérénice is prolonged in geographical space and in time, by the opposition between Rome and the Orient. Rome is the present; the Orient is the future and separation (V. vii. 1497). Departure from the stage acquires extra significance from this geographical dimension.

Bajazet

The double spatial structure, scenic and geographical, mimetic and diegetic, which operated in *Alexandre*, *Andromaque*, and *Bérénice*, is exploited again in *Bajazet*. In turn Racine plays upon geographical location and the place represented by the stage set. Along the axis Babylon–Byzantium are ranged the hopes and fears of the conspirators, according to news of the sultan's defeat or victory and according to his remoteness or proximity. In the early scenes we learn: 'A long distance separates his camp from Byzantium' (I. i. 26); 'he intends to transfer his throne and presence far away from Byzantium' (I. ii. 245). Then the distance narrows. Amurat 'is returning with great strides' (IV. iii. 1176); the sultan 'is approaching and returning as victor' (IV. vi. 1353).

At the end of this journey is the stage, representing the most secret place in the seraglio. The vizier, Acomat, explains to Osmin that Roxane 'herself has chosen this private spot [. . .] a slave brings me here by a little known route' (I. i. 207). The secret spot, according to the scene-painter, is a 'saloon in Turkish style'. The Turkish décor was doubtless intended to evoke for the spectator that foreign atmosphere in which Racine found the justification for choosing the subject for a tragedy from modern history: 'ordinary people hardly distinguish between that which is [. . .] a thousand years away and that which is a thousand miles away' (second preface to *Bajazet*, pp. 548–9). The first

---

[15] Lawrenson (p. 161) equates Laurent's description of the décor of *Bérénice* with a *palais à volonté*, but this does not do justice to the precision of Racine's stage set; Hourcade (p. 71) sees only splendour in the *festons* and interprets Bérénice's reference to them simply as 'What good is all this luxury if I am unhappy?'

words spoken by Acomat and Osmin, coming on stage to start the tragedy, transport the spectator a thousand miles away from a *palais à volonté*: Osmin asks anxiously of Acomat 'since when, my lord, can one enter this place? [. . .] Such audacity formerly merited a speedy death' (I. i. 3). Courville suggests how the two actors should make their entrance: 'Acomat advances, sure of himself, but treading warily; Osmin keeps to the wall, exercising even more prudence' (p. 21). These stage directions plausibly evoke the emotions which this place inspires in the two men. The Turkish saloon specified for Racine's *Bajazet* differentiates it from the *palais à volonté* which is all that Michel Laurent indicates for the scenery of La Thuillerie's *Soliman* (1680) which is none the less set in Constantinople 'in the courtyard of the first seraglio' (*Mémoire de Mahelot*, p. 126).

Racine, however, does not allot this space specifically to a single character. The stage may be interpreted as predominantly Roxane's space in Acts I and II, Atalide's space in Acts III and IV, various spaces in Act V (Voltz, pp. 66–70). The Cornelian convention of ambiguous place, whereby the location implicitly changes according to the needs of the characters, reappears to some extent in *Bajazet* and Scherer argues with some justification that *Bajazet* seems to be a return to Cornelian 'composite place' (*Bajazet*, pp. 189–90).

Mithridate

After three consecutive tragedies—two Roman, one Turkish—in which the décor represents an enclosed space, facilitating entrances and exits which are laden with significance, Racine in *Mithridate* allows himself the freedom of a *palais à volonté*, yet still achieves analogous theatrical effects from his choice of a specific geographical setting. One example only: 'The scene is in Nymphaeum, a port on the Cimmerian Bosphorus.' To this place, believing their father dead, come the sons of Mithridate to pay court to Monime and to win the hand of their father's prospective wife. Mithridate, back from the dead, reproaches his sons with their presence in this city: 'Your duty should not have brought you here' (II. ii. 424), and the suspicious father questions Arbate on the reasons that may have brought his sons to this spot (Act II, Scene iii). All this leads up to the moment when Mithridate tests Pharnace's intentions with regard to Monime, by ordering his son to leave the city at once to marry a Parthian princess. Pharnace's refusal to leave Nymphaeum convinces his father of his guilty designs upon Monime, in the same way that Xipharès's offer to leave Nymphaeum to fight against the Romans renders the younger son innocent in his father's eyes (III. i. 854–951). The precise geographical framework gives the scenic place its significance. Racine succeeds in focusing the spectator's interest on the stage space to see if Pharnace will exit or not. Mithridate threatens Pharnace: 'You, who have no cause to stay, depart this minute [. . .] I ordered you to leave just now. But after this moment [pause] . . . Prince, you understand me, you are lost if you reply' (III. i. 964). The audience see Pharnace hesitate. He does not exit. He wants to stay in Nymphaeum to be near Monime. This momentary hesitation followed by defiance of his father leads to Pharnace's arrest and intensifies his peril.

Iphigénie

Taken together, Racine's specification of place and Laurent's scenery requirements give a clear picture of the décor of *Iphigénie*, which accords with many allusions to it in the text. Racine specifies: 'the scene is in Aulis, in Agamemnon's tent'. Laurent notes that the stage requires 'tents and in the background sea and ships'. The front of the stage must represent the interior of Agamemnon's tent with an opening to reveal upstage the other tents mentioned by Laurent as well as the backdrop of sea and ships. This arrangement also emerges from the text. Awakened by Agamemnon, Arcas asks hopefully 'Have the winds tonight responded to our prayers?' Arcas listens for the sound of wind and the movement of soldiers. Then, to verify the silence, he looks outside the tent before replying to his own question: 'But all is asleep, army, winds, and the sea' (I. i. 7). This line 'Mais tout dort, et l'armée, et les vents, et Neptune' has been praised for its poetic qualities: 'the most breathtaking line in the play' (Lapp, p. 94); 'with each regular rhythmic pause (3/3/3/3), Arcas seems to apprehend dimensions of stillness wider than in either Euripides or Rotrou' (Pfohl, p. 15). Yet its links with the static backdrop of sea and ships have been passed over. According to Ubersfeld this line may have some *meaning* but cannot *signify* anything unless the scenery provides a mimetic referent (pp. 259–60), but she does not add that the backdrop at the Hôtel de Bourgogne did provide that mimetic referent. Speech and scenery interact again a moment later when Arcas, to convince the unhappy king of his good fortune, invites him to contemplate 'the imposing spectacle which these shores provide, these thousand vessels laden with twenty kings, which only await the winds to sail at your command' (I. i. 26). The backdrop of sea and ships excites quite different sentiments from Clytemnestre when she is at the height of her distress: 'Ah sea! will you not open new abysses to engulf the Greeks and their thousand ships?' (V. iv. 1684).

So, as performed at the public theatre of the Hôtel de Bourgogne, for which Laurent's scenery specifications were written, there is no doubt about the correspondences between the text and décor of *Iphigénie*. Yet the première of *Iphigénie* was in the avenue of the Orangerie at Versailles. There the scenery was different. A contemporary account reveals that the tents were placed amidst the green foliage and the backdrop was not sea and ships but a marble portico.[16] Few links therefore between the text and the Versailles décor. Was this Racine's intention? Or did he acquiesce in circumstances beyond his control? Doubtless the latter. For the Versailles performance the inventive dramatist took second place to the supple courtier.

Geographical place dominates most of Acts I and II. Agamemnon strives to keep his daughter from Aulis, and fails. In Acts IV and V Agamemnon's tent becomes the focus. Agamemnon expects to find her there (IV. iii. 1155). When Iphigénie accepts to die, Achille attempts to save her by urging her to leave Agamemnon's tent: 'Come, madam, follow me. Fear not the clamour nor the crowds who surge around this tent [. . .]; let them seek you in Achille's tent' (V. i. 1516). Achille's speech derives its meaning from being spoken in a precise place—Agamemnon's tent—in exchange for which he offers Iphigénie the safety of his own, thus underlining how Agamemnon has forfeited his paternal role.

---

[16] Félibien, *Les Divertissements de Versailles* (Paris, 1674), 63–4; *NCR* 80; discussion in Vanuxem, 'Racine, les machines et les fêtes'.

Phèdre

The scenery poses a problem. Is the action outside or indoors? Racine is less explicit than usual in his specification of stage space: 'The scene is in Troezen, a town in the Peloponnese.' For Laurent 'the stage is a vaulted palace', which seems to suggest an indoor scene, but the text of the play leaves some uncertainty. Le Bidois opts for out of doors on the grounds that 'the desire expressed by Phèdre to see the sun [. . .] and above all her apostrophe to the sun, make it quite clear that the action takes place in the open air'. Le Bidois (pp. 62, 73) inexplicably rejects as irrelevant the mention of the vaulted palace in the *Mémoire de Mahelot*.[17] Jean-Louis Barrault accepts the vaulted palace without any comment on the problem posed by Phèdre's apostrophe to the sun in Act I, Scene iii, but his suggested décor would reconcile inside and outside: 'On the one hand—light, sun, sea air; on the other—dark corners of walls and vaults' (pp. 30, 68). This would work, provided that the backdrop and wings represent the interior of a vaulted palace, and that for Act I, Scene iii, Phèdre facing the audience is deemed to apostrophize the sun in front of her, which could be achieved in a modern production by Barrault's proposed spotlight (p. 83 n. 9). This scene, when Phèdre emerges from the darkness into the sunlight, is one in which mimetic space is important.

The one other reference to scenery occurs in Act III when she says 'Already it seems that these walls, these vaults, might start to speak and accuse me' (III. iii. 854–5). This is the only line in which the vaults specified by Laurent for the scenery are mentioned. Whatever may be the emotional or descriptive value of the reference to vaults in this line, they do not involve any practical consequences for the unfolding of the action, in the way that the doors in *Britannicus* and *Bérénice* or the sea in *Andromaque* and *Iphigénie* do; but the delusion that the walls might speak brings the scenery into play as an element portraying Phèdre's hallucinatory state. Elsewhere and more frequently it is geographical place—Troezen, Athens, Crete—which serves as the framework for the action. Hippolyte seeks to leave Troezen to find his father, to escape from Phèdre and to avoid

---

[17] Hubert claims that the décor for *Phèdre* lacks specificity and is the same that spectators had seen in a host of tragedies such as *Cinna, Venceslas*, and *Bérénice* (p. 83).

Aricie (Act I, Scene i). Phèdre's love for Hippolyte would never have rekindled if Thésée had not brought his wife to Troezen (I. iii. 301). At the news of his father's death, Hippolyte, heir to Troezen, abandons Crete to Phèdre and hastens to Athens to protect Aricie's claims to that city (II. ii. 505). Victim of his father's unexpected return and of Œnone's calumny, Hippolyte is subjected to his father's rage and sentence of exile. Here stage space is transformed into geographical place. Thésée starts by ordering Hippolyte to leave the palace. Soon the perspectives broaden—'Purge my dominions of your loathsome sight'—to end up with: 'Were you already beyond the pillars of Hercules, I would still feel too close to such a traitor.' Finally Thésée's last words to Hippolyte bring attention back to stage space: 'Get out of my sight. Away, traitor! Do not wait for your frenzied father to expel you ignominiously from this place' (IV. ii. 1064–1156). At the very end of the play the geographical place is kept in focus. Hippolyte urges Aricie to accompany him: 'At the gates of Troezen [. . .] is a holy temple' (V. i. 1392). Théramène's narration is similarly linked to geographical place: 'Scarcely had we left the gates of Troezen' (V. vi. 1498).

Esther

After resting from the public theatre for twelve years Racine was enticed back by powerful patrons to write for private performance. *Esther*, commissioned by Madame de Maintenon for the schoolgirls of Saint-Cyr, was an unexpected theatrical challenge. Racine decided to give each of its three acts its own décor. Nothing better illustrates Racine's manner of handling stage space than to compare his *Esther* with Du Ryer's tragedy on the same subject published in 1644, whose last two acts correspond to the three acts of Racine's play.

It is in a neutral place that Du Ryer's Mardochée announces to Esther the decree for the massacre of the Jews (Act IV, Scene i). On the other hand for Act I of Racine's play the text specifies that 'the stage represents Esther's apartment'. He has combined the idea of retiring to one's closet to pray and the Old Testament notion of a central sanctuary. She 'utilizes the privacy of these rooms [. . .] to create a sacred space in which she can reassume her true identity as a Jewess and pray' (Gethner, p. 32). The sacred precinct is a source of strength. Moreover, this apartment is forbidden to men. Hence the dramatic entrance of Mardochée and Esther's horror: 'What sacrilegious man dares intrude upon us in this place?' (I. ii. 155). She attributes Mardochée's presence to divine intervention (I. ii. 157) thus linking the spatial setting with the religious background. That Mardochée's entrance is intended to be of theatrical interest is attested by the fact that Racine has included it even though it has no biblical authority. This attracted adverse comment at the time from Pontchâteau, writing to Arnauld: 'I wish the author had not made Mardochée enter the palace, for that is contrary to scripture.'[18] Apprised of the fatal edict against the Jews, Du Ryer's Esther immediately agrees to plead the Jewish case with Assuérus (Act IV, Scene i), whilst Racine makes his heroine hesitate a long time, because the royal throne room is a prohibited spot, even to the queen (I. iii. 191–204). Finally Esther resolves to intrude upon the forbidden spot, in spite of the peril (I. iii. 246; I. iv. 285). This peril is recalled at the start of Act II where 'the stage represents Assuérus's throne room'. Aman is amazed to be admitted there by Hydaspe: 'Do you make bold to admit me to this dreaded place?' (II. i. 374). All this prepares the spectator for Esther's entrance and Assuérus's anger: 'Without my leave someone is entered here?' (II. vii. 631) and this anger is emphasized later by the chorus of young Jewish girls (II. ix. 717). Esther collapses in a faint but, touched by the royal sceptre, she recovers her senses. Nothing so dramatic nor so theatrical in Du Ryer. The place where Esther meets Assuérus has no significance. All that the audience sees in Du Ryer's play is Esther's gesture as she 'places at the king's feet her crown and sceptre' (SD, V. iii. 1685).

The throne which dominates Act II of Racine's *Esther* illustrates an important aspect of theatrical semiology. It passes from being a physical object on which a king sits and which defines the actor as the king (Pl. 13), to become a symbolic backdrop to the chorus of young girls who are ordered to shelter by it. Esther says: 'Do not fear the gaze of a profane court, but in the shelter of this throne, await my return' (*Est.* II. vii. 712). The throne changes its denotative function, to assume a wider symbolic function as an ambiguous seat of power which

---

[18] Letter in B. Neveu, *S. J. de Pontchâteau* (Paris, [1969]), 685, *NCR* 245.

may protect the Jewish girls, even as they are singing of the perils arising from the spiritual blindness of the profane Assuérus. In this way Racine contrives a visual link between the action in Assuérus's throne room and the singing of the chorus which completes Act II of *Esther*. The change of semiotic function derives from the temporal flow of the action. From being a passive sign the throne at a particular moment becomes an active sign.

Aman's disgrace is postponed by Racine until Act III to take place in Esther's saloon and gardens in conformity with the biblical narrative. The commentary by the chorus on Aman at Esther's table endows the physical actions of eating and drinking with lyrical religious fervour (III. iii. 946–54).

For once in his life Racine was too modest when he attributed these changes of scenery to his desire 'to render this entertainment more pleasing to children' (preface to *Esther*, p. 831). In fact he succeeded in extracting powerful theatrical effects from the three places specified for the three acts of his drama, and the Prologue spoken by the figure of Piety invests Saint-Cyr itself, the wider setting of his tragedy, with the aura of a sacred place: 'I come down to this place inhabited by Grace' (Prologue, l. 2).[19]

Athalie

Writing again for the schoolgirls of Saint-Cyr, but reverting to a single precise setting, Racine placed all five acts of *Athalie* 'in the temple of Jerusalem, in a vestibule of the high priest's apartment'. Sainte-Beuve's comment is at first perplexing: 'I seek in vain in Racine this marvellous temple built by Solomon', but as far as strict décor is concerned, textual references in *Athalie* are actually rather scanty. The curtain which first hides Joas and then reveals him is not specific to the temple. The celebrated stage direction 'Here the back of the stage opens; the interior of the temple is seen' (V. v. 1730) is somewhat imprecise, and the visual effect, though striking, is confined to a hundred verses at the end. What does the spectator see? The

---

[19] Lapp maintains that in *Esther* 'space nowhere exists dramatically' (p. 76). For a more positive view, see Woshinsky, '*Esther*: No Continuing Place'.

engraving to the first edition shows a perspective of Corinthian columns (Pl. 14). No need, says Le Roy, for us to see the temple, 'but it must be there and we must feel its presence intensely; the problem is delicate' (p. 19). In the text there are a few details concerning décor, but they are meagre: a reference to the marble floor which Athalie's feet have touched and to the temple door being shut (II. viii. 750; V. iv. 1704). *Athalie* can be sumptuously staged, but it is not a necessity.

Yet the stage does indeed represent a part of the temple, centre of all the action. The danger is announced by Abner: Mathan aims to destroy the temple (I. i. 40); Athalie is planning an attack (I. i. 60). Propelled by her dream, Athalie desecrates the temple by entering it (II. i. 395). Act II, Scenes iii, iv, and v show Agar, Abner, and Mathan in turn urging her to depart. Under interrogation Eliacin replies to Athalie: 'This temple is my home' (II. vii. 640), and he rejects the invitation to leave it for Athalie's palace (II. vii. 679). Mathan sent in search of the mysterious child is confronted by Zacharie: 'Beware of advancing beyond this spot' (III. ii. 850). Mathan formulates Athalie's demands, which are the key to the action: the temple will be destroyed if the Jews do not hand over the child as hostage (III. iii. 899). Mathan's presence excites Joad's anger: 'With what impudence this enemy of God comes to infect the air we breathe in this place' (III. v. 1025). Joad's prophetic vision sees the murder of his son Zacharie in the temple itself (III. vii. 1143). Josabet trembles at Athalie's intrusion into the temple (V. iii. 1701). Even Athalie's death sentence is pronounced with reference to the scenic place: 'Let her at once be led from the temple; let not its sanctity be profaned' (V. vi. 1791). Certainly the action of *Athalie* is closely linked with the place represented by the stage. It has been suggested that here 'for the first time, place is linked to the action' (Picard in *Œuvres*, i. 887). Not so. The single precise setting does not distinguish *Athalie* from the earlier plays. It is what links *Athalie* to them.

(e) Lighting and Sound Effects

Flickering candle flames were the only source of illumination in the public theatres where Racine's plays were performed. The lighting of candles signalled the start of the performance.[20] The candles were replaced in the intervals between acts:

The scene-painters also have the task of providing two candle snuffers for the lighting [. . .] It must be done promptly so as not to let the audience lose interest between acts, and cleanly so as not to cause a bad smell. One man snuffs the front of the stage, the other the back, and they must be vigilant that the canvas scenery does not catch fire. (Chappuzeau, p. 149.)

There is no direct evidence for lighting effects being employed for Racine's plays, but it is hard to see why he should not have availed himself of the techniques attested for other plays at the Hôtel de Bourgogne. From the early seventeenth century it had been customary to give lighting cues in the text of the play. Desmarests's *Mirame* (1641), sumptuously produced for Cardinal Richelieu, seems to have benefited from a combination of machines and lighting effects: 'Night seemed to come on by the imperceptible darkening both of the garden and of the sea and sky, which was illuminated by the moon. Night was succeeded by day, which came on equally gradually with the dawn and the sun which rose and set (*soleil qui fit son tour*).'[21] An attentive study of the sky in the engravings to the folio edition of Desmarests's *Mirame* reveals the presence or absence of sun or moon in the sky to indicate the passage of time. Illustrations to Puget de la Serre's *Martyre de Sainte Catherine* (1643) show a lighted chandelier appearing back stage for Act II and then visibly extinguished in Act III (Lawrenson, p. 159). The use of lighting effects to show sunrise, midday, sunset, and dusk with exact regularity provoked the ironic comment: 'It's surprising they don't put a sundial on stage to mark the passage of time, so that the spectators can see that the play observes the twenty-four-hour rule.'[22]

The clear links between Racine's text and the scenery specified for his plays at the Hôtel de Bourgogne gives weight

[20] The *décorateur* is told to light the candles just before the play in Rotrou's *Saint Genest*, Act II, Scene v. Mascarille applauds the play even before it has started 'devant que les chandelles soient allumées' (Molière, *Les Précieuses ridicules* (1659), Scene ix, p. 278).

[21] *Gazette de France*, (1641); Scherer, pp. 120–3.

[22] Sorel, *De la connaissance des bons livres* (1671), 209.

to the hypothesis that the references to time of day in his text may also have been intended as lighting cues to be translated into visual terms. Racine is fond of starting his plays with an implicit reference to the transition from night to day, usually by mentioning sleep and waking. Jocaste rushes on stage reproaching herself for inopportune slumber: 'That sleep should close my eyes amidst such dread alarms!' (*Thé.* I. i. 4). Agrippine waits at Néron's door to catch him as soon as he awakes (*Bri.* I. i. 1). Agamemnon is shown actually waking Arcas up (*Iph.* I. i. 1). In *Athalie* dawn is signalled by Joad's reference to the increasing light: 'Already dawn lights up the temple top' (*Ath.* I. i. 160). These references hint that the tragic day is dawning and that the play will observe the unity of time. *Britannicus* is scattered with reminders of the precise time of the action. Junie was abducted in the middle of the night which preceded the action on stage (*Bri.* 54, 386, 699). The tragic day ends with Junie's fears that the oncoming night may cloak Néron's vengeance (*Bri.* V. i. 1543). There is a variant of the tragic day in *Esther*, where the onset of night occurs at the end of Act I: 'Already sombre night begins its course' (I. iii. 243) and Act II starts with reference to the dawning day: 'What! hardly has light of day begun to dawn' (II. i. 374).

In the age of electricity and neon it is hard to recapture the impressions of life in earlier centuries where flames were the only source of artificial illumination and when darkness could only be relieved by their tremulous glow. Yet such were the conditions of performance in Racine's time. The spectators always had the possibility of associating flames mentioned in the play with the flames of the candles which lit the stage and the auditorium (see Pls. 1 and 3). When Racine's characters narrate scenes of fire in the night there were real flames present to reinforce the word-pictures. Andromaque reminds Céphise of the cruel night when Pyrrhus invaded their flaming palace (*And.* III. viii. 997). Néron evokes Junie in terms which are even closer to the physical reality of attending a theatrical performance. He saw her brought to his palace by night, her beauty enhanced by the interplay of shadows and the light of fiery torches (*Bri.* II. ii. 386). Bérénice evokes the Emperor Titus at his father's funeral, dwelling on the splendour of that 'nuit enflammée' with its chiaroscuro of shadows and flames (*Bér.* I. v. 301).

Racine may on occasion have sought to exploit these visible contrasts for symbolic purposes. In *Britannicus* Junie's innocence is undoubtedly associated with obscurity and with the shadows of night, whilst the dazzling splendour of Néron's court is a place of corruption. To Néron's annoyance Junie's virtue lurks in the shadows and she protests that even from her obscure retreat she could not withstand the dazzling light of Néron's majesty (II. ii. 415; II. iii. 613). The spectator has seen Néron come on to the candle-lit stage surrounded by his courtiers and sees the innocent Junie emerge from darkness only to be confronted by the incipient monster basking in the light. *Britannicus* reverses the usual association of light with good and darkness with evil. Traditional symbolism can be seen in *Phèdre*. 'Men loved darkness rather than the light because their deeds were evil. For every one that doeth evil hateth the light lest his deeds should be reproved' (John 3: 13). Phèdre has shunned the light because she is consumed by guilt. For her first entrance Racine engineers an extraordinary blend of pagan and Christian symbolism. Phèdre comes on stage for one last look at the sun, but she is dazzled and shrinks back. 'You hate the daylight which you came to seek?' asks the bewildered Œnone (*Phè*. I. iii. 168). Through her confidant's insistent questioning Phèdre's sin is brought to light. Only when Phèdre finally dies and sinks back into darkness is the light of day cleansed of defilement (*Phè*. V. vii. 1641).[23] References to night and day in Racine's text have been exploited as lighting cues by directors. The 1870 Comédie-Française production of *Bérénice* under the aegis of Edouard Thierry picked up 'we still have enough daylight' and 'the queen leaves [. . .] this evening' (*Bér*. III. iv. 949; V. ii. 1262) to show Bérénice making her final exit in darkness escorted by torches (Chevalley, p. 109).

Sounds off-stage are frequently mentioned in Racine. The cries of the dying and the shouts of victory evoke the atmosphere of war and suffering (*Ale*. III. i. 700; IV. i. 957). Agrippine hears noise and tumult just before Burrhus rushes in

---

[23] Barko's view of the development of Racine's light symbolism, based on Goldmann, is perhaps over-schematic, and in his discussion of *Phèdre* he does not mention the possible biblical connotations of darkness, nor does Lapp, p. 132; see also Zimmermann, 'Lumière', for light/dark symbolism in *Britannicus*.

with news of Britannicus's murder (*Bri.* V. iii. 1609). Mithridate tells Monime: 'You hear shouts' (*Mit.* III. v. 1046). Achille urges Iphigénie not to fear the shouting crowds (*Iph.* V. ii. 1517).[24] Entrances are repeatedly marked by the phrase 'I hear noise' (e.g. *Pla.* I. ii. 60; *Bri.* I. i. 125). More specifically and dramatically Clytemnestre hears thunder which she interprets as the intervention of avenging gods (*Iph.* V. iv. 1697). None of these need to be represented mimetically; indeed the sometimes rowdy conditions of performance in the public theatres may have rendered useless any attempts to imitate undefined noise or mere shouts. Yet there were precedents for requiring sound effects. Boisrobert's *Palène* (1640) has a chariot race for which the stage directions read: 'After the sound of trumpets and some noise, a curtain opens and two chariots are seen' (Scherer, p. 170). Stage directions in Corneille's machine play *Andromède* (1650) specify for Eole's entrance: 'Here thunder begins to roll' (Act II, Scene iv). There is a similar stage direction in *Psyché* (1671), Act V, Scene vi. The affinities between Racine's *Iphigénie* and machine plays make it plausible that a thunder effect was intended at the climax of the play.[25]

Neglect of these cues can distort Racine in performance. According to Larthomas, Oreste's final madness is nowadays usually played for the words alone as a solitary virtuoso display by the actor; but Pylade is trying to save Oreste: 'Let's leave this palace now or lose our chance. Our troops defend the door but only just. The crowd is up in arms and after us' (*And.* V. v. 1583). Larthomas protests: why should Pylade efface himself so that the actor playing Oreste can hog the limelight? Why neglect the real violence of the theatrical situation? 'What!' exclaims the French scholar, 'in this palace surrounded by people, no shout is heard? No banging at the door?' (p. 141).

---

[24] Lapp (p. 80) suggests that Racine was too timid to specify actual off-stage shouts for *Alexandre*, since Axiane says only 'Le cri des mourants vient *presque* jusqu'à moi' (III. i. 700); but that a more confident Racine intended off-stage shouts for *Mithridate* and *Iphigénie*.

[25] Thunder effects were sometimes created by pistol shots (*Mémoire de Mahelot*, introduction, p. 39 n.). Mahelot specifies thunder effects frequently, Laurent never, even for Molière's *Dom Juan*. So the absence from Laurent's list of any thunder effect for Racine's *Iphigénie* is not evidence against the hypothesis that a thunder effect was intended.

(f) Interpreting the Décor

Did Racine collaborate with the stage-managers? It is plausible, though it remains speculative. But suppose that Racine played no part and that the scene-painter alone scrutinized the text for references to the décor. Where did he find the 'palace with columns' for *Andromaque*? For the single word *voûtes* in the text of *Phèdre* did he go to the trouble of constructing a vaulted palace? Why should Racine's tragedies, unlike the majority, have the benefit of special scenery if the stage designer could simply use the conventional *palais à volonté*? Paradoxically, the fact that some of the scenery details are not strictly necessary to the action seems to be best explained by the intervention of Racine in his anxiety to procure certain effects which the stage designer on his own could not gather from the text. There is evidence for Racine's personal interest in the declamation of his verse by his leading actress and for his involvement in the production of *Esther*.[26] It is plausible that he should also have been concerned with the scenery at the Hôtel de Bourgogne, and perhaps even have dictated the precise décor in order to distinguish himself from his rivals.

What is the importance of the references to scenery in Racine's text? The alert reader will neglect nothing which can stimulate his imagination. He will find that Racine's characters, just as they are conscious of their own culture and have lived their own individual lives, are also familiar with the places they inhabit. For the spectator and the director the matter is more delicate. Theatrical illusion floats between reality and fiction. Words can be substitutes for things. Le Bidois rejects what he calls the 'artifices of painted canvas'. In his opinion 'the material scenery of Racinian tragedy [...] is merely a setting of little significance'; the true décor is to be found in the watchful eyes of the protagonists, ever alert to interpret facial expression and to seize upon revealing gestures (pp. 73–6). Such stage business is certainly essential to Racine's theatricality, but the evidence of the *Mémoire de Mahelot* is decisive: it was with backdrops of painted canvas that Racine's tragedies were staged at the Hôtel de Bourgogne, the theatre which Racine himself favoured from

---

[26] Louis Racine, *Mémoires*, pp. 58–9, 89.

the moment when he transferred *Alexandre* from Molière's company to the more prestigious Comédiens du Roi.

Margaret McGowan has evoked the social significance of the court performances of Racine's tragedies. They could show to the courtiers a familiar world: magnificent décor, dazzling displays of absolute power, the constraints of protocol, the host of attendants always surrounding the prince. Her conclusion insists on the allusive style of Racine: 'Assumptions about his spectators' familiarity with the place of the action allowed him great scope for the elaboration of a style which was essentially allusive' (p. 183). There is certainly a network of courtly allusions but there are also precise details of place and décor which verge on a kind of mimetic realism which paradoxically can create distance between spectator and the spectacle. Whilst for courtiers the palace in *Mithridate*, the imperial apartment in *Britannicus*, the closet in *Bérénice*, could well be the prolongation of their real environment, it was not so at the Hôtel de Bourgogne where the backdrops of other plays representing sea, ships, or tents, a Turkish saloon or a vaulted palace, had little connection with the daily life of most spectators. In these cases the objective was another kind of theatrical illusion, a kind of local colour, designed to appeal to the imagination of Parisian spectators and to transport them into a world far distant from their own; an unfamiliar world, but one which was intended to be convincing in so far as Racine's text was supported by the scenic resources available to the stage designers of the period.

Today, of course, there is no need for the textual references to scenery to be necessarily accompanied by mimetic equivalents. The modern director will exercise his right to interpret Racine according to his own scenic imagination. Some idea of this freedom can be gained from photographs of modern productions of Racine, for example in the edition of Racine's theatre by Morel and Viala. Such considerations, however, do not justify dismissing Racine's references to scenery entirely.[27] Of course *Phèdre* can be performed without a vaulted palace. Of course one can dispense with the sight of sea and ships in *Andromaque* and *Iphigénie*—provided their importance is not forgotten. But

---

[27] Issacharoff implies that Racinian characters do not refer to scenic place at all (p. 83).

the drama will be misunderstood if one takes no account of the movements of Agrippine, Burrhus, or Britannicus in front of Néron's door, if one forgets the decoration and the special character of the closet in *Bérénice*, if one is unaware of the significance of the secluded room in *Bajazet*. Neither *Alexandre* nor *Iphigénie* make sense except in tents and in the middle of an army. To reduce *Esther* or *Athalie* to a *palais à volonté* would be to distort them completely.

Not that everything is impeccable. There was a price to pay for setting the action in a single precise place. It is strange that *Bérénice* should start with Antiochus penetrating Titus's closet in order to pay a visit to Bérénice (Act I, Scene i), and the abbé de Villars, a contemporary spectator, picked on this implausibility with facetious glee: 'Could Antiochus only visit Bérénice through Titus's closet?' (p. 244). Moreover, Racine has such trouble in explaining Antiochus's movements between Acts IV and V that he finally jettisoned his feeble explanations by suppressing Act IV, Scene ix, altogether in 1676. But at the cost of a few implausibilities Racine succeeded in creating scenic spaces which were truly theatrical. This was an advance on Corneille's fictitious locations which had only a verbal existence, though the conventions of ambiguous place do not disappear entirely in Racine.

Racinian stage space is predominantly precise but never simple. Barthes outlines a useful tripartite structure which suggests possible symbolic connotations. First, just off-stage the 'Chamber', the seat of authority. Secondly, the stage itself is the 'Antechamber' where characters wait in fear. Dividing them is the 'Door', a threshold across which is transgression. For the 'Door' can be substituted the 'Curtain', hiding the eye of authority. The third element in Barthes's structure is the 'Exterior', the place of death, of escape, or of recounted events (pp. 15–20). However, this schema can only really be applied to *Britannicus, Bajazet, Esther*, and *Athalie*. As far as it goes it is a useful concept, but it does not embrace the diversity and individuality of Racinian stage space in all twelve plays. Each play is characterized by a different relationship between mimetic and diegetic space. *La Thébaïde* represents a hesitant experiment with spatial dynamics. Mimetic space is strongest in *Andromaque*,

Les Plaideurs, *Britannicus*, *Bérénice*, *Esther*, and *Athalie*; diegetic space predominates in *Mithridate* and *Phèdre*; the relationship is more or less evenly balanced in *Alexandre*, *Bajazet*, and *Iphigénie*.

2

On Stage, Off Stage

J'ai cru le voir sortir tel qu'il était entré
(*Bajazet*)

Racine's characters are constantly coming or going. Even the longest scene lasts only about five minutes. The quick succession of characters entering and leaving gives the drama an agitated and restless air. The restricted number of characters on stage at any one time—rarely more than four—was an invitation to achieve maximum effect with minimum means. According to seventeenth-century French conventions it was the entrance or exit of a character which created scene divisions. A new scene did not signify a new place or a different setting, but a change in the group of characters on stage. Convention also required that from scene to scene at least one character should continue on stage to serve as a link. This was called *liaison des scènes*. The stage should not be left empty except at the end of each of the five acts. Most dramatists, including Racine, cheerfully disregarded *liaison des scènes* when it suited them.[1]

'Entrances and exits mark key junctures in a play [. . .] The timing, manner and direction of these comings and goings are fully in the control of the playwright, and his disposition of them may well signpost the way to our understanding of what he is about' (Taplin, p. 31). These comments help for French drama. The manner of getting characters on and off stage is a good measure of the theatrical imagination of seventeenth-century French dramatists. If the dramatist conceived his tragedy merely as a string of verbal encounters, he had only to whisk his characters on and off stage at whim. D'Aubignac complained of incompetent dramatists who 'put a man on stage to recite

---

[1] e.g. *And.* Act IV, Scenes i–ii; *Bér.* Act IV, Scenes ii–iii; *Iph.* Act II, Scenes i–ii; Act IV, Scenes i–ii. The break was disguised as *liaison de fuite*.

whatever they had dreamed up, and took him off when their inspiration was exhausted' (*Pratique*, iii. 7, p. 223). Such entrances and exits betrayed the dramatist who merely manipulated his characters like puppets.

The ideal was formulated by Corneille, though he did not observe it in practice: 'One must, if possible, provide a reason for the entrance and exit for each actor; I hold this rule indispensable for exits'; but he allowed that the first entrance in each act need not be motivated (*Discours des trois unités*, p. 69). D'Aubignac was more flexible, and warned against laborious explanations: 'The spectator must discover, almost without realizing it, the reason which brings an actor on stage' (*Pratique*, iv. 1, p. 253). These recommendations fell short of requiring the moment of entrance or exit to be a source of theatrical excitement in itself. Of course, the entrance of a new character is in itself a source of interest. In a dull play it may be the only source of interest; a new face, a new costume, a new body can break the monotony. One finds weak attempts at motivation when the entrance is welcomed by some comment on its opportuneness, or, in the case of an exit, when characters ran out of things to say, they could be snatched away with a complaint that the discussion was not getting anywhere. None of this amounts to much. Corneille tended to pay little attention to motivation. He simply engineered a series of meetings which showed characters 'grappling with a changing situation occasioned by their comings and goings, by their encounters'.[2] The real theatrical challenge was to make the visual effect of entrances and exits striking, significant, or suggestive. Racine deployed a varied arsenal of devices to heighten the theatrical impact of getting his characters on and off stage.

(*a*) Significant Entrances

The start of the play was the moment of keenest anticipation. The front curtain opened to reveal an empty stage. The audience waited for the actors to appear from behind the back-drop and make their way to the front of the stage.[3] The first lines had to

---

[2] Barnwell, '"They Have Their Entrances and Exits"', p. 56.
[3] These details are implicit in Corneille's discussion of the opening scene of *Cinna* (*Disc. des trois unités*, pp. 69–70); see also Scherer, pp. 279–84.

be arresting. Racine favoured the convention of representing a conversation in progress. All his tragedies start in the middle of a conversation which is deemed to have started before the play begins. This crucial first entrance is made dynamic by expressions of surprise, often in the very first line: 'What? will you resist this powerful king'; 'What? while Néron stays asleep, you wait for him to wake?'; 'Is it you, my dear Elise? Oh thrice blessed day!' These are the first lines of *Alexandre, Britannicus*, and *Esther*. The remainder of Racine's first entrances present variants of this technique, the expressions of astonishment being implied or slightly delayed.

For later entrances suspense and anticipation could be created by announcing the imminent arrival of a protagonist. Etéocle waiting for Polynice discloses to his confidant: 'The closer he comes, the more odious he seems to me' (*Thé*. IV. i. 933). The spectator is prepared for the hostile meeting and is alerted to the significance of the physical distance between the brothers when they come together on stage. A whole scene may serve as preparation. Œnone appears a few moments before Phèdre's first entrance to clear the path for her mistress (*Phè*. Act I, Scene ii). In a longer anticipatory scene, Zacharie announces that Athalie has profaned the temple. The horror of his mother, his sister, and the chorus of Levite girls scattering before the odious queen reinforces the drama of Athalie's entrance on stage (*Ath*. Act II, Scene ii). Another form of preparation is a long postponed entrance which finally satisfies protracted curiosity. The spectator has to wait for half the play before being accorded sight of the radiant Alexandre (*Ale*. Act III, Scene iv).

In contrast to entrances which were prepared, surprise entrances, embellished by the agitated reactions of the characters already on stage, also created excitement. Jocaste almost collapses at the sight of Etéocle appearing with blood on his clothes (*Thé*. Act I, Scene iii; Pl. 24). Such an effect is further enhanced if a character enters who has been believed dead. The entrances of Porus, Mithridate, and Thésée acquire added piquancy from such resurrections (*Ale*. Act V, Scene iii; *Mit*. Act II, Scene ii; *Phè*. Act III, Scene iv). The surprise entrance of an unwelcome character is full of theatrical potential. Racine revelled in this device, repeatedly ringing the changes. The exultant Hermione greets her rival's untimely entrance with a cruel aside: 'What have I to say to her!' (*And.* III. iv. 858). A surprise entrance is especially unwelcome when it interrupts a declaration of love before it has elicited a clear response and so leaves the lover in agonized suspense. Xipharès is interrupted by Pharnace's entrance; Hippolyte by Phèdre's (*Mit.* Act I, Scene iii; *Phè.* Act II, Scene iii). The rules of gallantry required that the woman should make some response to the formal declaration of love (Garaud, p. 21). The unwelcome entrance frustrates the desire of Xipharès and Hippolyte to learn the feelings of their mistresses, Monime and Aricie respectively. An unwelcome entrance catches some lovers *in flagrante delicto* or its equivalent. Britannicus kneeling at Junie's feet is caught off guard by Néron's sudden appearance (*Bri.* Act III, Scene viii). Roxane catches Bajazet and Atalide talking together (*Baj.* Act III, Scene v). In similar vein Roxane surprises Atalide while she is reading an incriminating letter from Bajazet (*Baj.* Act IV, Scene ii), echoing a similar scene in comic register when Chicanneau caught Isabelle reading a letter from her lover (*Pla.* Act II, Scene iii).

Danger associated with the place represented by the stage could illustrate aspects of character or the deeper significance of the situation. Britannicus dashes on stage, in front of Néron's very door, startling and alarming Agrippine: 'Ah Prince, where are you running to? What restless zeal propels you blindly amongst your enemies?' (*Bri.* I. iii. 287). So Britannicus's first entrance establishes his character in theatrical terms (McAuley, p. 352). It is the visual embodiment of Racine's conception of his young, courageous, and credulous hero (first preface to *Britannicus*, p. 404). Britannicus's peril is magnified by his next entrance, where there is even greater danger, because Néron is spying on him from behind a curtain (Act II, Scene vi). There is danger, too, for Esther. She braves the peril of Assuérus's throne room, supported by Elise and escorted by four Israelites holding her train. She faints at Assuérus's anger but is revived by the touch of his kindly sceptre. Le Brun's illustration depicts this symbolic entrance, which advances the plot, creates excitement, and carries symbolic significance, for it is a visual representation of Assuérus's ferocity giving way to tenderness for Esther, the key to the whole play (*Est.* Act II, Scene vii; Pl. 13).

Kings and emperors entered in majesty surrounded by their
suite or guards. The audience would expect it of them. Powerful people did not wander around alone. Attendants were a
visible sign of power. The entrances of Néron, Titus, and
Mithridate follow convention in this respect. Each starts Act II
with a splendid entry. Alexandre has a similar entrance even
later in his play (*Ale.* Act III, Scene iv). The reader of these
scenes may wonder why the suite is dismissed almost immediately. It seems wasteful, but there were practical reasons. 'Five
or six people get in each other's way when they appear on our
stage' said D'Aubignac (*Pratique*, iv. 1, p. 246). The speedy
dismissal of the suite cleared the stage of the encumbering
bodies. At a stroke it also created an atmosphere of privacy,
giving the audience the illusion of eavesdropping upon the
secrets of the mighty.

Dramatists ignored royal etiquette at their peril. Something in
the barbaric air of Buthrotum made Racine's King Pyrrhus
wander round his palace seeking out his social inferior.
Subligny's ready wit ridiculed Racine for not knowing the
protocol: 'I haven't seen anyone who did not laugh when
Pyrrhus says to Oreste "I was looking for you everywhere"
instead of summoning him to his private room' (*La Folle
Querelle*, p. 44, referring to *And.* Act I, Scene ii, and Act II,
Scene iv). Almost as a riposte to this criticism, Racine in his next
tragedy exploited the unattended entrance of the Empress
Agrippine to proclaim her restless ambition. The empress is
reproached by her confidant for 'wandering in the palace without suite or escort' and the confidant's words invite the spectator
to join in the astonishment that the 'mother of Caesar should
wait alone at his door' (*Bri.* Act I, Scene i). Perhaps the previous
critical reaction to the breach of etiquette in *Andromaque* alerted
Racine to the possibilities of exploiting such breaches for
dramatic purposes.

The inversion of majestic entrances was also seen when
pitiable entrances occurred late in the play as part of the
dénouement. Here the visual effect is enhanced by the entrance
of a dying protagonist who cannot walk unaided. According to
Racine's stage direction 'Guards who support Mithridate'
accompany the king (SD, *Mit.* Act V, Scene v). Mithridate is
'covered with blood and dust'; he is 'bloody and carried by

soldiers'. Monime cries with horror at the sight of 'the blood of the father and the tears of the son' (*Mit.* V. iv. 1595, 1553, and 1646). Chauveau's illustration conforms to these textual indications and shows the guards supporting Mithridate, who is in evident distress, while Monime weeps (Pl. 11). Porus has a similar entrance in Act V, Scene iii, of *Alexandre*. The text gives less guidance on visual appearance than in the case of *Mithridate*, but Chauveau plausibly depicts a physically enfeebled Porus half carried by Alexandre's soldiers with Cléofile weeping behind Alexandre (Pl. 5).

Life off-stage erupts into the visible action when a character enters pursued by another. Eriphile and Doris are startled by the entrance of Agamemnon fleeing the embraces of the daughter whose ghastly fate he is endeavouring to conceal (*Iph.* Act II, Scene ii). Bérénice is equally determined to tear herself from the hands of those restraining her (*Bér.* Act IV, Scene v), and she later makes a second irruption on stage pursued by Titus (*Bér.* Act V, Scene v). Such entrances are full of both physical and mental agitation. They are especially striking in *Bérénice*: 'So much for the view that nothing happens in this "elegy" [. . .] Racine prefers the vehemence of bodily action' (Voltz, pp. 60–1).

Finally, the entrance of messengers bearing news produces a vivid theatrical effect. It had pitfalls. They had to play the part well. D'Aubignac is sensitive to the difficulties:

The first time an actor comes on stage he can enter in three states of mind, either without passion, or with strong passion or somewhere in between. The two extremes are easy, since a good actor will know what voice and gesture is required to express violent passion. The difficulty lies with half passion (*demi-passion*) when a third or fourth actor comes, usually with good or bad news. This is often spoken with either too much or too little passion and so the audience laugh at the most serious parts of the play. The remedy is to give the actor a few words of calm, then work up to the half passion so that his voice rises by degrees and his gestures become more animated with his speech. Or like Mondory, who would walk up and down the stage before speaking, shaking his head, raising and lowering his eyes and striking different attitudes according to the feeling he had to express. This allowed him to hit the right degree of half passion. (*Pratique*, iv. 1, pp. 258–9.)

Racine sometimes indicates when the messenger enters in a state of 'full passion'. In *La Thébaïde* news of the broken truce is brought by a soldier whose demeanour must correspond to Hémon's description: 'But what does this soldier want? He is full of agitation' (*Thé.* II. iii. 563). There is a similar instruction for Zatime announcing the insurrection of Acomat (*Baj.* V. vi. 1626). More frequently the entrance of messengers is not marked by precise indications of demeanour. The actor is left to employ discretion and possibly to use Mondory's non-verbal warming-up techniques described by D'Aubignac in order to give the entrance its appropriate theatrical impact.

A rapid sequence of entrances often creates cumulative tension. This is especially evident in *Bajazet*, where the successive entrances of Acomat, Bajazet, and Roxane in Act III, and of Acomat, Zaïre, and Osmin in Act V, accelerate and intensify the dramatic pace.

Some characters never enter. One of the most significant is Octavie, Néron's spurned wife in *Britannicus*. Her ghostly presence dominates the play. For Junie she is a source of consolation; for Néron she is an obstacle; for Agrippine she is a stick with which to beat her undutiful son. Her presence is evoked by phrases such as 'Let us go and see Octavie' (*Bri.* V. ii. 1568). Racine never went as far as Corneille, who entitled *Pompée* with the name of a character who never appears, but *Octavie* as an alternative title for *Britannicus* would not do violence to Racine's subject.[4]

(b) Costume

Costume can be a significant element in the entrance of a new character. In Racine's time tragedies set in Greece or Rome were costumed in what was described as 'ancient dress' or 'Roman-style dress'. What exactly this meant is not clear. There was certainly no attempt at authentic period costume. In this respect the illustrations of Moitte, Peyron, Girodet, and Chaudet in the Didot edition of 1801 are misleading (Pls. 24–31). Actors in

---

[4] For a discussion of other non-appearing characters, especially Pallas in *Britannicus*, Amurat and Orcan in *Bajazet*, Calchas in *Iphigénie*, see Prophète, *Les Para-personnages*.

Racine's time wore wigs, hats with plumes, and sometimes gloves. What is certain is that the costumes were spectacularly rich. Real gold and real silver trimmings adorned a *habit à la romaine* according to Chappuzeau (p. 111). The inventories of actors' costumes confirm this opulence (Lough, pp. 71–5). La Champmeslé, leading actress in Racine's tragedies, owned seven Roman-style costumes, one valued at the huge sum of 1,100 *livres*. But the verbal descriptions in the inventories, though detailed, give little help in visualizing the costumes. Nor can the illustrations to Racine's published theatre be relied on. However, the engraving representing a scene from Corneille's *Cinna*, with the spectators actually present (Pl. 1), may give an impression of the mixture of Roman and French dress which was worn by the actors in this play, and which would also have been appropriate for Racine's *Britannicus* and *Bérénice*.[5] There is some external evidence for costume in performances of Racine's *Alexandre*. Cléofile appeared to be wearing 'pearls, rubies and all the precious stones which India could provide' whilst Axiane 'glittered like Diana' in rich clothing.[6] Each first entrance of a protagonist was at the very least an opportunity for the spectator to relish a dazzling display of extravagant luxury.

But Racine exploited conventional costume for dramatic effect. At the start of Act IV *Bérénice* makes an entrance characterized by the disorder of the rich costume. Phénice alludes to these visible signs of distress: 'Let me arrange these veils which are detached, and these stray hairs which hide your eyes' (*Bér.* IV. ii. 969). Bérénice is not sorry to let her distraught appearance plead with Titus in her favour, yet the splendour of her royal finery is no compensation for her emotional anguish: 'Let him see what he has wrought, Phénice. What use, alas, are these vain ornaments to me?' (*Bér.* IV. ii. 973). Rich clothes also adorn and fret Phèdre, Thésée's queen. At her first entrance they signal the royal status of which she is unworthy: 'How these vain adornments, how these veils weigh down upon me' (*Phè.* I. iii. 158). Monime's diadem visible at each entrance elevates her as Mithridate's wife, yet enslaves her person and her passions.

---

[5] For La Champmeslé's inventory and comments on the *Cinna* engraving, see Heuzey, p. 30.

[6] Robinet, i. 537–8; Lyonnet, pp. 40–1; Heuzey, p. 30.

Oppressive finery on stage mirrored the alienations of richly clad nobility and royalty. Elisabeth-Charlotte, duchess of Orléans, applied Monime's phrase 'crowned slave' to the restricted lives of the royal family under the later years of Louis XIV (letter of 17 August 1710; Moureau, p. 275). She also quoted Agamemnon's 'slaves that we are' (*Iph.* I. i. 365) to illustrate the same point (letter of 14 August 1707).[7] In *Esther* the Jewish queen of the Persian realm is raised to royal and lonely eminence, yet sees herself as slave to the king who has elevated her (*Est.* II. vii. 663). The costumes for the private performances of *Esther* exceeded even the customary luxury of public theatres. Madame de Maintenon 'had magnificent costumes made for all the actresses' and they used 'the same sumptuous ornaments which the king had worn formerly in the ballets'.[8] Esther refers frequently to her costume in Act I in order to emphasize her horror of vain luxury. In Act II the grandeur of her costume is augmented by a train supported by four young Jewish women, in conformity with the biblical account (SD, *Est.* Act II, Scene vii; Pl. 13). The ambivalence of royal accoutrements is common to *Bérénice, Mithridate, Phèdre,* and *Esther.*

In addition to visual effects derived from conventional costume, most plays furnish an example of Racine's care in specifying some particularity relating to costume. Such effects do not have to be reproduced mimetically on stage. In terms of production, any visual effect permits of maximal or minimal or sometimes purely verbal representation. A theatrical reading, however, highlights the places where Racine is appealing to visual imagination in the performance text. Whilst costume has a close link with entrances because it strikes first when a character enters, the implications of special details of costume often develop during the action on stage and can reinforce the significance of the play as a whole.

Blood on king Etéocle's clothes inaugurates *La Thébaïde*, this tragedy of bloodbond and bloodshed. Is it Etéocle's blood or his brother's? asks the anguished mother, jumping to the worst conclusion. It is neither. Etéocle casually dismisses his mother's fears. The blood belongs to some insolent soldiers he has killed

---

[7] I am grateful to Professor Yarrow for assistance with the correspondence of the duchess of Orléans.

[8] Picard, *Carrière,* pp. 396 and 404, quoting memoirs of Manseau and Mère Du Pérou; Lyonnet, p. 186.

(*Thé.* I. ii. 53). The action of *La Thébaïde* works towards the moment when the king's blood is really shed. Créon reports how it spurts to the ground. It is not essential that blood-stains on Etéocle's clothes should be seen by the spectator when he first enters. They may be as spotless as in Moitte's illustration (Pl. 24), but Racine creates the image of bloodstained costume and the image is reinforced by the constant references to blood throughout the play.[9]

The significance of costume is established in *Les Plaideurs* when Dandin contrasts his lawyer's robes with the frivolous ribbons worn by his son (*Pla.* I. iv. 88). Act II starts with L'Intimé entering disguised as a court usher, though Léandre is still wearing the costume of a fashionable young man about town complete with 'blond wig', which, says L'Intimé, he should exchange for sober black hair (*Pla.* II. i. 304). Léandre's next entrance (Act II, Scene v) is enhanced by his disguise as a *commissaire*, his blond wig now indeed exchanged for black hair. He reappears later in normal clothes (Act II, Scene x), the quick changes making mockery of Dandin's eulogy of the lawyer's robes in Act I, Scene iv. The contrast between gentlemanly and legal costume is clearly depicted in Chauveau's illustration (Pl. 7).

Everything suggests that *Bajazet* offered not only an evocation of a Turkish saloon but also a series of Turkish-style costumes to delight the audience at the first entrance of each character. Chauveau's illustration of Atalide fainting may offer a seventeenth-century French view of Turkish costume (Pl. 10). The portrait of La Champmeslé attributed to Mignard is said to represent her in the costume of Atalide (*Album*, p. 153) and it has some affinities with the costume in Chauveau's illustration. Corneille is reported to have spoken of 'Turkish dress' in *Bajazet*. Louis Racine recorded that the Comédie-Française played *Bajazet* in 'long robes and turbans', and this tradition may go back to the first performances in 1672.[10] However, the

---

[9] In earlier versions l. 46 was 'Ah! mon fils, de quel sang revenez-vous taché?' In 1697 Racine amended this to 'Quelles traces de sang vois-je sur vos habits?' Edwards comments 'L'expression *sur vos habits* [. . .] localise l'image et la rend encore plus visuelle' (introduction to *La Thébaïde*, p. 86), His introduction mentions other cases where Racine's revisions reinforce visual or theatrical effects.

[10] Corneille anecdote in J. R. de Segrais, *Œuvres* (1755), ii. 43; L. Racine, *Œuvres* (1743–7), ii. 283, both quoted by Lough, p. 72.

most significant aspect of costume is Bajazet's sword. His
entrance in Act II without a sword signifies that he is Roxane's
prisoner, whilst in Act III he enters 'with weapons in his hand'
(*Baj*. III. iv. 947). It will be shown later how important Bajazet's
weapons are (Chapter 7, section *b*).

Racine's prose sketch for the first act of *Iphigénie en Tauride*
shows his interest in costume. There is a reference to the Greek
costume which fatally betrayed Oreste and his campanion (Act
I, Scene ii); this would probably have been represented on stage.
He also refers to Iphigénie's costume when she was first brought
to Tauris (Act I, Scene iv).

The possible scandal in *Esther* of seeing schoolgirl actresses
play male parts in male clothing was averted by Racine's appeal
to historical accuracy. He reassured his readers: 'These [male]
characters were none the less played by girls with all the
seemliness of their sex. This was all the easier for them because
in the old days the costume of Persian and Jewish men was long
robes falling to the ground' (preface to *Esther*, p. 831). The most
striking male costume in *Esther* is Mardochée's 'frightful hair-
shirt' and hair covered in ashes (I. iii. 159). It is an arresting
visual contrast to the finery of the Persian court. Mardochée's
costume and unexpected entrance represent visually the religious
and geographical contrast between rich Persian Susa and Jewish
Sion reduced to ashes. The chorus sings: 'Pitiable Sion, what has
become of your glory? [. . .] You are now but dust' (*Est*. I. ii.
132). Sébastien Le Clerc, who engraved the frontispiece to
Esther from sketches by Le Brun, may have drawn on accounts
of the actual performance by the girls of Saint-Cyr, for by
comparison with Le Brun he seems to have softened Assuérus's
features (Guibert, p. 37). The somewhat effeminate Assuérus in
the engraving seems inappropriate for the terrifying monarch.
This is a hint that the illustration may be closer to actual
performance than is usual.

Athalie was performed at Saint-Cyr without special scenery
and in regulation school clothes.[11] Yet the text emphasizes the
importance of Joas's long white linen robe. It sets him apart
from the adult characters crowded on stage for his first entrance

---

[11] Manseau, *Mémoires*, ed. Taphanel (Versailles, 1902), 157–8, *NCR* 265;
Lyonnet, p. 204.

when summoned by Athalie for interrogation (*Ath*. Act II, Scene vii). There are clear indications of further symbolism. Athalie invites the child to exchange the white robe for rich clothes (*Ath*. II. vii. 694), whilst Joad urges him to remember the white robe as a symbol of poverty and orphanhood (*Ath*. IV. iii. 1407).[12]

(*c*) Significant Exits

The exit of a character marks the end of a scene. Many scenes are verbal duels and may end with a whimper or a bang. Weak exits are rare in Racine. Assailed by two women, mother and daughter, Créon laboriously disengages himself: 'I will do this, madam, and spare you my very presence. My obligations reinforce your contempt for me. I must make way for your beloved son. You know the king did bid me wait upon him. Adieu. Let Hémon and Polynice come' (*Thé*. I. v. 284). It is rare for Racine to end a verbal battle so lamely. Much more characteristic is Achille's exit in *Iphigénie*. When he has angered Agamemnon into breaking off his betrothal to Iphigénie, Achille fires one last shot before storming off stage—the father will have to reckon with Achille's valour before he lays his knife upon his daughter's heart. This insolent exit and threat is exactly the event which makes Agamemnon more determined than ever to sacrifice his daughter to the gods (*Iph*. IV. vii. 1431), though he later changes his mind when full horror of the act dawns upon him. In *Phèdre* Thésée's accusations against Hippolyte all but extort from Aricie the revelation of the horrible truth, but she exits saying: 'I imitate your son's restraint and flee your presence, so that I am not forced to break my silence' (*Phè*. V. iii. 1449). Aricie's physical departure takes from Thésée his last chance to learn the truth before Hippolyte's death.

When the verbal battle is in the form of an interrogation, Racine excels at engineering an economical yet meaningful exit. When Titus can no longer endure Bérénice's questions, his parting words invest his departure with an emotional charge as

---

[12] Phillips, however, claims that in Racine there is 'complete disregard of physical appearance (apart from Bérénice's dishevelled hair and Phèdre's veils)' ('Theatricality', p. 37).

profound as the words are simple: 'Let us go, Paulin. I can say nothing to her' (*Bér.* II. iv. 624). Agamemnon is harassed by Iphigénie's anxious enquiries. After a few simple questions and doom-laden answers, she makes her final innocent request: 'May I join your prayers at the altar?' It is too much for Agamemnon. He is dumb with emotion, and can only flee the stage with the celebrated ambiguity of 'You will be there, my daughter. Adieu' (*Iph.* II. ii. 578). Such exits frustrate the interrogator's desire for knowledge and invest their ignorance with emotional intensity.

Other exits depict frustrated physical desire. Antigone evades Créon's grasp. Her exit deprives him of the object of his passion (*Thé.* Act V, Scene iii). The pathos of Monime's command that Xipharès must never see her again is intensified by her exit: 'I must leave. Remember, Prince, to avoid me and so be worthy of the tears you will cost me' (*Mit.* II. vi. 745). Monime slips away from Xipharès and leaves him in suicidal torment.

For the exit to be significant it does not have to involve a protagonist. The discreet exit of a confidant marks the turning point in relations between Andromaque and Pyrrhus. 'Go and await me, Phoenix', says Pyrrhus, ridding himself of a hostile presence. He gives Andromaque one more chance, and so brings about his own death (*And.* Act III, Scene vi). Act IV of *Iphigénie* is rich in a sequence of exits which mark significant developments in the plot. The visual background of soldiers causes Agamemnon to repent of ordering the death of his daughter. His monologue concludes: 'Eurybate, summon the princess and the queen. They need fear no more.' Eurybate's exit means safety for Iphigénie (*Iph.* Act IV, Scene viii). At the end of the act Eriphile's path diverges from that of the royal family, and signifies her treachery. She goes by another exit to betray Agamemnon's rescue bid: 'That's not our way [. . .] Come, I tell you. I shall uncover everything to Calchas.' Her words imply that she and Doris leave the stage by a different exit from that taken by the characters at the end of the preceding scene (*Iph.* Act IV, Scenes x and xi).

When an attempted exit collides with an entrance, it can change the course of the drama. This theatrical contrivance can be camouflaged by generating excitement to divert the spectator from seeing the hand of coincidence too obviously at work. The plot of *Britannicus* would collapse if Britannicus, on the point of leaving Narcisse, were not detained by the arrival of Junie (*Bri.* Act III, Scene vii). Without Junie's entrance keeping Britannicus on stage at that precise moment, Néron could not have caught Britannicus kneeling at Junie's feet. In *Bajazet* Atalide's peace of mind might have been preserved if she had left the stage before Acomat's arrival with his exaggerated account of the reconciliation of Bajazet and Roxane. A second coincidence in the same act is Bajazet's entrance which prevents Atalide's exit. The sequence of entrances which prevent exits bring about the tragedy (*Baj.* Act III, Scenes i and iii).

Steps off stage can be steps leading to death. Racine's first tragedy has a striking example. Jocaste's exit highlights her despair at the implacable enmity between her sons and takes her to suicide (*Thé.* Act IV, Scene iii), The movement is repeated in later plays. The steps which take Britannicus through Néron's door are the steps which lead Britannicus to his death (*Bri.* Act V, Scene i; McAuley, p. 353). Racine prepares the spectator to interpret Bajazet's exit as his death warrant, when Roxane pronounces her single word 'Depart' (*Baj.* Act V, Scene iv). She uses her power to destroy him, and to destroy herself.[13] Iphigénie leaves the stage in an atmosphere of unbearable emotion, begging her frantic mother not to cause an undignified scene and disengaging herself with a final: 'Eurybate, conduct your victim to the altar' (*Iph.* V. iii. 1666). In the prose draft of *Iphigénie en Tauride* Iphigénie's exit is the signal that the two Greeks shipwrecked in Tauris must be sacrificed by her. This prompts a passionate debate between the king and his son, who pleads for the life of the two Greeks (Act I, Scenes iii–iv). Athalie's death is conveyed to the spectator by Joad's command that the temple be not defiled by the shedding of her blood. She too makes a last exit to death (*Ath.* Act V, Scene vi). In each of these cases Racine has invested exits with fatal significance.

(*d*) Choruses

No amount of commentary can convincingly evoke the effect of the choruses entering and leaving in *Esther* and *Athalie*. The

---

[13] See Brody's commentary on 'Sortez': pp. 288–90.

twenty-four bodies on stage for about two-thirds of each play, as melodious singers or mute spectators, makes these two musical tragedies quite different visually from the earlier tragedies.[14] The most striking feature is the entrance of such a large number of people. The Jewish children in *Esther* make an appropriately disordered entrance in Act I. Racine specifies that 'the chorus all enter on stage from several different places' (SD, *Est.* Act I, Scene ii). It is not the formal entrance of a Greek tragic chorus but a crowd of shy children. Elise's astonishment reinforces the stage direction: 'What a numerous crowd of innocent beauties crowd in before my gaze, appearing from every side' (*Est.* I. ii. 122). The chorus have a simple, natural role in *Esther*. The children's vocal talents are shown off to Elise. Their innocent singing throws Mardochée's dramatic entrance into relief. Later they underscore the issues raised by the massacre edict and Esther's prayer. Some of them attend their mistress in the throne room. They sing to entertain the guests at Esther's banquet.

The entrances and exits of the chorus have a quite different function in *Athalie*. Whilst in *Esther* the three acts take place in three settings, so that the exits of the chorus signal the end of each act, in *Athalie* the chorus links the five acts by its presence on stage. Racine explained: 'I have tried to imitate from the ancients that continuity of action which ensures that the stage never remains empty, the intervals between the acts simply being marked by hymns and moral observations of the chorus relating to the action' (preface to *Athalie*, p. 892). This is a striking departure from the intervals in the public theatres of Paris, which were filled by violin-playing and refreshments. It is almost as though Racine, having challenged Corneille's views on the virtual impossibility of setting plays in a single precise setting, was now challenging Corneille's disapproval of the singing of the Greek chorus on the grounds that simple violin music allowed the audience to discuss during the interval what they had seen during the previous act (*Discours des trois unités*, p.

---

[14] Chorus of 24 attested for *Esther* by Donneau de Visé in *Mercure Galant* (1689), 382; *NCR* 231. Stewart reproduces photographs of the chorus from his production of *Athalie* ('Mise en scène d'*Athalie*'); Le Roy gives several diagrams of the positions of the chorus.

69). The theatrical problem in *Athalie* was to contrive a suitably motivated entrance for the chorus in each act and to keep them on stage until there was an opportunity to get them off in the subsequent act.

The chorus enter carrying garlands and bedecked with flowers. This is consistent with the joyful day of festival, but provides a visual contrast with the dark presages voiced by Josabet. Their first song spanning the interval between Acts I and II celebrates the religious feast. They exit in Act II terrified at the profane approach of Athalie and her suite. Le Roy suggests that the chorus can be got off stage in small groups to emphasize significant moments in their singing and he indicates appropriate moments for their departure (p. 127).

The second choral entrance in Act II, Scene vii, is to accompany Eliacin while he is interrogated by Athalie. After the interrogation choral recitative and singing convey the emotional states generated by the interrogation they have just witnessed—joy, anxiety, fear, sombre foreboding. The transition from these elevated sentiments to low plotting is rationally motivated by Racine, but bristles with the danger of laughter in performance. The enemy priest Mathan and his confidant Nabal come to demand that Eliacin be handed over and so disturb the choral singing. The girls scatter in fear. Nabal is surprised: 'What is this? they all scatter and flee without replying to you!' Le Roy is sensitive to the potential ridicule: 'One has to be as stupid as Nabal to be surprised that the young girls of the chorus should scatter and flee in silence. It is essential not to allow the whole atmosphere of the temple to evaporate. It will be prudent not to present Mathan and Nabal in costumes which could excite laughter' (p. 167).

In Act III, Scene vii, the chorus re-enter quietly. They listen to Joad's prophecy, for which Racine specifies a mixture of music, singing, and speaking. The quiet dignity of the last lines of the choral interlude between Acts III and IV are indissoluble from the dignified entrance of Eliacin to start Act IV. The ceremonial arrival of the sword, book, and diadem is embellished by the presence of the chorus, but they discreetly withdraw for Joad to prepare Joas for his coronation. The exit of the chorus here is analogous to the departure of the imperial suite of Néron or Titus. Ceremony gives way to the intimacy of private discussion. The visual change renews interest in what is to follow.

The final entrance of the chorus presents no problem of motivation. The high priest has revealed the identity of Joas to the chief Levites (Act IV, Scene iii). The chorus are summoned to see the new king. Their final sung interlude between Acts IV and V participates in the martial excitement generated by the forthcoming battle against Athalie, yet also emphasizes the ambiguity of God's action. This is the choral climax of the play; thereafter their significance progressively diminishes. They are used only to make ready the throne for the recognition of Joas (Act V, Scene iii). It is the band of Levites who take over the theatrical spectacle for the final ambush of Athalie.

This survey of entrances and exits reveals that these key junctures of Racinian drama are used for maximum theatrical impact instead of simply marking transitions in the realignment of the action as in Corneille. This is achieved by varying degrees of contextualization. The mimetic quality of Racinian stage space provides a context for the entrances signifying danger (*Britannicus, Esther*) and the mimesis of surprise or alarm which greets such an entrance has an immediate impact upon the spectator. The social context operates when richly clad figures enter to perform actions inconsistent with their status (Agrippine, Bérénice, Phèdre). The verbal context endows exits with the power of signifying either frustrated desire or death.

3

Physical Action

Il faut des actions, et non pas des paroles
(*Iphigénie*)

The common view is that Racine's theatre is poor in physical action and rich in speech; but physical action and speech have a complex relationship which this chapter will explore. It starts with a preliminary examination of stage directions, both explicit and implicit, to show how physical movements are conveyed by words, and how words and actions can have parallel theatrical functions. Then physical action is shown at work as an important element in Racine's visual language. An accumulation of evidence is offered in order to overcome the traditional reluctance to recognize physical action as a significant feature of Racinian drama. The survey starts with the human body, which can be seen standing, sitting, kneeling, collapsing, or prostrate. Racine also employs various forms of bodily contact such as supporting, restraining, constraining, and embracing. The handling of stage properties, such as letters or swords, also involves physical action. After this evaluation of features which recur from play to play, the connotations of visual language are examined in detail for the last two acts of *Athalie*.

(*a*) Stage Directions

It is commonplace to underestimate the nature and importance of the stage directions in Racine's drama: 'Racine is poor in indications for the actor: nothing on diction, nothing on décor, the occasional mention of a gesture' (Backès, p. 8). Descotes, even though his focus is theatrical, is equally dismissive: 'The stage directions [in Racine] are sparse compared with the wealth of detail in contemporary drama; they are fragmentary and only concern points of detail' (p. xiii). Such a view is puzzling. Even confining oneself to the italicized stage directions, one discovers that they are not as meagre in Racine as these critics suggest. Racine specifies a variety of bodily postures—sitting or rising for Ephestion, Dandin, Agrippine, Bérénice, Mithridate, Phèdre, Assuérus, Athalie; kneeling for Burrhus, Clytemnestre, Esther, Aman, Abner; prostration for Joad; falling for Créon and Esther. He indicates tone of voice in *Les Plaideurs, Esther*, and *Athalie*. In the case of Antigone, Titus, and Bérénice, he specifies whether lines are to be spoken in the normal position at the front of the stage or as characters are entering or exiting. The italicized directions designate actions involving stage properties such as letters in *Bérénice* and *Bajazet*, a cup of poison in *Mithridate*, a diadem in *Athalie*; they refer to stage décor such as a curtain and backdrop in *Athalie*, to window, door, and basement in *Les Plaideurs*. Racine carefully notes when Néron speaks without realizing that Burrhus is present, when Néron catches sight of Agrippine, and when L'Intimé catches sight of Chicanneau. Italicized stage directions require Créon to prevent Antigone's exit, Atalide to kill herself, Mithridate to enter supported by his guards, Esther to enter leaning on Elise, Aman to be led off by guards, Joas to rush into the arms of the high priest, Joad to speak while Joas and Zacharie embrace, Joad and Josabet to embrace Joas, Mathan to exhibit signs of disorientation. The list could be extended by including the abundant stage directions in *Les Plaideurs*: Petit Jean dragging a large bag, putting on his hat, and waving his arms; L'Intimé crouching to write and presenting puppies to Dandin; Dandin yawning. Italicized stage directions are inserted to avoid ambiguity by telling characters to whom to address their words when there are more than two actors on stage. Italics indicate whether verses are spoken or sung in *Esther* and *Athalie*, and whether a character is alone on stage.

The reader of French seventeenth-century drama is also given important information by means of the French typographical conventions whereby a new scene starts and finishes whenever a character enters or exits. The list of names at the start of each scene defines who is on stage for the duration of that scene. If these names are omitted, as they sometimes are in translations into English, then crucial points can be missed. The printed text of *Phèdre* indicates that when Thésée makes his first entrance in Act III, Scene iv, having returned from being presumed dead, he enters with Hippolyte and Théramène. Phèdre sees Thésée entering with Hippolyte and Théramène and interprets the expression on Hippolyte's face as a sign that he has told his father of her attempt to seduce her. In R. D. MacDonald's English translation the effect of the entrance of the three men is somewhat obscured by omitting the French typographical conventions and by failing to indicate that Thésée enters accompanied by Hippolyte and Théramène. Consequently the reader of the translation might overlook the importance of Phèdre's mistaken interpretation of the expression on Hippolyte's face as he enters with his father, and would certainly not realize that in Racine's text Théramène also enters at this point. But the list of names at the start of Act III, Scene iv, of *Phèdre* makes the theatrical situation quite clear. A theatrical reading of these indications suggests a solemn entrance of three men advancing upon the two women. It is the first time in the play that five characters have been on stage together. Above all Phèdre commits her fatal error of misinterpretation as she sees Hippolyte advancing towards her at Thésée's side. An attentive reading of the Racinian text reveals the importance of explicit stage directions in all their forms.

It is wrong to stop there. Haffter, in his analysis of Racinian stage directions, is too rigid in his use of the terms *narrateur* and *texte à dire* to draw a distinction between the dramatist as narrator giving explicit instructions for performance on the one hand and the text spoken by the characters on the other. Haffter does not take account of the incorporation of stage directions into the dialogue or *texte à dire*. Yet Racine's text abounds in stage directions embedded in the words spoken by the characters. Issacharoff, who ranges more widely in his general survey of stage directions, recognizes the importance of stage directions which are implicit: 'wherever stage directions are not given explicitly, they must be deduced by the director and by the reader from the logic of the text and from the allusions contained in the dialogue' (p. 29). This type of stage direction can also be termed 'internal'. Racine's practice in this matter was in accordance with the French conventions of his time, as well as with those of Elizabethan and Jacobean drama in England. These conventions are as important for a theatrical reading as they are for the actor in performance. 'Shakespeare's internal

stage directions [. . .] ensure that he can control the actions and
expression of the players precisely and permanently for as long
as his words are obeyed [. . .] By the internal directions,
Shakespeare grips our own attention, forcing us to see what he
wants us to see' (Slater, p. 33). D'Aubignac was particularly
strict in urging French dramatists to follow the ancient Greek
dramatists and use implicit stage directions as opposed to those
external to the dialogue: 'the movements of the characters, the
costume and gestures [. . .] must be expressed by the verses
which [the dramatist] causes to be recited' (*Pratique*, i. 8, p. 46).
So important did D'Aubignac consider this that he insists on it
again in the *Dissertation sur Sertorius* where he criticizes Corneille
for not observing this convention (p. 269). Corneille took the
opposite view and argued against implicit stage directions because 'the verses should not be cluttered up with little details of
performance (*menues actions*), which detract from their dignity'
(*Discours des trois unités*, p. 70). Racine, however, followed the
Greek example and D'Aubignac's advice. So he indicates sitting, kneeling, falling, tones of voice, and general demeanour
through explicit stage directions, but also, and more frequently,
through implicit stage directions. Indeed, a much wider range
of guidance for performance is given in this way, such as weeping, sighing, shouting, hurrying, or averting the eyes. The
incorporation of implicit stage directions into the text obviously
lent itself to ridicule from theatrically uncomprehending readers.
Flaubert, reading Voltaire's tragedies with a hostile eye, dismissed the words 'I shudder, I tremble' with the comment 'Do
people *say* they shudder and tremble? They shouldn't say it,
they should just do it' (i. 49). Flaubert's strictures on Voltaire
would strike at Racine as well.

Implicit stage directions are most commonly inserted at the
moment they are required so that action and speech are concurrent. Agrippine to Britannicus: 'Where are you rushing to'
(*Bri.* I. iii. 287); Bérénice to Titus: 'You turn your eyes away'
(*Bér.* II. iv. 596); Roxane to Bajazet: 'You are sighing' (*Baj.* II. i.
559); Monime to Phoedime: 'See my face in tears' (*Mit.* II. i.
394). Even the prose sketch for *Iphigénie en Tauride* is rich
in implicit stage directions indicating passion and movement.
Iphigénie's companion is 'astonished at her sadness' (Act I,
Scene i); Iphigénie asks the Prince: 'Why are you still so dis-

turbed and upset?' (Act I, Scene ii). Examples could easily be
multiplied from any of Racine's plays. There is also a less
obvious technique for implicit stage directions. It was used by
Shakespeare, recommended by D'Aubignac, and practised by
Racine. This is the retrospective stage direction employed when
a scene requires such an economy of words that concurrent
stage directions would overload the dialogue. In such cases the
actions are described after the event instead of concurrently.
Slater explains Shakespeare's directions for the assassination of
Julius Caesar: 'there is no room for directions in the rush of
action [. . .] As the play progresses, however, Shakespeare
gradually leaks Plutarch's details [. . .] If these speeches are to
have any dramatic force, they must describe the scene as the
audience actually saw it' (p. 25). D'Aubignac insists on the
need to incorporate stage directions at the most appropriate
moment either concurrently or retrospectively: 'Often things
are not explained at the time they are acted, but long afterwards,
according to the poet's judgement of their appropriateness to
his subject. Those who read the [dramatic] poets or who wish
to perform the plays must pay special attention to this point.'
D'Aubignac goes on to give an example from Corneille's
Andromède where Phinée is struck by a thunderbolt 'without
anything being said at the time, but this is made known in the
following act'.[1] In *Alexandre*, Act IV, Scene i, Racine gives
Axiane a monologue recalling her farewell to Porus with details
which provide stage directions for the farewell scene in Act II,
Scene v, which has already been witnessed by the spectator.
Phèdre and Œnone retrospectively provide directions in *Phèdre*,
Act III, Scene i, to supplement the concurrent stage directions
for Phèdre's declaration of love to Hippolyte in Act II, Scene v.
And whilst the link between action and retrospective description must be recognizable to the spectator, the dramatist can
slant the later description so that it reveals the bias of the
character who relates the actions witnessed by the spectator in
the earlier scene. Œnone, for example, stresses the odious
contempt with which Hippolyte watched Phèdre humiliate
herself: 'If only Phèdre could have had my eyes at that moment'
says Œnone (*Phè*. III. i. 780). Retrospective stage directions are

---

[1] *Pratique*, i. 8, pp. 53–4; *Andromède*, II. v. 743–60; IV. iii. 1206–11.

less frequent than the concurrent ones, but they play their part in Racine's theatricality.

Finally there are breaks in speeches which require non-verbal interpretation in performance. Ubersfeld calls these 'textual holes'; they leave space for performance but make the dramatic text uncomfortable for the reader (p. 54). They are most obvious when ellipsis stops are employed for a pause or change of direction in a character's speech:

AGRIPPINE Et ce même Sénèque, et ce même Burrhus,
    Qui depuis . . . Rome alors estimait leurs vertus.

(Bri. IV. ii. 1166)

The break at 'depuis' demands a change of tone, perhaps a gesture of contempt. Racine sometimes breaks the logical sequence of words without advertising it by ellipsis stops. In such cases the actor is forced to supply some gesture or facial expression to create sense. Céphise probably employs visual language to persuade Andromaque to make her final appeal to Pyrrhus. One moment Andromaque is addressing her confidant in despair, the next moment she has decided to appeal to Pyrrhus. The lines follow without any typographical break, but there is a break in the sequence of argument, which must be filled by the actors in performance or the reader in his imagination. Andromaque's lines imply some stage business. The following suggestion is only one possibility:

CÉPHISE
    Madame . . .
ANDROMAQUE
            Et que veux-tu que je lui dise encore?
    Auteur de tous mes maux, crois-tu qu'il les ignore?
    [*Céphise, by a look, persuades Andromaque to speak to Pyrrhus*]
    Seigneur, voyez l'état où vous me réduisez.

(*And*. III. vi. 927)

Alternatively Andromaque notices that Pyrrhus, despite saying to his confidant 'Let us go', has remained on stage, a piece of stage business which anticipates Vladimir and Estragon in Beckett's *Waiting for Godot*. This may prompt Andromaque to renew her plea. In *Alexandre*, Act V, Scene iii, Axiane addresses Porus, who without replying to her declaration, abruptly addresses Alexandre instead. In the earlier version of this scene Racine did write lines for Porus's reply to Axiane, but he suppressed them in his final revision of the text so that the break requires some *jeu de scène*. In *Mithridate*, Act V, Scene i, Monime breaks off an apostrophe to herself to address some women attendants who are nowhere else mentioned in the play. Verbal breaks are cues for performance. 'Don't play the words, play the situation.' Sartre the dramatist learnt this from Charles Dullin (*Théâtre de situations*, p. 228). Racine's text requires the theatrical reader to keep this in mind.

A deeper understanding of the nature and function of stage directions in Racine can open the eyes of reader and performer to the full impact of Racine's theatrical language. At the same time, the fact that stage directions for physcial action are expressed in words, and that implicit stage directions usually require action and speech to function simultaneously in performance, illustrates one of the many aspects of the symbiotic relationship between action and speech in theatrical language.

(*b*) Visual Language

Visual language includes the décor of the plays as well as the entrances and exits of characters. These have been discussed above in Chapters 1 and 2. Once actors were on stage, physical action could take place. Often the term physical action evokes duels or battles or grandiose spectacles, but it also embraces all movements of the human body even down to the twitch of an eyelid. Fighting on stage or grandiose spectacle usually require crude mimetic representation. Voltaire, in one of the few helpful remarks in his *Discours de la tragédie*, pointed out that 'the more majestic or terrifying the spectacle is, the more insipid it becomes if it is frequently repeated' (p. 83). The really imaginative dramatist exploits the natural movements of the body for visual variety and for symbolic significance. Seventeenth-century actors usually remained standing but there were three postures which departed from this: sitting, kneeling, and falling to the ground. Such variations are exploited to the full by Racine as part of his theatrical language. They also served the artists who illustrated the plays. They seized on scenes which provided variety of bodily posture and which carried suggestions of physical action. Racine's text provided no shortage of material.[2]

Sitting

In eight of his twelve plays Racine includes explicit or implicit stage directions which require characters to sit and then rise. In each case the visual effect is suggestive or significant.

Ephestion, a mere ambassador seated on the inferior *tabouret*, rises unbidden in the presence of the two Indian kings seated on the superior *fauteuils*, thus conveying the insolent arrogance of Alexandre and a declaration of war (*Ale.* Act II, Scene ii). *Fauteuil* is a chair with arms and a back for a king; *tabouret* is a stool or seat without arms or a back for subordinates. Courtin's manual of etiquette is quite explicit about the social hierarchy of seating: 'the *fauteuil* is the most honourable seat; next the *chaise à dos*; then the *siège pliant*' (p. 51). He condemns people of inferior rank who take the initiative in rising from their seat when superiors remain sitting, or who remain seated when their superiors rise (p. 53). That these social conventions were reflected on stage can be seen from the *Mémoire de Mahelot* where the different types of seat are clearly specified: 'two armchairs and a stool' for *Alexandre*; 'two armchairs in the fourth act' for *Britannicus*; 'an armchair and two stools' for *Mithridate* (pp. 112–13).

Agrippine in an inopportune display of quasi-judicial authority takes her seat first and then commands her son, the emperor, to sit, with a peremptory 'Take your place' (*Bri.* IV. ii. 1115). Her command implies that the emperor should not only sit, but also know his place in relation to her. Perhaps there is a further metaphorical connotation. Néron is like the defendant in the lawcourt being required to sit on the *sellette* (Barnwell, p. 202). Racine was clearly conscious of the significance of this feature of judicial seating when he wrote in the preface to *Les Plaideurs* of 'putting a real criminal on the *sellette*' (p. 328). Agrippine's action betrays the bossy, accusatory mother where-

---

[2] See the plates in this book and the descriptions of other illustrations in Guibert, 'Iconographie de Racine'.

as she should be ingratiating herself with her adolescent son. Vauvenargues observantly commented that the prejudice in favour of grandiloquent words led people to underestimate or overlook Racine's skill in using this simple visual effect to portray Agrippine's haughtiness (i. 154).

Bérénice, Phèdre, and Athalie sit to show degrees of mental turmoil and physical collapse, though Athalie also shows determination by planting herself in a chair in the vestibule of the high priest's apartment (*Bér.* Act V, Scene v; *Phè.* Act I, Scene iii; *Ath.* Act II, Scene iii). Phèdre's collapse into a chair, accompanied by words of emotional turmoil, allowed a satirist to immortalize this theatrical moment in a cruel sonnet, which starts with a reference to her chair: 'In a gilded armchair Phèdre, trembling and pale, makes a speech which at first no one can understand . . .' ('Dans un fauteuil doré', *NCR* 96).

In *Esther* Assuérus on his throne is menacing to the timid Esther who approaches him without permission, but the throne may become a source of protection to the Jewish girls who remain in its shelter (*Est.* II. vii. 713). In *Athalie* a significant visual contrast is established through reversal of roles, when the child Joas, who stood before the seated Athalie in Act II, Scene vii, is himself seen seated upon his throne in Act V, Scene v, signalling God's victory over Queen Athalie (Pls. 14 and 30). In comic vein Léandre and Isabelle by force of words argue Dandin into sitting down, thereby expressing his assent to their marriage (*Pla.* III. iv. 859). Racine is economical in his indications of this nature. Only in the case of Bérénice does he specify the exact moment of both sitting and rising (*Bér.* Act V, Scene vii). Elsewhere Racine's text specifies only one of the two elements, either 'he sits' or 'rising'. The text must be read theatrically to ascertain a plausible or significant moment for the action which is not specified to be inserted. In *Mithridate*, Act III, Scene i, Racine indicates only the moment when Mithridate rises from his deliberation with his two sons. One may presume that they all took their seats to commence the deliberation in a conventional manner, but Racine creates a significant effect by specifying the moment for Mithridate to rise, namely to lift Xipharès from his knees, and to signal where his sympathies lie between his two sons.

Kneeling

On fifteen occasions Racine requires characters to kneel. Sometimes the posture simply reinforces the pleading of the suppliant character. This is the case when Burrhus kneels to Néron, or Esther to Assuérus (*Bri.* Act III, Scene iii; *Est.* Act III, Scene iv). Kneeling may be a sign of homage as when Abner abandons Queen Athalie for the new King Joas by 'throwing himself at Joas's feet' (SD, *Ath.* V. vi. 1740). Yet even this banal gesture of allegiance has added significance here, because it represents the moment of choice for Abner, caught between loyalty to Athalie and loyalty to his religion; he decides for the latter. In other cases the text draws attention to the special humiliation of the suppliant's posture. Andromaque kneeling to Hermione asks: 'Is it not sweet for you to see Hector's widow weeping at your feet?' (*And.* III. iv. 859). Similarly the Queen of Argos startles a subordinate warrior by falling at his feet. Achille is bewildered: 'A queen at my feet humiliates herself!' (*Iph.* III. vi. 952). Racine took this from Euripides, but his rival Le Clerc who composed his *Iphigénie* at the same time seems to shrink from the full physical action, because his stage direction reads: 'Clytemnestre, attempting to kneel' (SD, p. 35), which implies that Achille prevents her from actually sinking to the ground. Le Clerc's timidity is a hint that Racine was deliberately using kneeling in a significant way to portray the intensity of Clytemnestre's distress by a posture which, though natural for a mother, was incongruous for a queen. Louis Racine approved of the theatrical effect of this special humiliation (*Remarques*, p. 59).

As with sitting and rising, Racine does not necessarily specify both the moment of kneeling and the moment of rising. He leaves scope for reading into the text the best way of exploiting the beginning or end of the visual effect. Andromaque must surely be kneeling to Pyrrhus when she says to him: 'Without you, Andromaque would never have knelt to an oppressor' (*And.* III. vi. 915). But when exactly did Andromaque fall to her knees and when does she rise? The most likely moment to kneel is at 'Ah my Lord, stop. What are you doing?', when the distraught mother attempts to restrain Pyrrhus as he threatens to depart and hand over her son to the Greeks (*And.* 901). This is the moment that the 1736 edition of Racine's theatre inserts the stage direction 'Throwing herself at Pyrrhus's feet'. This edition may preserve details of performances at the Comédie-Française.[3] No doubt Andromaque rises when she says 'Let us go and rejoin my husband' (*And.* 925), in order to emphasize her moment of decision. She has been on her knees for about twenty lines (Pl. 6).

From this perspective, Atalide's supplication to Roxane reveals a significant feature. Atalide almost certainly falls to her knees at the beginning of the scene. 'I place my heart and my crime at your feet' (*Baj.* V. vi. 1576) could be wholly meta-phorical, but Courville's stage direction for this line 'She kneels upon the ground' (p. 139) is probably correct. At the end of the scene she is bidden rise by Roxane's peremptory 'Get up' (*Baj.* 1626). Atalide's long speech is delivered in this suppliant pos-ture. So not only does an Ottoman princess kneel to a upstart slave, but Atalide's humiliation—some fifty lines, compared with twenty lines for Andromaque—is strikingly long.

In *Phèdre* Racine leaves discretion to determine how best to exploit Œnone's kneeling to Phèdre, and Hippolyte's to Thésée (*Phè.* I. iii. 243; IV. ii. 1121). However, in *Esther*, the precise effect of Aman kneeling to Esther is made explicit, for Aman's posture is interpreted by Assuérus as an assault upon his queen, and leads to Aman's speedy condemnation to death (*Est.* Act III, Scene vi). The dramatic effect of Aman's misinterpreted sup-plication is made possible by the act of grasping the knees, an action which is described explicitly in Œnone's supplication of Phèdre: 'By your knees which I hold embraced' (*Phè.* I. iii. 243). In almost every case therefore the visual effect of kneeling carries connotations beyond simple supplication.

On the Ground

Modern productions of Racine enjoy showing the actors on the ground. In Michel Vitold's *Britannicus* of 1961 Narcisse squats with a consoling arm on the neck of a nearly prostrate Néron (Backès, p. 32). Many a Phèdre has writhed upon the floor to

---

[3] According to claims in the editors' preface; see Mesnard in Racine, *Œuvres*, i, pp. vii, xiii.

signal her degradation, as can be seen in the illustrations of the productions by Antoine Vitez and by Jean Gillibert (in *Phèdre*, ed. C. Geray). All of this produces pleasurable variety, and may, appropriately or not, throw some aspect of the tragedy into sharp visual focus. Racine himself is of course alert to visual variety but is sparing in throwing his characters to the ground. The only unambiguous example of a character on the ground occurs in *Athalie*. Joad signals his homage to Joas by suddenly 'prostrating himself at his feet' (SD, *Ath*. IV. ii. 1290). The astonished child asks: 'My father, what is this posture I see you in?' Joad replies: 'I render you the respect I owe my king.'

Fainting and Supporting

The other occasions on which Racine may envisage characters falling to the ground are when they faint or lose consciousness. Atalide's plight is the most spectacular. Holding the letter which contains Bajazet's death warrant she faints in the hostile presence of Roxane. Zatime, Roxane's confidant, exclaims 'She falls, there is scarcely life in her.' Roxane orders her attendants to remove the inert body: 'Go (*allez*), take her to the adjacent room' (*Baj*. IV. iii. 1206). The presence of additional attendants is implied by the use of the *vous* form in *allez*; Roxane addresses Zatime alone as *tu*. It would be consistent with these lines that Atalide should fall to the ground, but it is possible she may be caught by Zatime before she collapses entirely, as depicted in Chauveau's illustration (Pl. 10).

Oreste's faint at the conclusion of *Andromaque* may also end upon the ground, unless Pylade catches him as he says 'He has lost consciousness' (*And*. V. v. 1645). The other examples of losing consciousness in Racine are accompanied by directions which do require the actor to be supported in the arms of another. When Créon goes mad, Racine specifies 'He falls into the arms of the guards' (SD, *Thé*. Act V, Scene vi). When Esther confronts Assuérus's anger, Racine first specifies that she enters 'leaning on Elise's arm' (SD, *Est*. II. vii. 631), then, as Esther 'falls in a faint' (SD, II. vii. 635), the explicit stage directions are reinforced by the actions implicit in the words 'Maidens, support your queen in her distress' (l. 635). Le Brun's illustration shows the fainting Esther supported by Elise, with other attendants assisting. This is probably the posture in which the reader may imagine, or the spectator may see, Jocaste when she is thrown off balance at the entrance of Etéocle, and calls to her confidant: 'Olympe, support me, my anguish is extreme' (*Thé.* I. iii. 44). Moitte's illustration shows Jocaste recoiling into Olympe's arms rather as Esther collapses into Elise's (compare Pls. 13 and 24).

Analogous with the supporting of a character in a faint are the occasions when a character makes an entrance in a state of collapse. The dying Mithridate has to be carried on by his soldiers (SD, *Mit.* Act V, Scene v). Porus probably enters in a similar state (SD, *Ale.* Act V, Scene iii). For an exit in *Athalie* Racine specifies Mathan's mental derangement as he reels away from Joad's imprecations: 'he becomes confused' (SD, *Ath.* Act III, Scene v) and Nabal's words strongly imply that he assists Mathan with a guiding hand: 'Where are you straying? [. . .] your way is over here' (*Ath.* III. v. 1042). Le Roy envisages Nabal leading Mathan off (p. 183). Confounded by Jehovah's priest, the impious Baalites clutch each other for support.

Bodily Contact

It is clear from the above examples that, contrary to popular belief, characters do make bodily contact in Racinian tragedy. This occurs in a more violent form when one character physically restrains another. The stage direction 'Créon restraining (*arrêtant*) Antigone' (SD, *Thé.* Act V, Scene iii) presumably signifies that Créon lays a hand upon Antigone in an attempt to prevent her exit. It is the only time in Racine's tragedies that bodily contact is suggested between a man and the woman he is in love with. There is an analogous situation between the lovers in *Iphigénie* which implies that Achille lays hands upon Iphigénie, although, if interpreted minimally, the visual effect may be limited to a sketched gesture on Achille's part as he makes to conduct Iphigénie forcibly to the safety of his tent, thereby eliciting from Iphigénie the indignant retort: 'What! would you go as far as to constrain me by force?' (*Iph.* V. ii. 1586).

It is more usual for the restraining or constraining hand to be that of a person of the same sex. Atalide pleads with Zatime for news of Bajazet. In despair she asks Zatime to kill her. Then in

an abrupt change of tactics, she tries to escape from Zatime. All
this is conveyed by the following lines:

ATALIDE

> Ah! c'en est trop cruelle. Achève, et que ta main
> Lui [Roxane] donne de ton zèle un gage plus certain.
> Perce toi-même un cœur que ton silence accable,
> D'une esclave barbare, esclave impitoyable,
> Précipite des jours qu'elle me veut ravir;
> Montre-toi s'il se peut, digne de la servir.
> Tu me retiens en vain; et dès cette même heure,
> Il faut que je le voie, ou du moins que je meure.
>
> (*Baj.* V. viii. 1647)

The most probable theatrical interpretation of 'you restrain me
in vain' (*tu me retiens en vain*) is that Atalide struggles with
Zatime. Courville suggests: 'Atalide tries to pass. Zatime prevents her. They struggle' (p. 143). Lejealle in his edition of
Bajazet also interprets it in this way: 'Atalide tries to escape from
Zatime's grasp' (p. 93). There is an analogy in *Les Plaideurs*
when Dandin tries to escape Petit Jean's grasp (*Pla.* I. iii. 65).
Another case of bodily restraint occurs in *Mithridate* and seems
to have escaped the attention of commentators on this play.
Monime is attempting to elude Phoedime's importunate solicitude but finds her exit barred by other female attendants who
appear to lay hands upon her:

MONIME

> Oui, cruelles, en vain vos injustes secours
> Me ferment du tombeau les chemins les plus courts,
> Je trouverai la mort jusque dans vos bras mêmes.
>
> (*Mit.* V. i. 1497)

Although female attendants are not indicated either in the list
of actors nor in the names of those present during the scene,
Monime always addresses Phoedime as *tu* and here the plural
cruelles implies more than one woman, just as Roxane addressed
unnamed women in *Bajazet*, Act IV, Scene iii.

Monime's implied struggle with female attendants can be elu-
cidated by comparison with the more explicit struggle between
Clytemnestre and the guards who prevent her from following
Iphigénie as the latter is led to her death:

CLYTEMNESTRE

Ah! vous n'irez pas seule; et je ne prétends pas . . .
Mais on se jette en foule au-devant de mes pas.
Perfides! contentez votre soif sanguinaire.

(Iph. V. iv. 1667)

Louis Racine commented that this incident showed the intensity of Clytemnestre's maternal love, since she was only prevented from following her daughter by the violence of the soldiers who throw themselves in her path (*Remarques*, p. 63).

The very fact that these lines of Atalide, of Monime, and of Clytemnestre do not offer a complete verbal picture of the physical movements suggests that Racine may have had such a clear picture of the stage business when he wrote the lines that he did not need to spell every detail out in his text . He may simply have relied on instructing the actors of the Hôtel de Bourgogne during the rehearsals which authors attended for this purpose (Chappuzeau, p. 72; Grimarest, *Traité*, p. 78).

So far, the examples have mainly been of physical restraint used in an attempt to prevent a character from leaving the stage. On other occasions the restraint may be more specifically directed towards preventing a suicide. In *La Thébaïde* Créon is intent on killing himself. Attale and the guards restrain him. Créon says 'Let me die . . .'. Attale and the guards riposte 'Ah, my lord, what cruel desire . . .' (*Thé.* V. vi. 1493). Moitte's illustration is a good commentary on this scene (Pl. 25). A grim-faced Créon has drawn his sword. Attale kneels beside Créon with one hand on the blade of the sword, the other outstretched in supplication. The stage direction added to the 1801 edition specifies that Attale tries to wrest the sword from Créon. This is not explicit in Racine's text but is certainly implied when Créon reproaches Attale and the guards 'Ah, to save my life is to assassinate me!' (l. 1494).

The same kind of physical movement, though more subdued, is implicit at the end of *Bajazet*. Zaïre probably restrains Atalide as she plunges a dagger into her heart. The stage direction, 'She stabs herself', is followed by Zaïre's exclamation: 'Ah, madam . . . She breathes her last' (*Baj.* V. xii. 1747). The break after 'madam' suggests that Zaïre attempts to prevent Atalide from stabbing herself, then realizes that she has not acted quickly enough and that the mortal blow has been struck.

A more complex series of physical movements accompanies Phèdre's attempt to have Hippolyte kill her on stage. Racine's text permits some freedom of interpretation regarding the extent of the bodily contact, but obviously Hippolyte's sword cannot leap spontaneously from its scabbard into Phèdre's hand. Subligny, who saw *Phèdre* performed during its first run, in fact criticized the violent physical action which spectators witnessed when Phèdre drew Hippolyte's sword from its scabbard, and he blamed the incident on Racine's desire for theatrical effect: 'M. Racine can only have exposed this violent action to our eyes, in order to embellish his play with a fine piece of stage business' (*Dissertation*, p. 379). Gravelot's illustration shows the snatching of the sword (Pl. 19). Goldmann, picking up the retrospective stage directions in Act III, Scene i, envisages Œnone restraining Phèdre from stabbing herself with Hippolyte's sword (p. 435) and Sève depicts this with allegorical figures (Pl. 21). Then Œnone hurries her mistress off stage. Contemporary spectators saw 'Phèdre fainting and dragged off stage by Œnone' (Subligny, *Dissertation*, p. 381). Girodet's illustration depicts this exactly: he shows Œnone supporting Phèdre with one hand, whilst with the other she propels her mistress off stage (Pl. 29). Barrault's stage directions convey the same picture: 'Phèdre almost faints and allows herself to be manœuvred like a puppet [. . .] Œnone drags her off' (p. 123). This bodily contact is necessary to give point to Théramène's question 'Is Phèdre fleeing or is she being dragged?' (II. vi. 714).[4]

There is similar scope for flexibility regarding bodily contact when characters are placed under arrest. Physical contact is not necessary. Dignified acquiescence would be appropriate in most cases; but a character surrounded by soldiers creates a powerful visual effect and occurs in every tragedy except *La Thébaïde, Bérénice*, and *Phèdre*, though the scene in *Andromaque*, when Andromaque appeared under arrest at the end, was deleted by Racine from later editions. Three men are seen to be under arrest: Britannicus (*Bri.* III. viii. 1084), Pharnace (*Mit.* III. ii. 989), Aman (*Est.* III. vi. 1175). Racine has a partiality for

---

[4] Descotes, however, claims that 'strictly speaking the text of *Phèdre*, only offers the actor the words "She sits down"' (p. xiii).

showing women in this situation: Andromaque (*And.* V. iii. 1494*a*, text of 1668 only), Junie (*Bri.* III. viii. 1080), Atalide (*Baj.* V. ii. 1453), Iphigénie (*Iph.* V. iii. 1666), Athalie (*Ath.* V. vi. 1791).

Potential arrest can also be significant. Roxane orders Bajazet's arrest but does not carry it through. This is interpreted as a visual sign of Roxane's irresolution by Atalide (*Baj.* II. ii. 568; II. v. 780). The guards waiting to escort Iphigénie to her death are the visual backdrop to Agamemnon's deliberations, and help to bring home to him the enormity of his decision to have his daughter sacrificed to the gods. Racine is precise about the presence of characters on stage in the scenes which lead up to this decisive moment. In *Iphigénie*, Act IV, Scene vii, Agamemnon is alone and reaches his decision to send Iphigénie to her death. To put this into effect he calls Eurybate and his guards. They are present during Act IV, Scene viii, and their presence is the backdrop for Agamemnon's change of heart to clemency.

The gap between potential and actual bodily contact can generate theatrical tension. Suspense is created when an arrest is anticipated, because the spectator has a visual image of actual arrest, conditioned by his previous experience. The same kind of tension can be generated in the case of embraces, which may be seen on stage or may be the focus of expectant anticipation.

The embraces seen on stage in Racine's drama are all of a parental or fraternal nature. There can be little doubt that when the dying Mithridate invites his son to embrace him and to receive his last breath, Racine intended the dutiful son to obey, thus investing the conclusion of tragedy with a predictable atmosphere of tranquil melancholy. This physical embrace is the most plausible interpretation of the interval between Mithridate's command to Xipharès: 'In this embrace receive my spirit' and Monime's exclamation: 'He breathes his last' (*Mit.* V. v. 1696–7). Chauveau shows the embrace about to take place (Pl. 11).

When Iphigénie embraces her father, the atmosphere is filled with much greater tension. Agamemnon is shrinking from the embarrassment of kissing a daughter whom he has determined to sacrifice, but reluctantly accords her the sought-for embrace: 'Well then, my daughter, embrace your father. He loves you as always' (*Iph*. II. ii. 537). Not that this embrace was universally admired. Pierre de Villiers records the disapproval of spectators who felt it unseemly that a girl of the age of Iphigénie should chase after the caresses of her father; but he also records the opposing view that this was 'exactly what created the whole effect on stage (*tout le jeu de théâtre*), and which represented the full extent of Agamemnon's tenderness and embarrassment' (p. 22). Villiers's testimony clearly relates the visual effects on stage to the response of the spectators. On the next occasion of embracing in *Iphigénie* Racine's text leaves scope for an imaginative response by reader or director. Iphigénie certainly asks her mother for an embrace: 'Deign to open your arms to me for the last time, madam.' But it is likely that Iphigénie quickly disengages from a potential embrace which might lead to an embarrassing scene (*Iph*. V. iii. 1664).

In *Athalie* Racine exploits the fact of having a child on stage to include four embraces, each of which carries an additional charge of significance. After Joas's interrogation by Athalie, the high priest Joad, absent during the questioning, re-establishes his presence by congratulating the child's courage 'whilst embracing him' (SD, *Ath*. II. viii. 742). This provides a sudden release of tension after the interrogation. Later the anxious child Joas is seen 'rushing into the arms of the high priest' (SD, *Ath*. IV. ii. 1264) and then, a minute later, in sudden visual contrast, Joad's prostration at the feet of the child signals the high priest's allegiance to the king (SD, *Ath*. 1290). The final two embraces in *Athalie* form a complementary pair. Joas as the new king is embraced loyally and maternally by Josabet and then fraternally by Zacharie (SD, *Ath*. IV. iv. 1412, 1416). The latter embrace is laden with irony since one day the king turned idolater will murder this brother figure, as Joad prophesied (*Ath*. III. vii. 1142–3). Racine underlines the irony of the embrace between these brother figures by specifying that 'while they embrace' (SD, *Ath*. 1416), the high priest pronounces his wish for the two children always to be united. This, the last of the four embraces in *Athalie*, crystallizes the tragic irony of the whole drama. Inspired by God, the high priest casts down Athalie to replace her with a child who will become as evil and bloodthirsty as his grandmother. The embrace between Joas and Zacharie shows good and evil as interconnected parts of God's plan for human salvation.[5]

In the six scenes just mentioned from *Mithridate, Iphigénie*, and *Athalie*, parental or fraternal embraces are actually seen on stage. The tension of potential embraces is evoked in three other scenes from *La Thébaïde, Mithridate*, and *Phèdre*. Jocaste urges her sons to embrace fraternally (*Thé.* Act IV, Scene iii). In *Phèdre* Racine evokes his only embrace between husband and wife. Thésée, miraculously returned from presumed death, holds out his arms to Phèdre. She recoils in shame (*Phè.* III. iv. 914). In each case there is scope for a high degree of expectancy and suspense as the spectator watches to see whether the physical action will take place or not. Mithridate tests Pharnace with the command to give his father a farewell embrace but Pharnace refuses (*Mit.* III. i. 957). This is mirrored in Xipharès's acceptance of his father's final embrace at the end of the play: the visual symbolism differentiates the two brothers.

The spatial relationships between human bodies have been analysed by the anthropologist E. T. Hall under the term 'proxemics' (see Elam, pp. 62–9). In the theatre the proxemic codes which operate in society are inevitably modified by the demands of performance, though the dramatist and actors will have to observe social codes as best they can if they are to create the illusion of reality. Courtin's manual of etiquette contemporary with Racine recommended that when two people of unequal rank were in discussion, they must not sit side by side but 'in front of each other, so that the superior person can see that he is being listened to; one must turn one's body a little to the side to show a profile, because that posture is more respectful than full face' (pp. 51–2). Evidence is lacking for the manner in which this was translated into stage conventions in Racine's day but Servandoni's *Observations sur l'art du comédien* (London, 1776) comes close to Courtin's recommendations: 'It is neither polite nor gentlemanly to engage in dialogue face to face with or too close to someone of higher social standing

---

[5] Starobinski, however, asserts 'his characters do not embrace [. . .] each other on stage' (p. 90).

[. . .] Now one should do on the stage what one would do in society.'[6]

The dramatist, however, may infringe social codes to achieve special effects. This has been seen in Racine's stage directions for sitting or kneeling. Other aspects of Racine's identifiable proxemic vocabulary have been illustrated in the examples of bodily contact such as support, restraint, constraint, arrest, or embrace. Racine also varied the proxemic conventions of theatrical performance. Normally characters came to the front of the stage to speak. It is likely that the speaker stood slightly upstage from the listener. They then changed places when the listener became the speaker (Barnett, 'Ensemble Acting', p. 160). Racine's stage directions occasionally indicate a more 'three-dimensional' positioning of the actors: Créon pursues Antigone as she leaves the stage (SD, *Thé.* Act V Scene iii); Bérénice speaks 'as she makes her exit' (SD, *Bér.* Act IV, Scene v); Titus speaks 'as he enters' (SD, *Bér.* Act V, Scene iii). Néron speaks 'without seeing Burrhus' (SD, *Bri.* Act III, Scene ix); Assuérus 'moves away' (SD, *Est.* Act III, Scene iv). This last stage direction is especially significant. As Assuérus moves away, but before he exits, an Israelite speaks one line, praying for truth to descend. The fact of this line being spoken whilst Assuérus is still visible, implies that the prayer is focused upon him. He exits for one scene (Act III, Scene v) and then returns to the stage. Exit rapidly followed by re-entrance was most unusual. When he returns he is a changed man. Truth has descended. Assuérus is enlightened and Aman is sent to his death (Woshinsky, pp. 264–6). Racine showed particular interest in how the characters on stage related physically to each other. His explicit or implied proxemic vocabulary often conveys a wealth of meaning, either through bodily contact or physical separation.

Eyes and Tears

When characters stand apart, they watch each other. Racine alerts the spectator verbally to the importance of being watched by constantly reminding his actors and his audience that eyes

---

[6] Quoted in D. Barnett, 'Ensemble Acting', p. 165.

and facial expression are an eloquent language. Oreste knows that eyes can betray (*And.* II. ii. 575). Atalide, hearing that Roxane is to test Bajazet by offering him marriage, is in despair: 'If only I had been able to prepare his countenance!' (*Baj.* I. iv. 397). She even considers waylaying him before he meets Roxane. She might warn him by a word, or even by a look (*Baj.* I. iv. 398).

Having alerted the spectator to the significance of the language of eyes and facial expression, Racine makes it part of the spectacle he offers to his spectators, even though some of them may have experienced difficulties in getting a clear view of the actors' faces in the public theatres of Paris (see Chapter 1, Section *a*). In *Britannicus* Néron watches behind a curtain, while Junie is forced to respond coldly to Britannicus's protestations of love. Néron warns Junie: 'I'll read those looks that you will think are mute [. . .] When you see him, remember I'll be watching you' (*Bri.* II. iv. 682 and 690). On stage the characters are all alert to read the signs conveyed by eyes and face. Axiane sees love in Porus's eyes (*Ale.* IV. i. 971). Bérénice is distressed by Titus's averted eyes (*Bér.* II. iv. 596). Sometimes the signs are misinterpreted: Pyrrhus sees only disdain in Andromaque's averted eyes (*And.* Act III, Scene vi). Racine's strong sense of theatre leads him to exploit the theatrical possibilities of characters engaging with each other on stage by means of eye contact and watchfulness.[7]

The eyes were also a source of tears, which were avidly watched and eagerly interpreted. Racine specifies tears again and again, though he is not precise about the way in which this must be shown on stage. In Shakespeare's time an onion could assist the dry-eyed: 'An onion will do well for such a shift' (*Taming of the Shrew*, i. 135 ff.; Slater, p. 101). Good actors could weep at will and trickle their cheeks with real tears simply by the force of their imagination (Grimarest, *Traité*, p. 114). Chauveau's illustrations show Cléofile, Bérénice, and Monime raising a fold of their dress to their eyes, the same gesture used to identify the allegorical figure of Pity in his frontispiece (Pls.

[7] Watchful eyes are discussed by Le Bidois, pp. 78–86; and by Starobinski in 'The Poetics of the Glance'; by Van Delft, 'Language and Power'; R. L. Barnett, however, asserts that 'visual' terminologies do not function on any level of literality ('Non-Ocularity', p. 116); for the tragic significance of the eyes, see Ch. 7, sect. *d*.

4, 5, 9, and 11). A plausible substitute would be a gesture of the arm hiding an averted face, or hands covering it. The illustration of Moreau le Jeune for *Iphigénie* shows Agamemnon seated, elbow on table with hands hiding his eyes. This would be apt for Clytemnestre's accusation: 'Why feign for us sham grief? Do you believe your tears will prove your love?' (*Iph*. IV. iv. 1257).[8] In the same play Racine seems to suggest that Iphigénie should lower her eyes to indicate weeping through Agamemnon's words: 'You weep and lower your eyes' (*Iph*. IV. iv. 1172). When Mithridate accuses Monime with 'I see in spite of your efforts your tears are ready to flow' (*Mit*. II. iv. 581), his words require Monime to show herself on the verge of tears. Racine sometimes does specify tears visible to the characters as opposed to a suggestively lachrymose demeanour. Thésée says of Théramène: 'Wherefore these tears I see you shedding now?' (*Phè*. V. vi. 1490). The very fact that some spectators might see a physical sign of weeping, be it tears or a gesture, whilst others might only hear the words, indicates the value of the implicit stage directions spoken by the characters, as opposed to the italicized stage directions available only to the reader of the printed page. Through implicit stage directions the dramatist can require the actor to communicate visually to the spectator, whilst at the same time stimulating the imagination of those in the audience who cannot see. For the reader of the printed page, the implicit directions have the advantage of not distracting him from his involvement with the speeches of the characters in the way that italicized stage directions do (D'Aubignac, *Pratique*, i. 8, p. 48). The possibilities mentioned above for representing weeping on stage—actual tears or gestures of the arm—are plausible historical reconstructions of performance in Racine's time. However, visual signs can become clichés or contaminated with unacceptable associations or simply impractical. This may lead a director to substitute one visual sign for another whilst preserving the syntagmatic paradigm. Thus in Vitez's *Phèdre* (Paris, 1975) tears were represented by characters bathing their cheeks in water from a basin (Ubersfeld, p. 32). Similar considerations led to the discarding of Phèdre's chair in Stefan Stern's production of *Phaedra* (Oxford, 1988). Instead, Phèdre

---

[8] Illustration reproduced in Achach's edn. of *Iphigénie*.

sat upon the ground to signal distress. By exploiting visual synonyms or, in the case of Vitez, inventing a visual periphrasis, the image can be rejuvenated and the visual dimension of the text reinforced.

Stage Properties

The letters which occur in five of Racine's twelve plays can function on different levels of significance. Mimetically the piece of paper denotes a letter, but also in Racine it may be a symbolic conveyer of truth. The written word can cut through the tangle of deceiving speeches. Titus snatches the letter which Bérénice has written to confirm her departure from Rome (*Bér.* Act V, Scene v). It is a moment of truth. Racine expanded on the use of letters in *Bajazet*. The two letters seen on stage, one from Amurat to Roxane, the other from Bajazet to Atalide, also contain truths like those in Bérénice's letter to Titus, but in *Bajazet* their effect is deceptive. Amurat's letter contains the order for Bajazet's death, but used deceitfully by Roxane it elicits evidence of Atalide's love for Bajazet (*Baj.* Act IV, Scene iii). Bajazet's letter to Atalide contains his profession of love for her, but is folded back into the action to become Bajazet's death warrant when Roxane gets possession of it (*Baj.* Act IV, Scenes i–vi; Act V, Scene iv). It is also used to represent Roxane's wavering between illusion and enlightenment (Brody, pp. 283–8). There is further complexity in *Iphigénie*. Agamemnon's letter is a deception warning his wife and daughter away from Aulis on the spurious grounds that Achille has withdraw from his proposed marriage to Iphigénie. The fraudulent missive makes a dramatic entrance brandished in Clytemnestre's matronly hand: 'Daughter, we must depart [. . .] I am not surprised your father seemed to greet us with regret, and feared to expose you to the shame of rejection. He had sent me this letter by Arcas's hand' (*Iph.* II. iv. 625–30). The false letter becomes a source of mortification for Agamemnon on top of his other woes (*Iph.* Act II, Scene iv; Act III, Scene i; Act IV, Scenes iii–vi). Only in *Esther* does a written document serve a simple verificatory function. Mardochée, to prove the truth of the projected massacre of the Jews, thrusts the document under Esther's eyes: 'Read, read the cruel and execrable edict' (*Est.* I.

iii. 163). The letters of Bérénice and Bajazet contain truths, but fall into the wrong hands at the wrong time. Amurat's letter contains truth but is used by Roxane to deceive Atalide. Agamemnon's letter to Clytemnestre is a deception which provokes fatal misunderstandings with Clytemnestre, Iphigénie, and above all, Achille, whose reactions open Eriphile's eyes (*Iph.* Act II, Scenes iv–vii, and ll. 761–5). Eriphile's treachery, however, recoils upon her. The letters can be as treacherous as the spoken words.

In *Les Plaideurs* as well as letters there are lawyer's brief-bags, stick and torch, chicken's head and legs, and live puppies, all of which are the focus of physical action. The list of stage properties is one of the longest of any comedy appearing in the *Mémoire de Mahelot*, and involved extra expense. The puppies in their basket were preferably live, and cost thirty sous to hire for performances at Versailles and Fontainebleau in 1696 (*NCR* 396, 397). Live animals were relatively rare on the Parisian stage, and limited to docile species, such as dogs and sheep. The more unruly species were constructed of wicker or represented by actors wearing animal skins (Lancaster, iv. 35). Corneille prudently confined himself to showing only the head of a restive horse in *Clitandre*, Act II, Scene iv, probably stuffed. Dealing with live animals, dramatists could ensure reasonable control of the situation provided they wrote parts which accorded with the animals' natural proclivities. For example a dog licks the wounds of a leper in *Le Mauvais Riche*, not a difficult effect to engineer. The shepherdess in Troterel's *Aristène* enters upbraiding her wandering sheep for doing what came naturally: 'Where are you off to!'[9] Racine was a more intrepid entertainer and exploited the propensity of puppies to urinate: 'Ils ont pissé partout' (*Pla.* III. iii. 826; Pl. 7).

Detaching themselves from their passive denotative function, items of costume can be involved in physical action and temporarily assume the kind of significance associated with stage properties such as letters. The sword, which identifies a male nobleman, can be unsheathed engage in a conflict. Racine originally had his characters draw their swords in Act IV of *La Thébaïde* but revised this to expunge the direct representation of

---

[9] Lancaster, i. 263; *Mémoire de Mahelot*, p. 37, for live sheep.

the clash of steel on stage. He wrote to the abbé Le Vasseur in November 1663: 'Unfortunately neither I nor others relished all the drawn swords; so they had to be sheathed and more than two hundred lines deleted, which is not so easy' (*Œuvres*, ii. 457). All that remains of the swords in *La Thébaïde* is Etéocle's defiant acceptance of Polynice's challenge to single combat: 'Now I believe you worthy of the crown, and bear it to you on this proferred blade' (*Thé.* IV. iii. 1076). Etéocle's sword, probably only partially drawn as an accompaniment to these words, becomes an oblique hint of the incipient fratricide. Much more frequent is the use of the sword or dagger as a potential instrument of self-immolation in scenes of persuasion or accusation. Burrhus invites Néron to kill him so that he is not obliged to witness his master's crime; presumably Burrhus proffers his sword (*Bri.* IV. iii. 1378). A desperate Atalide invites Zatime to stab her (*Baj.* V. viii. 1649). Phèdre tries to kill herself with Hippolyte's sword (*Phè.* Act II, Scene v). Only Atalide uses such a weapon on stage to kill herself in the view of the audience. The text does not specify how she puts into practice 'Elle se tue' (SD, *Baj.* Act V, Scene xii), but the *Mémoire de Mahelot* lists two daggers for *Bajazet*, one of which is presumably used by Atalide at this point.[10] Swords and lances appear in *Athalie*, incongruous in the hands of priests and Levites, who, if assimilated in the minds of seventeenth-century spectators to French clerics, would be forbidden to carry swords or engage in fighting (*Ath.* III. vii. 1179 and 1193; IV. v. 1461). A ceremonial sword is carried on stage for Joas's coronation in a ceremony to be discussed below.

The French word *bandeau* means a diadem or headband which is a sign of royalty. Esther detests her headband (*Est.* I. i. 107; I. iv. 277), in the same way that the royal finery of Bérénice or Phèdre importunes them in their distress. In *Athalie* the *bandeau* is associated not only with royalty, but also blindness and sacrifice. In *Mithridate*, too, Monime's headband becomes more than an item of apparel; it crystallizes the main movements of the action. Monime at her first entrance confesses herself a

---

[10] The other may be used by Zatime and Atalide in Act V, Scene viii. It is not always clear which weapons appeared in the various scenes of *Bajazet*; for a discussion, see Scherer, 'Mise en scène de *Bajazet*', pp. 211–13.

'crowned slave' (*Mit.* I. iii. 255). The *bandeau* binds her dutifully
to Mithridate, who reminds his betrothed that it is 'a pledge of
my faith' (*Mit.* II. iv. 541). Wearing it, Monime protests that it
symbolizes the impossibility of Xipharès's love (III. v. 1111),
and pointing to it she tries to convince a suspicious Mithridate
of her loyalty to him (IV. iv. 1331). But in the final act the
headband joins with a cup of poison, Mithridate's other gift to
his prospective wife, to become a potential instrument of death.
Monime enters having tried unsuccessfully to strangle herself
with the flimsy headband (V. i. 1458). Desperate for a means of
escape into death, she welcomes the cup of poison, only to have
it dashed from her hand by a countermanded order (*Mit.* Act V,
Scenes ii–iii). Peyron gave both objects prominence in his illustration of this scene, though they are more conspicuous in the
handsome full-size engraving than in reduced reproduction.
The headband lies abandoned on the ground as Monime grasps
eagerly at the cup of poison borne towards her by Arcas.
Symbol of royal power, symbol of death, the headband and
poisoned cup unite to encapsulate the poisoned relationship
between Monime and Mithridate (Pl. 28).

So far it has been possible to categorize those elements of
Racine's visual vocabulary which occur in more than one play
and which acquire different meanings in different contexts.
Some of these visual elements relate to the actions of the human
body: sitting, kneeling, embracing, supporting, restraining,
constraining, assaulting; others relate to the handling of inanimate objects: letter, sword, or diadem. These could be seen as
relatively common elements of Racine's visual vocabulary. In
his one comedy and the two biblical plays the visual vocabulary
and accompanying physical action is richer, more specialized,
and produces more varied and complex effects. The last two
acts of *Athalie* call for particular consideration. This also has the
advantage of highlighting the continuum of speech and action
which categorization necessarily obscures.

(c) *Athalie*

A cluster of three stage properties imparts to Act IV of *Athalie*
its individual shape. The three objects—book, sword, and

diadem—have a double function in evoking the coronation of Joas and at the same time functioning symbolically with connotations of sacrifice. Nor does Racine merely portray an arid ceremonial, but uses its appurtenances and gestures for the visual representation of intense human emotions.

The book, sword, and diadem are brought on stage in solemn procession by three youths. Eliacin anxiously questions Josabet as to their significance. The spectator's curiosity is aroused by the mystery. Racine heightens the emotional tension by planting a false clue. A tearful Josabet, anticipating the coronation, tries the diadem upon Eliacin's head; but the child interprets her sobs as a sign that he is to be a human sacrifice: 'Princess, what pity moves you? Am I to be sacrificed like the daughter of Jephthah?' (*Ath*. IV. i. 1258). The high priest Joad enters, seemingly come to sacrifice Eliacin. The child leaps into the adult's arms in a poignant mixture of submission and terror: 'rushing into the arms of the high priest' (SD, *Ath*. 1264). A minute later the child is looking down upon the prostrate adult as Joad swears homage and signals his allegiance to the king by 'prostrating himself at his feet' (SD, *Ath*. 1290). The peril of sacrifice is passed.

The ceremony continues. The book becomes the focus. Five chief Levites enter and stretch their hands to the book to swear loyalty to the newly revealed king. The high priest then asks the child to swear fidelity to God. Eliacin-Joas does not do so immediately. Has Racine written a significant pause into his text? Joad's question is: 'And you, king, do you swear to be ever faithful to the law, your eternal rule?' The child's reply is equivocal: 'How could I not comply with this law?' There may be here on stage a slight but significant hesitation, which would be consistent with the boy king's future guilt lurking beneath his present innocence; and the point would be reinforced by the high priest's next eighteen lines warning against the perils of evil counsellors and concluding with: 'Alas, they have led astray the wisest of kings.' This line marks the moment that the high priest renews his command for an oath: 'Promise on this book, and before these witnesses, that your first duty will always be to God.' Then, at last, Eliacin-Joas takes his oath, presumably placing his hand upon the book as shown in Chaudet's illustration (Pl. 31; *Ath*. IV. iii. 1381–1409). A more exemplary king might have placed his hand on the book more promptly.

Underneath the coronation ceremonial of book, sword, and diadem lie darker connotations.[11] The book is the voice and will of God. It is mentioned six times in *Athalie*, qualified by the epithets 'divin', 'saint', 'redoutable', 'auguste'. In Act IV it is brought on stage physically veiled and placed on the table— God's will present on stage. The sword is an instrument of purification and also of God's vengeance. Joad had alerted Abner to God's desire not for the blood of goats and sheep, but implicitly perhaps for human sacrifice: 'banish crimes from amidst my people, then you will come and offer sacrifices' (*Ath.* I. i. 91). At the end of the play the exterminating angel is at hand (*Ath.* V. iv. 1698). Athalie becomes the human sacrifice: 'The blade has expiated the horrors of her life' (*Ath.* V. viii. 1808–9). The third object brought for Eliacin-Joas's coronation is the *bandeau*, the multivalent object which can mean royal headband, bandage, or blindfold. Racine had already used the *bandeau* verbally in *Iphigénie* where blindfold, fire, and knife were reported to be ready for the sacrifice of Iphigénie (*Iph.* III. v. 905). In *Athalie* Racine plays with these connotations of blindness, royalty, and sacrifice and introduces the physical object on stage. 'We shall see each other again', Athalie had said at the end of her interrogation of Eliacin-Joas, 'Adieu, I leave content. I wished to see. I've seen' (*Ath.* II. vii. 736). She saw nothing then, her eyes were blindfolded in error and impiety. In Act V Josabet prays to God that Athalie's vision may again be obscured as she walks into the ambush:

> Remets-lui le bandeau dont tu couvris ses yeux,
> Lorsque lui dérobant tout le fruit de son crime,
> Tu cachas dans mon sein cette tendre victime.
>
> (*Ath.* V. iii. 1670)

Athalie will indeed walk blindly into the trap, wearing a meta-phorical blindfold, but when she finally sees Joas crowned with the diadem, the visible *bandeau*, her eyes will be opened. Josabet's prayer will be answered: Athalie will go to her death as a human sacrifice. In support of Yashinsky's interpretation (p. 72) could

---

[11] Analysed by Yashinsky, '"Pourquoi ce livre saint, ce glaive, ce bandeau?": Commentaires textuels sur *Athalie*'.

be added the reference to the sacrifice of Jephthah's daughter which causes such alarm between Joas and Josabet when she tries the *bandeau* on him (IV. i. 1256–61). In this way the three objects of Act IV, sword, book, and diadem, are the visual embodiment of a web of associations central to the whole play.

Act V offers the spectacle of a staged anagnorisis which is unique in Racine's theatre, yet employs a visual language in many respects familiar from his earlier plays. Joad is a stage-manager like Créon, Léandre, Néron, or Acomat.[12] The high priest puts Joas behind a curtain 'He draws a curtain' (SD, *Ath.* V. iv. 1701), just as Néron hid behind a curtain to spy on Junie and Britannicus. Joad's armed Levites are concealed—'they all hide' (SD, *Ath.* V. iv. 1692)—like the guards waiting in the wings for the behest of kings and emperors, such as Néron or Agamemnon. Athalie is lured into the ambush and stands on stage in front of the hidden throne. 'The curtain is drawn back' (SD, *Ath.* V. v. 1717). Joad shows the child king seated upon his throne. To prove the identity of the child, Joad points to the scar inflicted by Athalie herself: 'Recognize at least these marks of your dagger' (*Ath.* 1720), and then as further proof he points to the nurse whom Athalie must recognize (*Ath.* 1723). The scar and the nurse are unique to *Athalie* though familiar in the tradition of anagnorisis, but when Joad summons his Levites to arrest Athalie, the sight is similar to that of Néron or Agamemnon ordering the arrest of their victims (*Bri.* III. viii. 1069; *Iph.* IV. vii. 1433). However, in *Athalie*, the effect is enhanced by the stage direction: 'Here the back of the stage opens. The interior of the temple is seen, and armed Levites come on stage from all sides' (SD, *Ath.* V. v. 1730). Athalie cries out, 'With weapons and enemies I am surrounded' (*Ath.* 1732). Jean-Baptiste Corneille's frontispiece conveys these tumultuous moments: the high priest's arms pointing heavenward; Athalie with terror drawn upon her face, hands raised to the height of her head; Abner kneeling to the enthroned Joas, his armoured back to

---

[12] Créon brings the warring brothers together in *La Thébaïde*, Act IV (see Edwards, 'Créon: Homme de théâtre'); Léandre in Act II, Scene xiv, of *Les Plaideurs* prepares to stage the trial in Act III; Néron gives Junie her role to play when she meets Britannicus (*Bri.* II. iii. 679); Acomat has an energetic, though not always successful, role as the impresario of the rising against Amurat, e.g. *Baj.* I. i. 93, 135, and IV. vi. 1333; on Acomat, see Cave, pp. 349–58.

Athalie signalling his change of allegiance; Levites brandishing swords, lances, and shields. Stretching dimly in the background is a perspective of Corinthian columns (Pl. 14). Within minutes, Joad has ordered the queen to be led to her death. Athalie's steps off stage, like those of Britannicus or Bajazet, are steps to death. Almost all the elements of the visual language of the last act of *Athalie* can be paralleled in earlier plays, but Racine has here combined them in a special way. The visual vocabulary is largely familiar, the syntax is unusual, the connotations are unique.

The drama of *Athalie* is neatly concluded. In a literal sense the spectators have been privileged participants in the recognition of Eliacin-Joas. The curtain which hid him is like the curtain which hides the stage at the start and the end of the performance. A white-robed orphan has been royally placed upon the throne. Jews have rejoiced in the spectacle. Athalie has been cast down. But the visual signs can be read on other levels. The sight of Joas enthroned explains Athalie's dream, which has been succeeded by 'an awakening, full of horror', words with a biblical resonance, evoking the punishment of the powerful (Psalm 73; *Ath.* II. ix. 835). Cave offers more levels of interpretation. Joas, like Christ, is recognized by his scar. The high priest is 'not only master-plotter but also master-exegete' (p. 363). The visibly artificial veiling and unveiling is a contrivance by Joad, and does not arise out of the preceding action. Racine lets Joad take responsibility for the artifice, but the dramatist can take credit for reconstructing in dramatic terms an implicit Pascalian argument 'that since man is fallen, only fallen means can help him; he can only know the truth by artifice, never directly (except by grace)' (Cave, p. 365).

Athalie illustrates in a particularly vivid way how Racine's visual language can be as eloquent and suggestive as his words. However important words are, Racine the dramatist cannot be fully understood without exploring the theatrical dimension. In his theatre the words are not everything: in many passages they are subordinate to the visual language. Sometimes, indeed, the words are unintelligible without visualizing what is being seen on stage. The written text must be translated by theatrical reading into the performance text.

The visual language and physical action so far examined—décor and costume, movements of the human body, and stage properties—is the most striking theatrically. There remains the more elusive language of gesture and facial expression. This has a much closer relationship with verbal language. Here action and speech are more intimately combined.

4

Verbal Action

Et peut-être déjà sait-il persuader
(Britannicus)

Theatricality does not consist only in physical action or visual effects. It embraces verbal language as well. It would be pointless to emphasize Racine's visual language at the expense of his verbal language. But how do words constitute action in the theatre? In the first section of this chapter the key is D'Aubignac's formula 'parler, c'est agir' (speech is action), though this formula is not nearly as simple as it seems, because of the various connotations of the word 'action' in a theatrical context. 'Parler, c'est agir' offers the notion of 'verbal action through persuasion' as a way of explaining the theatricality of speech in Racine. This concept of verbal action will be analysed within the framework of traditional rhetoric, which, though associated with the training of the orator, is relevant to drama because of the persuasive role of the characters in Racinian drama. The exploration of this aspect of Racine's theatricality begins with three sections which are primarily expository. First, a discussion of the concept of speech as action. Secondly, under the heading 'the art of persuasion', there is a rapid survey of the various rhetorical skills requisite for effective and persuasive speech. Thirdly, a more detailed account of the fifth part of rhetoric, namely *actio*, the art of delivering the speech with appropriate tone of voice and gesture. Here the craft of orator and actor converge. Evidence for contemporary acting styles is examined, including Racine's own, since he himself was considered to have had a powerful acting talent. This discussion of speech as action, the art of persuasion and acting styles will serve as the basis for the exploring Racine the director in the following chapter.

(a) Speech as Action

'The theatres of other countries assemble *spectators*; but an *audience* is only to be found in France.' In these terms Lady Morgan voiced the British view of French classical tragedy—all for the ears, nothing for the eyes. In the light of the preceding discussion of Racine's visual language, such a view seems untenable. Lady Morgan continues her indictment of the performance of *Britannicus* she had attended (one dare not say seen): 'Long and cold recitals, and a succession of antitheses, points, and epigrams, were relieved only by a declamation that froze, and by dialogues where each interlocutor was permitted to speak alternately for half an hour, in all the monotony of recitation.' She confesses 'it was with the greatest difficulty, and only, I believe, owing to the exquisite acting of Talma and Mademoiselle George, that I could sit it out' (Morgan, p. 90). It was fashionable in early nineteenth-century France to contrast the visual action of Shakespearean drama with the interminable declamation of French classical tragedy. The view may be prevalent today: 'What strikes the modern English-speaking reader of Corneille, Racine and their contemporaries perhaps most is the apparent absence—or the whittling down to an absolute minimum—of physical movement in tragedy, the priority which seems to be given to words over deeds' (Gossip, p. 94). There was certainly a tradition in seventeenth-century France which privileged hearing over sight, and which relegated visual effects to the taste of the common people:

Even in tragedy [. . .] it is undesirable especially in the eyes of educated men that things should be represented by concrete visual representations, which often do not correspond to the majesty of the subject and deprive the action of much of its dignity. I say educated men, because the vulgar people whose minds and intelligence do not rise very high, do demand visual entertainment in the theatre, and not pleasures which come through the ears.[1]

Caussin's view doubtless satisfied those who hoped education would raise them above the common people. It also provides a

---

[1] N. Caussin, *Eloquentiae sacrae et humanae parallela* (Paris, S. Chappelet, 1619), 'De affectibus', viii. 317, quoted in Fumaroli, p. 232.

good strategy for denigrating the visual in favour of the verbal and the intellectual. The matter seems to be clinched by the dictum of the seventeenth-century theorist of drama, the abbé D'Aubignac, when he wrote: 'the whole representation consists only in speeches' (*Pratique*, iv. 2, p. 260).

Yet the eyes were not without their supporters. Racine himself in the first preface to *Britannicus* repeated the rule that the dramatist should 'only put into a narration, what could not be represented in action' (p. 404). All the visual effects described in the preceding section argue against the view that Racinian drama is purely verbal. And D'Aubignac himself emphasizes in unambiguous terms that drama is something to be seen, spelling out the visual implications of the Greek and Latin terminology in current use:

Tragedy [. . .] is *drama*, that is to say, action not recital. Those who perform the action are actors not orators; those who are present are called spectators or watchers (*regardans*), not hearers (*auditeurs*); the place which serves for performances is called a theatre not an auditory (*auditoire*), that is to say, a place where one watches what is done and not where one listens to what is said.

D'Aubignac goes on to quote Donatus on actors, who are so called because their performance is 'more in gestures than in words' (*Pratique*, iv. 2, pp. 259–60).

In this theoretical battle between the ears and the eyes, it is easy to extract quotations which support the primacy of either words or of physical actions. The truth, however, lies in the complex relationship between these two components of the theatrical language of seventeenth-century French drama.

D'Aubignac's remarks on the etymology of the word *théâtre* and his insistence on the visual and performative nature of drama are preliminaries to his formulation of the concept that, in the theatre, to speak is to act, or speech is action. This formulation is a bridge between D'Aubignac's apparently contradictory statements that the theatre is a place 'where one watches what is done and not where one listens to what is said' and 'the whole representation is in speeches'. The second statement is a concession to the first. The concept of speech as action is an elusive one, not helped by the different senses of the French word *action* as it was used by seventeenth-century writers on theatre including D'Aubignac, Corneille, and Racine.[2]

In the context of discussion about the nature of drama, the French word *action* could mean: (1) the subject of the drama; (2) episodes forming part of the plot; (3) a physical act; (4) the technical rhetorical term *actio*, meaning the delivery of a speech; (5) a piece of public speaking such as a sermon, harangue, or pleading in the lawcourts. One or more of these five connotations may be at work when the French word *action* is used in theatrical contexts. To elucidate what he means by *parler, c'est agir*—D'Aubignac's concise formulation of his preceding sentence: 'speech in the theatre must resemble the actions of those who appear on stage'—he gives three examples: (*a*) the narration of Hippolytus' death in Seneca is 'the *action* of a man terrified by a monster which he has seen rise out of the sea, and terrified by the fatal adventure of this prince'; (*b*) in Corneille's *Cinna* the lamentations of Emilie are the *action* of a daughter torn between vengeance and love; (*c*) in Corneille's *Le Cid*, when Chimène speaks to the king, 'it is the *action* of a bereaved daughter who demands justice' (*Pratique*, iv. 2, p. 260). In theatrical terms these examples constitute three important types of dramatic discourse prevalent in seventeenth-century French drama: Hippolytus's death is a *narration*, Emilie's lamentations are a *monologue*, Chimène's pleading before the king is a piece of *judicial oratory*. What then, according to D'Aubignac, is the nature of the action which the spectator is watching when a narration, a monologue, or a piece of judicial oratory is enacted on stage?

It is not entirely clear. Obviously D'Aubignac is not here referring to the general meanings of *action* as dramatic subject or episode (senses 1 and 2 above). His concept seems to partake of the three other senses. A piece of persuasive public speaking, such as a speech in the lawcourts (sense 5) is especially relevant to Chimène instigating judicial proceedings against Rodrigue. The rhetorical term *actio* (sense 4), which involves depicting emotion by gesture and facial expression, is indeed applicable to these speeches when delivered by actors on stage. D'Aubignac's characterization of his three examples lays special emphasis on the expression of emotion or passion—'a man terrified . . . a

---

[2] See Hawcroft's discussion of these issues, pp. 17–36.

daughter torn between vengeance and love ... a bereaved daughter', all of which would be given visible expression when performed by an actor. Physical act (sense 3) seems most inappropriate to a speech, but once it is realized that the speech is public, and that it involves gesture, movement, and a display of emotion, then it clearly does appeal to the eye as well as to the ear.

D'Aubignac's concept of *parler, c'est agir*, his concept of speech as action, could be summed up in the phrase *verbal action*, meaning that the speech is active in that it both seeks to persuade by acting on another person, and also has a physical dimension, being delivered with appropriate gesture or actions in public. The notion of speech being active is clarified by another statement on the subject, this time from Corneille, who says 'the actions are the soul of the tragedy, in which one should only speak actively (*en agissant*) and in order to act (*et pour agir*)' (*Discours du poème dramatique*, p. 19). The phrase *en agissant* implies that the characters are activated by emotion or self-interest, whilst the phrase *pour agir* implies that the speaker intends to use the words to achieve an effect on someone else. Even the monologue falls into this pattern because D'Aubignac specified that the single person is divided into two, being 'torn between vengeance and love', and Emilie in his example has to decide which of these emotions will determine her course of action. An earlier passage of the *Pratique du théâtre* spells out further implications of this notion. Throughout the play, says D'Aubignac, speaking of continuity of action, 'the principal characters must be always active (*agissants*); there must be shown on stage an uninterrupted succession of schemes, expectations, passions, troubles, anxieties, and similar agitations' (*Pratique*, ii. 4, p. 79).

The Protean senses of the French word *action* undoubtedly confuse the issue of sight and sound in D'Aubignac's discussion of speech and action. One cannot neglect the importance of words alone in signifying action to the imagination of the audience. Murray rightly stresses the role of this in D'Aubignac's theory, and supports it by reference to the statement: 'the poet brings very few actions on stage, [...] the actions are only in the imagination of the spectator, who conceives them as visible through the ingenuity of the poet' (*Pratique*, iv. 2, pp.

260–1). Murray, however, seems to go too far in concluding: 'The significant actions are *not visible* on the stage [. . .] By *substituting words for actions*, D'Aubignac displaces vision as the guiding principle of dramatic practice' (p. 72, his italics). In the quotation from D'Aubignac, with which Murray supports this, the word *action* is used in the sense of subject of the drama or those physical actions which take place off-stage; but the other senses of *action* undermine the notion that D'Aubignac completely displaces vision as the guiding principle of dramatic practice.

Verbal action can therefore be explained as a verbal exchange of a persuasive and emotional nature in a situation where personal interests are at stake and which requires a decision to be taken. The exchange is usually between two characters representing different views, but in a monologue the exchange can be between conflicting viewpoints of a single character. This appears to be the sense in which D'Aubignac's 'parler, c'est agir' conveys a concept of speech as action which is vital to an understanding of the theatrical language of Racine and his contemporaries.[3]

It is a peculiarity of theatrical language that it operates simultaneously on two axes: (*a*) the character axis, when characters engage with each other in the fictional situation; and (*b*) the spectator axis, when the dramatist acts through his fictional characters upon the spectator. The effects of the verbal action will vary according to the axis chosen for analysis. The simplest case is when the verbal action is an exciting oratorical joust. A vivid description can be found in D'Aubignac's *Dissertation sur Sophonisbe* (pp. 143–4) where he praises Corneille for

those fine debates which he so often put on our stage, which pushed human ingenuity to the limit; where the last speaker seemed to have

---

[3] Verbal action could be approached through the terminology of the speech act theory of John Austin and John Searle, which distinguishes between performative and constative utterances and qualifies speech acts as locutionary, illocutionary, and perlocutionary (see Elam, pp. 156–70). Full-scale application of this terminology would result in a philosophical or linguistic rather than a theatrical analysis. For some examples, see Felman's extended discussion of Molière's *Dom Juan* in *Le Scandale du corps parlant*; Aragon, 'Étude de quelques actes de langage dans *Bajazet*'; and a brief reference to performative and constative acts in Romanowski, 'Circuits of Power and Discourse in Racine's *Bajazet*', p. 857. Ekstein uses the concept of performative utterance to elucidate the dramatic function of narrations (pp. 20–6).

been so completely in the right that one would have thought it was impossible to make any reply; where speech and counter speech excited such great applause that one was repeatedly frustrated by losing a good part of them; and this compelled everyone to return several times to the same play which always led to some new enjoyment.

It is clear that, where oratorical jousts are concerned, the character axis predominates, though excitement is also generated on the spectator axis when the spectators feel the pressure exerted by the persuasive force of the protagonists' speeches. On the other hand, when the dramatist writes only with the spectator axis in mind, and does not pay sufficient attention to the plausibility of the character axis, then the theatrical effect is undermined. Poorly motivated scenes of exposition, such as Act I of Corneille's *Rodogune*, illustrate this. There, two minor characters exchange long historical narrations concerning events with which both are familiar. D'Aubignac is severe: 'The poet gets a character to repeat what the other knows already [. . .] This defect is noticeable in *Rodogune*' (*Pratique*, iv. 3, p. 276). Even Corneille made only half-hearted attempts to defend himself on this score in his *Examen* of *Rodogune* (pp. 132–3). D'Aubignac summed up the need to balance the two axes: 'Everything which seems deliberately directed towards the spectator is thoroughly defective (*vicieux*)' (*Pratique*, i. 6, p. 32).

How can the dramatist achieve the necessary expertise and vigour in verbal action? How can he ensure that in his plays speech is action? D'Aubignac has a clear answer: 'I recommend that poets should become skilled in the art of good speaking. [. . .] The poet must have good knowledge of all the passions, of the mechanisms which activate them, and of the manner of expressing them in a well-organized, energetic, judicious manner.' D'Aubignac has no need to encumber his own treatise with all the details. He refers his budding dramatist to the many treatises already written on the art of rhetoric (*Pratique*, iv. 2, pp. 263–4).

(b) The Art of Persuasion

There are obstacles to accepting rhetoric as a guide to theatrical reading. The pejorative connotations of 'rhetorical' as something artificial or extravagant in language seem to take us back to Lady Morgan's indictment of *Britannicus* for its 'long and cold recitals, and a succession of antitheses, points, and epigrams' (p. 90). This seems the very opposite of theatre as something to be seen. Even sympathetic analyses of Racine's rhetoric stress above all its stylistic features. Butler says 'the first characteristic which links Racine's style to that of his predecessors is the place still accorded to rhetoric, not necessarily in a pejorative sense [. . .] The speech of Oreste is constructed upon a series of parallels and antitheses' (pp. 127–8). Peter France's study, *Racine's Rhetoric*, certainly takes account of the spectator in the theatre, and he examines the importance of 'stirring the passions of one's audience' (p. 164). He acknowledges the active oratorical dimension (p. 213), but his analysis is 'chiefly concerned with *elocutio*, the stylistic devices used by Racine on his audience' (p. 205). This is a legitimate concern when dealing with a poetic text which was written to be read as well as performed. Indeed the textbooks of rhetoric seem far removed from the concerns of poetic drama. They concern the training of a Greek or Roman orator for three principal situations: for debating issues in public life (deliberative oratory), for pleading in the lawcourts (judicial or forensic oratory), and for composing panegyrics or invectives (epideictic oratory). Yet the apparent gap between the training of the seventeenth-century French playwright and the training of an orator for public life in ancient Greece and Rome was no problem to D'Aubignac's contemporaries, since the art of rhetoric formed an important part of the education of the time. Racine as a schoolboy copied out extensive extracts from Quintilian.[4] He annotated copies of Cicero's rhetorical treatises.[5] These ancient works, sometimes published in French adaptations, taught schoolboys and adults the skills necessary for speaking and writing persuasively on all occasions.

The relevance of the art of rhetoric to a theatrical reading of Racine lies in the fact that by considering the drama on the character axis it becomes apparent that the characters do indeed

---

[4] Bibliothèque Nationale, fonds français, 12888; on the cover is written: 'Extraits ecrits par Jean Racine des auteurs Latins qu'il lisoit à Port-Royal en 1656; il avoit alors environ 15 ans'; Hawcroft, p. 42.

[5] Text of the annotations in *Œuvres*, ii. 975–9; Racine's knowledge of rhetoric is discussed by France, pp. 37–57, and Hawcroft, pp. 40–6.

behave like orators when they engage with each other. The audience derives pleasure from seeing characters fighting their verbal battles, similar to those which Quintilian described as oratorical jousts (IX. i. 20–1). Racine shows characters in scenes of formal oratory, acting as ambassadors or counsellors: Oreste (*And.* Act I, Scene ii), Ephestion (*Ale.* Act II, Scene ii), Mathan (*Ath.* Act III, Scene iv). Other scenes are not strictly formal but characters engage with each other in a formal spirit, e.g. Agrippine and Néron (*Bri.* Act IV, Scene ii), Mithridate and his two sons (*Mit.* Act III, Scene i), Esther and Assuérus (*Est.* Act III, Scene iv). Of particular theatrical effectiveness are scenes where inquisitorial oratory, based on the examination of witnesses, is brought into play (e.g. *Baj.* Act IV, Scene iii; *Mit.* Act III, Scene v; *Ath.* Act II, Scene vii). Rhetoric was not only concerned with formal occasions. Its skills were valid for informal situations. The orator, wrote Quintilian, 'stands armed for the battle, ever ready for the fray, and his eloquence will no more fail him in the courts than speech will fail him in domestic affairs and in the daily concerns of his life' (XII. ix. 210). Racine shows this at work when he extends oratorical techniques into informal scenes where domestic concerns predominate and characters use the art of persuasion for private ends (e.g. *Iphigénie*, Act IV, Scenes iv–vii, and all through *Bérénice*). Even in encounters between protagonists and confidants, where there is no major conflict of aims, Racine engineers differences of opinion between them to endow these scenes with dramatic momentum (e.g. Agrippine and Albine in *Bri.* Act I, Scene i). Monologues may seem to be poetic interludes and narrations may seem merely to impart information; but here, too, Racine contrives to give them theatrical dynamism. Monologues often represent two sides of a character in conflict with himself; a narration often functions within a persuasive framework.[6]

To what purpose is the persuasion directed? Often to the act of speaking itself. In their confrontations characters press each other for a verbal response. A single word may suffice. Xipharès pleads with Monime: 'I beg you, one word' (*Mit.* I. ii.

---

[6] All the scenes mentioned are analysed by Hawcroft with special reference to their theatrical qualities. For Assuérus's deliberation, see *Est.* Act II, Scenes iii–v.

220). A character may try to avert an irrevocable pronounce-
ment, as when Andromaque begs Pyrrhus not to give the order
to have her son killed (*And.* I. iv. 275). The act of speaking may
be contextualized so that it is invested with momentous
significance. Acomat tells Osmin that on his report depends the
fate of the Ottoman empire (*Baj.* I. i. 14). Bajazet's life or death
will depend upon his reply to Roxane (*Baj.* I. iii. 326). Silence is
no refuge.[7] Racine directs persuasion towards the act of
speaking itself and invests that act with dramatic potential; but
his theatricality does not stop there. Persuasion is also directed
towards physical actions such as leaving the stage or staying. In
moments of intense conflict it can be focused on an embrace, a
beating, or a killing (see Chapter 5, section *f*). In response to
persuasion either speech or action may be a perilous commit-
ment.

Whilst the art of rhetoric is an indispensable tool for analysing
theatrical language, certain aspects of verbal action are more
prominent in drama than in formal oratory, because drama
consists of dialogue whereas the art of rhetoric concentrates
mainly, though not exclusively, upon the single speech. The
aside is a peculiarly theatrical device. Characters break off a
dialogue to speak to different person (*aparté dialogué*) or simply
to themselves (*aparté monologué*). The essence of the aside is that
the words are concealed from at least one character on stage.
This piece of verbal action is always associated with moments of
stress. Racine usually combines the aside with an entrance or
exit, thus rendering it more plausible because the characters are
on the move. As Monime exits, Pharnace's aside gives a
lightning glimpse of his real feelings as a prelude to his
deliberation with Xipharès (*Mit.* Act I, Scene v). Bérénice's
aside conceals her real distress from Antiochus and is uttered as
she staggers off stage with Phénice (*Bér.* Act III, Scene iii).
Other asides serve to punctuate a scene, marking its main
stages. The tense atmosphere of Athalie's interrogation is
structured and heightened by three asides (*Ath.* Act II, Scene
vii).[8]

Rapid exchanges between characters are another important

way of generating theatrical excitement. Greek tragedy provided models for *stichomythia*, where characters exchange
couplets or single lines with each other. Racine uses this
technique in most of his plays. Even more exciting is the
quick-fire exchange which divides the alexandrine line between
characters. They are almost absent from the three tragedies
which precede *Les Plaideurs*, but in *Britannicus* there are six such
passages (*Bri*. Act II, Scenes ii and iv; Act III, Scene vi; Act V,
Scenes i, iv, and vi). *Bérénice* has spectacular examples where
three or more exchanges are created from a single alexandrine
divided between Titus and Bérénice (*Bér*. II. iv. 623; V. vi.
1307). In the rest of the tragedies such exchanges are fewer,
though they always highlight crucial points of revelation. Both
Fournier (p. 178) and Flowers (p. 77) note that the experience of
writing *Les Plaideurs* seems to have been pivotal in the
development of Racine's dramatic technique with regard to
asides and quick-fire exchanges, both of which become more
common in the tragedies Racine wrote after his one comedy.
Whilst quick-fire exchanges are especially appropriate to the
theatre, they still represent in condensed form the persuasive
techniques of the orator.

In addition, the art of rhetoric acknowledged close connections between the performance of the orator and the actor.
Grimarest formulated a notion that was familiar to his contemporaries: 'the actor must consider himself like an orator, who
pronounces in public a speech composed to touch the audience'
(*Vie de Molière*, p. 162). It was also a commonplace of rhetorical
theory that the orator might learn from the actor. The two
professions were closely linked.

If one considers the character in Racinian drama as a kind of
orator who has to persuade other characters, then some aspects
of the combination of verbal and visual action can be highlighted using the framework of the five traditional categories of the
art of rhetoric:

1. Finding ways to persuade the listener (*inventio*)
2. Organizing the speech (*dispositio*)
3. Selecting the appropriate style (*elocutio*)
4. Memorizing the speech (*memoria*)
5. Delivering the speech (*actio*)

These five skills relate to the theatre in different ways. The most important in the theatre is *actio*. All the others are preparatory steps which look forward to the pronouncing of the speech before the audience. Each of the four preparatory steps has some specifically visual implications which tend to be overlooked in rhetorical analysis but which assume greater significance in a theatrical reading.

Inventio

At first sight *inventio* seems to be predominantly a matter of words, because it is mainly the art of finding persuasive things to say; but *inventio* can also include visual effects. The three traditional divisions of *inventio* were (*a*) character (*mores*), (*b*) passions (*affectus*), (*c*) proofs (*probationes*). Thinking about these categories would provide the orator with material for composing his speech; for the dramatist each has theatrical implications.

Mores meant finding ways to create a favourable impression of oneself. When Burrhus tells Agrippine that he is 'a soldier with no knowledge of how to dress up the truth' (*Bri.* I. ii. 174) he is trying to give a picture of himself as a bluff, sincere man. Such comments are designed to make Agrippine take seriously what he says. They also provide guidance for the actor who has to interpret the character on stage. Agrippine in turn uses *mores* to persuade Britannicus to ally himself with her, by saying she is not the type of person whose 'anger will remain impotent' (*Bri.* I. iii. 301). She is encouraging Britannicus to have faith in her. This also gives clues to the actress for performance.

Affectus was extremely important. The primordial role of passion or emotion in persuasion was ruefully acknowledged by La Rochefoucauld: 'Passions are the only orators which always persuade' (*Maximes*, no. 8). The passions defied neat classification. Those most commonly mentioned were love, hate, hope, despair, fear, and grief (Aristotle, *Rhetorica*, ii. 12–19). The portrayal of passion was the essence of good theatre. Passions were visible. Le Brun explained: 'Most passions of the soul produce bodily actions [. . .]; the eyebrows are the part of the face where the passions can best be recognized, though some say it is in the eyes' (pp. 3 and 13). Displays of passion created the impression that the character was in the grip of forces beyond his control. They are not hard to find in Racine as a means of persuasion. Hémon, reunited with Antigone after a year's separation, wants his impatient mistress to stay with him instead of rushing away to the temple. In his pleadings he exudes love in every speech (*Thé.* Act II, Scene i). Antiochus, on the other hand, is exposed to a blast of hatred when Bérénice urges him to reveal what Titus had said about her: 'Prince, this very moment content my desire, or be assured of my undying hate.' Antiochus immediately acknowledges the effectiveness of this display of emotion: 'Madam, with that I must unloose my tongue; and what you ask I now will satisfy' (*Bér.* III. iii. 885). The spectator has *seen* hatred displayed in Bérénice's demeanour and has *heard* Antiochus admit that he has been persuaded by it.

Probationes, meaning proofs, or, more accurately, probabilities, were the third division of *inventio.* The proofs could be 'real' (*inartificiales*) if they existed independently of the speaker, or 'contrived' (*artificiales*) if the orator constructed them himself. 'Contrived proofs', which are always verbal, can be classified by the *loci* or places where the orator might find them. 'Definition' is one such locus. Hippolyte defines Phèdre as 'the daughter of Minos and Pasiphaé' (*Phè.* Act I, Scene i) in order to explain more persuasively why he wishes to leave Troezen. This kind of argument is specially suited to poetic drama since from a stylistic aspect it involves the poetic figure of periphrasis. When the periphrasis contributes to the argument, it reveals the link between poetry and persuasion which Racine practised so skilfully.[9] Other sources of argument are cause and effect, consequences, antecedents, or adjuncts.[10] 'Real proofs' could also be of many kinds. In the verbal category are the citation of authorities, examples, or customs. Paulin warns Titus of the Roman dislike of queens to strengthen the emperor's resolve to abandon Bérénice (*Bér.* II. ii. 377). Roxane and Bajazet wield the customs of the Turkish sultans in their verbal battles. Roxane seeks precedents to persuade Bajazet to marry her; he finds contrary precedents to dissuade her (*Baj.* II. i. 462 and 487). In the theatre it is the concrete object or physical sign as 'real

---

[9] Vinaver, p. 149; see also Sayce, 'Racine's Style'.
[10] For a fuller account of the *loci*, see Hawcroft, pp. 59–69.

proof' which provides the opportunity for striking visual effects. Almost all Racine's stage properties are brought into play in a persuasive context. Etéocle points to his sword to persuade Polynice that he will only give the crown up after a fight (*Thé.* IV. iii. 1076). Roxane uses the letter Bajazet wrote to Atalide as proof of his infidelity (*Baj.* V. iv. 1487). The lawsuit in *Les Plaideurs* involves a dog who has eaten a chicken. Racine comically puts the dog in the dock as the accused. The judge calls for evidence of the misdeed. The prosecutor says: 'I have them in my pocket; here you are—the chicken's head and feet', and he produces them (*Pla.* III. iii. 720). Joad persuades the Jews and Athalie to recognize Joas as king by showing his scar and his nurse (*Ath.* V. v. 1720–5).

Dispositio

Having assembled his arguments from these sources, the orator organized them into a framework. The major divisions were *exordium*, *narratio*, *confirmatio*, and *peroratio*. These can be illustrated from Oreste's speech to Pyrrhus (see Hawcroft, pp. 74–8, 112–16).

The *exordium* was the place for the orator to gain the goodwill and attention of the audience and to guide their minds along the path desired by the orator. It is especially the place for *mores*. Oreste draws on *mores* and *definitio* to flatter Pyrrhus as a worthy son of Achilles 'Yes, we admire your deeds as we admired his exploits [. . .] only the son of Achilles could fill his place' (*And.* I. ii. 143–50).

The *narratio* was a relation of past events arranged in a way favourable to the orator's purpose. Oreste's *narratio* is short. He tells how Pyrrhus, by protecting Astyanax, the son of Hector, has given succour to the Trojan cause. This event is narrated so that its implications are spelt out: 'the Greeks see with grief'; Pyrrhus's pity is 'fatal' (*And.* 151–4). Simply by narrating what Pyrrhus has done with judiciously placed words of emotion, Oreste has placed Pyrrhus in the wrong.

The *confirmatio* is the part of the speech for arguments arising out of the case as stated in the *narratio*. Oreste urges Pyrrhus to consider the consequences of protecting Astyanax: the son of Hector is associated with the death of many Greek families.

What might the son of such a father as Hector do to the Greeks one day? (*And*. 155–64) Pyrrhus must consider the consequences for himself: he may be punished for preserving the life of Hector's son (*And*. 165–8). In these arguments Oreste is drawing on the *loci* of adjuncts and consequences.

The *peroratio* is the orator's opportunity to bring everything together by recapitulating the main points of his arguments and arousing a final burst of emotion. Oreste is quick to repeat his main point, which is that Pyrrhus must satisfy the Greek demands and have Astyanax killed. He ends by seeking to arouse fear when he warns Pyrrhus to expect vengeance from the Greeks for his protection of the son of the Trojan hero (*And*. 169–72).

Dispositio seems in some ways the least theatrical part of rhetoric, being concerned with the formal ordering of the speech. This aspect of Racinian tragedy attracted particular censure from Lady Morgan who commented on the characters taking turns to deliver formal set-piece speeches (p. 90). On the other hand it is the ordering of the speech which has the most potential for creating suspense in the audience. A narration which is part of a longer speech of persuasion raises the question 'How does this fit into the argument? What *confirmatio* will follow?' The divisions of a speech can engender suspense as they unfold. The textbooks of declamation also advised on the manner of delivery appropriate to each of the formal divisions of the speech, as will be seen when *actio* is discussed below.

Elocutio

Nor does *elocutio* seem theatrical either. Style, word patterns, and figures of speech have been the focus of predominantly literary interpretations of drama. Peter France devotes the major part of his analysis of Racine's rhetoric to decorative rhetoric and pattern rhetoric (pp. 58–163) but he also studies the way *elocutio* can offer guidance to the actors in the expression of passions (pp. 164–204). Since the passions were a particularly visible form of persuasion *elocutio* could have a theatrical effect. Interjections like 'Ah!' or 'Alas' can express surprise or grief, and by punctuating a speech give guidance to the actor for tone of voice for the whole speech. Choice of words can contribute to theatrical effect. The imperative denotes anger when Phèdre dismisses Œnone: 'Go, execrable monster, go, leave me' (*Phè.* IV. vi. 1317). A question expresses Mithridate's fear of defeat (*Mit.* II. iv. 555) or Monime's sad resignation (*Mit.* I. ii. 147). Apostrophe is used by Roxane to express fury at the absent Bajazet (*Baj.* IV. v. 1272 and 1298). Hyperbole in Racine is usually functional, expressing violent passion rather than being the form of decoration favoured by some of his contemporaries.[11] Verbal patterns, the other major branch of *elocutio*, were criticized as untheatrical by D'Aubignac, though they seem to have pleased some ignorant sections of the audience (*Dissertation sur Sertorius*, pp. 271 and 278). *Elocutio* could have theatrical effect in other ways. In forms of address, the switch from the polite *vous* to the contemptuous *tu* signals change of demeanour. Courtesy slips: passion breaks through. It is also characteristic of Racine to vary the style from poetic to prosaic. By expressing themselves on occasion in simple everyday language, in sentences which could almost be spoken in modern French conversation, his characters engage intensely at moments of crisis. Roxane has a striking line: 'Bajazet, écoutez; je sens que je vous aime' (*Baj.* II. i. 538). Atalide asks with fierce inquisitiveness: 'Parle. L'épouse-t-il?' (*Baj.* III. i. 811). Mithridate has a remarkable sequence of prosaic sentences: 'Non, Madame. Il suffit. Je vais vous l'envoyer. Allez. Le temps est cher' (*Mit.* III. v. 1113). Agamemnon rudely asks Achille 'Pourquoi le demander, si vous le savez?' (*Iph.* IV. vi. 1340). Such flashes of plain-speaking sharply contrast with the predominantly elevated style, and electrify the audience by their brusque intensity.

Enargeia is the figure of speech where words create visions: 'It makes us seem not so much to narrate as to bring to life the actual scene' says Quintilian (VI. ii. 32). All the examples he gives are rich in visual detail. Quoting one from Cicero he says 'Is there anybody so incapable of forming a mental picture of a scene that, when he reads the following passage, he does not seem not merely to see the actors in the scene, the place itself and their very dress, but even to imagine to himself other details that the orator does not describe' (VIII. iii. 64). In this same sense Racine's word-pictures transport the spectator from the visible

---

[11] Examples from France, pp. 171-8.

stage of the Hôtel de Bourgogne into scenes of violence.
Andromaque's narration of Troy's last bloody night (*And*. Act
III, Scene viii) is an example of enargeia which Quintilian's
enthusiastic comment seems almost to paraphrase: 'We may
move our hearers to tears by the picture of a captured town
[. . .] We shall see the flames pouring from house and temple,
and hear the crash of falling roofs and one confused clamour
blent of many cries' (VIII. iii. 67–8). A frequent device to signal
enargeia is the incorporation of the words 'I saw (*j'ai vu*)' into a
narration. It is particularly useful in heterodiegetic narrations,
where a narrator, who did not actually participate in the events
described, thereby lends authenticity to his *récit*. As part of their
persuasion of each other Racine's characters repeatedly conjure
up mental pictures which serve also to delight the spectators.
Indeed, the enterprise of theatrical reading treats the whole play
as a specimen of enargeia, when the written text is mentally
transformed into the performance text.

Memoria

The memorizing of the speech concerned the actor. Chappuzeau
records that a normal role could be learnt in a week if need be,
but that an actor blessed with a powerful memory could learn
even the longest part in three days (p. 72). The spectator was
involved only when lapses of memory occurred on stage.
Racine humorously evokes this predicament by introducing the
prompter in *Les Plaideurs* to supply Petit Jean's defective
memory when he is acting as counsel for the prosecution in the
trial of the dog (*Pla*. III. iii. 667). Titus's inability to speak to
Bérénice could be interpreted rhetorically as a lapse of memory
caused by his fear of Bérénice's likely reaction to being told they
must separate (*Bér*. II. ii. 473; II. iv. 624). Phèdre confesses to
this very fault: 'I forget as I see him what I came to say' (*Phè*. II.
v. 582).

Actio

The fifth part of rhetoric was the art of delivery. Here the paths
of the orator and the actor met. Grimarest is quite explicit. He
says that the part of rhetoric which concerns *actio* is a guide to
the art of acting. He adds: 'The actor must consider himself as

an orator, who pronounces in public a speech composed to touch the audience' (*Addition à la vie de Molière*, p. 162). Touching the audience was Racine's constant concern. The understanding of *actio* is therefore a major tool in a theatrical reading of Racine. Some historical considerations are a necessary introduction.

Quintilian's treatment of *actio* in Book XI of the *Institutio oratoria* illustrates the framework in which subsequent treatises on the art of public speaking were developed. He gives advice on voice control, on gestures of head, arm, and hands, on the face and the eyes, on body posture and movements, even on dress. He makes recommendations for the type of delivery suitable for each part of the speech: gentle delivery for the *exordium*, a sharper, colloquial, but more emphatic delivery for the *narratio*, variety in the *probationes*. Arguments should be lively, energetic, bold, and rapid. The *peroratio* should recapitulate with short clear-cut clauses. If pity is to be excited then gentle melancholy must prevail.

Even though Quintilian was writing primarily for the lawcourts he also has public recitations in mind (XI. iii. 57) and his references to poetry and drama show the links between the art of the orator and the art of the actor. To illustrate correct phrasing he shows how the pauses should fall in reciting the first lines of Virgil's *Aeneid* (XI. iii. 33–9). To stress the importance of the eyes and glance in conveying threats, flattery, sorrow, joy, pride, or submission, he points to the masks worn in tragedy and comedy, which convey character through expression—Medea is fierce, Ajax bewildered, Hercules truculent (XI. iii. 72–3). Other comments could easily be applied to the stage. Quintilian disagrees with Pliny on the problem of hair. Pliny thought the orator should endeavour not to disorder his hair when drying his brow with a handkerchief. Quintilian felt 'that dishevelled locks make an additional appeal to the emotions' (XI. iii. 148). Racine's dishevelled Bérénice may have this advice in mind as she prepares to appeal to Titus. Phénice says 'Let me arrange your hair which is hiding your eyes.' 'No,' says Bérénice, 'let him see the damage he has wrought' (*Bér.* IV. ii. 969). So the Queen of Palestine, dutiful disciple of Quintilian, appears with dishevelled hair before Titus to arouse more pity in him and to increase the anguish of their parting.

Since there is no treatise on the art of acting as such in seventeenth-century France it is necessary to draw in some measure on the treatises on the art of rhetoric to evoke the actors' performance. This is legitimate because of the acknowledged connections between the rhetorically trained orator and the actor. Moreover, a knowledge of the liberal art of rhetoric was held to be the mark of the actor who had risen above the status of mere entertainer, and many of the recommendations for *actio* shade off into recommendations for appropriate conversation in polite society. Not until the eighteenth century did works appear which dealt specifically with the art of acting. Grear has charted the evolution of acting techniques from the seventeenth century, when *actio* for the orator served as a possible basis for the actor's performance, to the mid-eighteenth century, when the actor was guided more by feeling and intuition (Grear, pp. 412–17). This evolution could be described as a transition from art to heart. Grimarest's *Traité du récitatif* (1707) stands at the crossroads in this evolution.[12] Although the treatise is based on precept, and so leans towards art, he made the distinction between the *comédien* with a knowledge of declamation, who 'animates his *actio* like a common artisan doing his job', and the *acteur*, who, 'master of his métier, gives his performance all the truth and delicacy which nature demands' (*Addition à la vie de Molière*, p. 164). Grimarest's treatise has the advantage of giving advice on how specific passages from the plays of Corneille and Racine should be delivered, whether in public readings or by the actors on stage. Another aid to visualizing performance is Le Brun's manual for artists, instructing them in appropriate ways of depicting passions through facial expression and bodily movement.[13] Both Le Brun and Grimarest are careful to stress that the different passions are often mixed. This mitigates the schematic nature of their treatment. The artist's visual repertoire had much in common with that of the actor. In both cases the real interest of facial expres-

---

[12] For 17th-cent. acting, see Capatti, pp. 137–52; for the 18th cent., see D. Barnett, 'The Performance Practice of Acting'; A. Blanc, 'L'Action'.
[13] Le Brun's links with Descartes and with Molière are examined in Powell, 'Making Faces'; Le Coat shows how *actio* applied not only to actors and public speakers, but also to musicians ('Mimique de l'acteur et du musicien'); Goodden explores the links between acting, the visual arts, and dance in '*Actio*' *and Persuasion*.

sion lies in its ability to convey a wealth of nuance within the broad categories of the primary passions, and interpretations might differ. Greuze's picture of a girl weeping over a dead bird (1765) provoked contradictory interpretations from Diderot and another critic. The actress, Mlle Clairon, was noted for her striking but sometimes enigmatic facial expressions (Goodden, pp. 153–4). *Actio* was a text to be deciphered as well as the mimesis of passion. The actor's performance was by no means rigidly controlled, and there is also evidence for a variety of styles of acting, illustrating different relationships between speech and action. Passing now from discussion of the art of persuasion to description of acting styles, we pass from active words to acted words.

(c) Acting Styles

Racine's plays were performed by two sets of actors in two theatres. Firstly by Molière's troupe for *La Thébaïde* and *Alexandre*. Then Racine transferred his allegiance. to the rival actors of the Hôtel de Bourgogne. The latter company performed all his plays between *Alexandre* and *Phèdre*. His last two plays, *Esther* and *Athalie*, were written for schoolgirls and never performed by professional actors in Racine's lifetime.

The wealth of evidence for acting styles in seventeenth-century France would make students of ancient Greek drama, or even of Shakespeare, green with envy. However, the abundance of evidence does not make the realities easier to grasp. Much of it is polemical. One often has to grope towards understanding through a fog of facetiousness. Molière puts himself on stage in a short play, *L'Impromptu de Versailles* (1663), showing himself directing his actors. He pokes fun at his rivals at the Hôtel de Bourgogne. In turn Molière's enemies made fun of Molière's own acting style. Their comments on each other are partisan, caricatural, and exaggerated. A different problem arises with Robinet's rhymed gazette which pays tribute to the actors and actresses, but conceals the reality beneath a mass of superlatives. Some evidence for Racine's training of his actresses comes from his sons, one of whom was concerned to present a wholesome public image of his father. Debate about acting styles for French tragedy echoed down into the eighteenth century, drawing

on fallible memories of the golden age of Louis XIV, sometimes distorted by new ideas on the actor's art. None the less,
some sense can be made of the styles of acting at the Hôtel
de Bourgogne, of Molière's innovations, and Racine's own
preferences.

The theatre called the Hôtel de Bourgogne was the chief place
for tragedy in Paris. There D'Aubignac had watched the French
theatrical renewal take shape through the efforts of Pierre
Corneille, Pierre Du Ryer, Georges de Scudéry, and Jean
Rotrou. Illustrious actors had brought this renaissance to life:
Mondory, Montfleury, Floridor. Their delivery was stylized.
The two halves of the alexandrine line were regularly accentuated. Actors conveyed moments of intense passion by loud
vehement delivery. They marked the climaxes. Their technique
was designed to elicit shouts of applause from the crowded
auditorium. There was a bond between actors and spectators.

There are no friendly accounts of this style. It was easy to
caricature; but as this was the theatre that Racine favoured for
most of his theatrical career, it is essential to explore its characteristics as a contribution to understanding Racine's own views
on acting and the theatricality of his text. Some details may be
gleaned from François Riccoboni, though he is a late and
unsympathetic witness who uses the term 'declamation' in a
pejorative sense to describe the kind of acting associated with
the Hôtel de Bourgogne: 'Declamation is a combination of
vehemence and monotony. Start low, pronounce with affected
slowness, drag out the sounds languorously without variation,
suddenly raise the voice on a syllable at the half pauses in the
sense, and immediately fall back to the tone from which one
departed.' This suggests how metre and punctuation governed
the phrasing and pitch of the voice. François Riccoboni continues with an account of how emotion was conveyed: 'In
moments of passion, express yourself with superabundant force,
without ever departing from this same kind of modulation.
That is how one declaims.' In another passage, Riccoboni
suggests that the range of emotion was limited to two broad
categories, 'a lamenting tone' and 'a forceful tone' (*ton pleureur,
ton emporté*).[14]

---

[14] Quoted by Grear, pp. 383, 386.

Such a style of delivery placed great strain on the actors, even in normal roles, let alone the taxing part of Oreste in Racine's *Andromaque*, whose madness Saint-Evremond called a strange frenzy, costing the life of actors who tried to represent it properly.[15] Guéret's humorous account of Montfleury's death as he played the part of Oreste does tally with Riccoboni's description of sudden shifts of pitch and the forceful delivery of passions. In a comic confession, Montfleury is made to say: 'I wore out my lungs in those violent movements of jealousy, love, and ambition [. . .] If you want to know what I died of, [. . .] it was *Andromaque*'.[16] One of the few commentators well disposed to this style of acting describes Montfleury as excelling in roles requiring 'transports and anger' and regrets that he died playing his 'frenetic Oreste' in Racine's *Andromaque* (Robinet, ii. 1120). Saint-Evremond, Guéret, and Robinet were all Racine's contemporaries, writing in the 1660s. A later and friendly testimony from Mme Paul Poisson mentions Montfleury's skill in 'delivering speeches of twenty lines at a time, emphasizing the last line with such vehemence that he excited wild and prolonged applause'.[17] All this attests Montfleury's success with audiences and in particular his interpretation of Oreste in Racine's *Andromaque*.

Some impressions of possible types of delivery for Montfleury's expression of love, jealousy, and anger are suggested by the treatises for public speakers. Though schematic, they are somewhat more varied than the two broad tones—lamenting and violent—which François Riccoboni mentioned so scornfully. René Bary's *Méthode pour bien prononcer un discours* (1679) is closest in time to Racine.[18] According to Bary:

Love is expressed in a voice which is either cajoling, cheerful, or lamenting (*voix flateuse, gaye, plaintive*). Jealousy has a bold voice (*voix hardie*). Anger requires a loud voice for one who has just received an affront; a growling voice (*grondante*) when anger is directed against someone of superior rank; an explosive voice (*éclatante*) and somewhat

---

[15] Saint-Evremond, *L'Amitié sans amitié*, iii. 285.
[16] Gabriel Guéret, *Le Parnasse réformé* (Paris, 1671), 86–8; *NCR* 43.
[17] Mme Paul Poisson in *Mercure de France* (May 1738), quoted in Molière, *Théâtre*, ed. G. Couton, i. 1299.
[18] Extensive extracts from Bary are given in Grear, to whom reference is made for this work.

indistinct, when on the verge of physical violence; controlled anger has a very agitated voice (*fort émue*) yet moderately loud. (Grear, pp. 418–22.)

These tones of voice are exactly those recommended by Grimarest for these passions in his *Traité* (pp. 81, 88, 91). Of the various tones appropriate to the figures of speech *gradatio* was the most demanding. According to Bary, it required 'first a bold voice, then an exclamatory voice, finally according to the degree of injustice, the voice must become louder and louder' (Grear, p. 421). Bary also gives advice on gesture. His examples are mainly sentences which come from sermons, but two could be applied to the role of Oreste as acted by Montfleury: '*Anger* requires the eyelids to be horribly elevated, the lower lip to be protruded' (Grear, p. 424). To illustrate astonishment, Bary quotes the sentence: 'What do I see? What do I hear? Ah! I see only blood, I hear only shouts' and recommends that this should be delivered 'looking at the audience with wide open eyes, turning the head slowly from side to side, spreading the arms as they fall to the side and opening the hands' (Grear, p. 422). This would be appropriate to Oreste's final madness.

Obviously this is conjecture, an extrapolation from contemporary texts of what might be appropriate to the acting style of the actors of the Hôtel de Bourgogne, in particular Montfleury playing the part of Oreste; but given the general picture of the Hôtel de Bourgogne's stylized and declamatory manner of acting, and the close relationship between treatises on public speaking and the performance of actors, such conjectures may legitimately flesh out the evidence, provided their speculative status is recognized.

A shorthand term for the acting style of the Hôtel de Bourgogne would be 'rhetorical acting'. This is appropriate, since it conveys the connection between drama and rhetoric— rhetoric being understood in its active sense as the art of persuasion. At the same time, the word 'rhetorical' has connotations of artifice and stylization, which are the key characteristics of the formal stylized delivery which derived from the sections on *actio* in the treatises. Such a style of acting is out of fashion in twentieth-century Europe, at least for drama which strives to create the illusion of everyday reality. The nearest approach to 'rhetorical acting' may survive in grand opera. The stylized facial expressions and the movements of arms and hands seen in productions of Mozart or Verdi may give some impression of the acting style of the Hôtel de Bourgogne, but this analogy only concerns acting style; there is little in common between the lyrical outpourings of operatic arias and the active use of words for persuasion in Racinian tragedy. Another analogy might be the acting style of the silent cinema of the early twentieth century. Such a style has universal appeal. Here one would look to the exaggerated yet eloquent facial expressions of Chaplin and his fellow actors which convey the passions in various combinations. Le Brun's depictions of Fear, Horror, or Desire (Pls. 15–17) would not be out of place in the silent cinema, provided that it is recognized that the individual actor's face generally renders the facial expression much more complex than its schematic depiction in the two dimensions of an engraving. Modern opera and silent cinema may have affinities with the acting style at the Hôtel de Bourgogne.

Such a style of acting was an easy target for parody and the parodies are illuminating. A shrewd observer was at hand ready to exploit the advantages, all the more since he had his own ideas for an alternative acting style. Molière in 1659 set up his troupe as rivals to the well established Hôtel de Bourgogne and it was Molière's troupe which launched Racine on his theatrical career. Molière fired his first salvo in *Les Précieuses ridicules* with a mock eulogy of the actors of the Hôtel de Bourgogne, known as the *grands comédiens*:

Only they know how to show off things to the best advantage; all others are ignoramuses because they recite as one speaks; and don't know how to make the verses boom (*ronfler*), nor how to pause at the high points (*au bel endroit*). How can you know where the fine verses are, if the actor doesn't pause, and thereby signal that this is the place for thunderous applause (*brouhaha*). (Scene ix, pp. 278–9).

This ironically couched criticism focuses on the sonorous dignity of the tragic actor and the way he controls his audience by clever timing so that they recognize the 'punch-line'. Molière has put his finger on the fact that the rhetorical acting style is very much a self-conscious artistic performance which draws attention to its own merits to solicit applause, rather than transporting the audience into an illusory world by the creation of character. This was exactly Tallemant's objection to Montfleury's style of acting: 'He is too affected in showing off his expertise' (ii. 777).

Molière took his caricature of the Hôtel de Bourgogne further in *L'Impromptu de Versailles* where he put himself on stage as a director of his troupe, and parodied the individual style of his rival actors of the Hôtel de Bourgogne (Scene i, p. 680). Montfleury is the first target for Molière's impersonation. Molière picks on his declamatory delivery, bodily posture, and the emphatic delivery of the final line of the speech designed to make the audience applaud at the right moment. Yet the style at the Hôtel de Bourgogne was not so uniform that Molière could not parody the idiosyncrasies of other actors, and he continues with impersonations of Beauchâteau and Hauteroche. Molière's text gives no indication of their individual foibles, as he does in the case of Montfleury; but there would be no fun for the audience if the several impersonations were not recognizably different for each actor. Moreover Molière omits Floridor, a leading actor of the Hôtel de Bourgogne, who is said to have been less declamatory in his delivery than Montfleury: 'He acts with such gracefulness that cultivated people are always saying that he acts like an *honnête homme*.'[19] This gives a clue to Molière's own ideas on acting style.

Molière, *enfant terrible* of the Parisian theatre world, conducted a revolution in acting style on two fronts. For the tragic genre he advocated a natural style; and for the comic genre he himself adopted a mixture of clowning, stylized acting, and naturalness. Both got him into trouble. What was the natural style? It seems to have been advocated in fiction even before Molière's time by the experienced actor, La Rancune, in the continuation of Scarron's *Roman comique* (1653): 'You must observe the punctuation of the sentences and not make it obvious that it is poetry. You must pronounce it as if it were prose. You mustn't sing the lines nor stop at the middle or end of the line like the common people do' (ch. 9, p. 835). One can glimpse what Molière himself means by a natural style of acting for tragedy from some of his recommendations to his actors in the *Impromptu de Versailles*, even though he is here depicting himself directing them in a comedy. The natural style requires the actor to put himself into the character he is to portray: 'You must all get a good grasp of the characters you are playing, and you must

---

[19] Donneau de Visé, *Nouvelles nouvelles* (Paris, 1663), iii. 261; Grear, p. 207.

imagine that you *are* what you represent.' His instructions to each actor for playing the parts of poet, prude, or *soubrette* do contain some suggestions for precise gesture, but the main thrust of his advice is always 'Enter into your character'. And he positively discourages gesture in the case of Brécourt playing the part of an *honnête homme* or the educated courtier, who comes closest to the characters whom one would expect to see in a tragedy: 'You must take on an air of composure, a natural tone of voice, and you must gesticulate as little as possible' (Scene i, p. 682). This notion of thinking the character through, and considering what is plausible in the situation in which he appears, is the basis of Molière's criticism of Montfleury playing the part of King Prusias in Corneille's *Nicomède*. All the loud declamation and exaggerated posture are not appropriate to a scene where the king is quietly consulting with his confidant. Molière explains the grounds for his criticism of Montfleury's technique by including the opinion: 'It seems to me that a king who is talking alone with the captain of his guards would speak a bit more moderately, and would scarcely take on this demoniacal tone' (Scene i, p. 680).[20] However, Molière's new ideas on a natural style for tragedy do not seem to have been much appreciated by audiences.[21]

There was another acting style, which will be shown to be paradoxically relevant to a theatrical reading of Racine: incompetent acting. The rivalry between the illustrious champions of 'rhetorical' acting and of natural acting during this golden age of French drama may give the impression that acting standards were uniformly high. Not so. D'Aubignac in his *Projet pour le rétablissement du théâtre français* lamented the lack of well-trained actors. Many, he says, mount the boards who 'express imperfectly what they are reciting, and often the opposite of what they should' (pp. 350–1). More trouble was in store if the actor was ignorant of the historical background and of the subject of the tragedies he was acting: 'He will make nonsense of it, in spite of himself, and he will often misinterpret his lines' (Scudéry, *La Comédie des comédiens*, II. i. 237–9). Grimarest

---

[20] For Molière the actor, see Bray, *Molière, homme de théâtre* (1954), 147–65; Howarth, *Molière: A Playwright and His Audience* (1982), 9–18; Powell, 'Making Faces'.

[21] Bray, pp. 162–5, citing Donneau de Visé, Tallemant, Montfleury, and Le Boulanger de Chalussay.

pinned down the precise awfulness of the incompetent actor whose delivery was quite inappropriate to the situation: 'some actors seem calm when they are quarrelling, angry when they are exhorting, indifferent when they are remonstrating, unemotional when they are denouncing' (*Vie de Molière*, p. 163).

Grimarest also castigated actors who did not act while they were listening to the actor who was speaking: 'Every day one sees these actors who let their gaze and their imagination wander towards anything that is outside the action' (*Traité*, p. 76). Gherardi conjured up a different fault, namely rushed delivery: 'An actor may play simply from memory; he only comes on stage to gabble what he has learned by heart. He is so preoccupied with this, that, with no concern for his partner's movements or gestures, he continues on his own sweet way, in a furious hurry to get through his part as if it were some exceedingly tiresome task' ('Avertissement').

Racine himself could have been a brilliant actor. 'Everyone knows my father's talent for declamation' wrote Louis Racine with justification. Racine apparently liked to try out his compositions aloud and with passion. Striding through the Tuileries gardens he thought he was alone, but his declamation of a speech from *Mithridate* startled the gardeners, who rushed to surround him, fearing he was a madman likely to hurl himself dementedly into one of the ornamental pools (Louis Racine, *Mémoires*, pp. 58, 84). Racine read Sophocles' *Oedipus* to some friends. 'He was so carried away, that those who heard him experienced the emotions of terror and pity with which this play abounds.' Valincour, who told this story, adds: 'I have seen our finest plays performed by our best actors; but nothing has ever approached the emotion I felt at his reading. Even as I write I can still picture Racine, book in hand, and all of us around him thrown into a state of high agitation.'[22] Independent testimony confirms this: 'If he were a preacher or an actor, he could easily outshine the lot of them in either genre.'[23] Grimarest was equally enthusiastic:

[22] Valincour, 'Lettre à M. l'abbé d'Olivet', in *Histoire de l'Académie française*, quoted by Louis Racine, *Mémoires*, p. 84.

[23] Ezechiel Spanheim, *Relation de la cour de France en 1690*, ed. Schefer (Paris, 1882), 402–3; *NCR* 263.

I recommend an actor to be guided by the author of a play, if he is still living and available. The author will always know better than anyone the distribution of the roles and the manner of executing them [. . .] M. Racine, who could recite better than anyone, would ensure that his actors understood all the subtleties requisite for delivery. (*Traité*, p. 78.)

Had Racine chosen to act rather than to write, he could have assumed some flowery stage-name and joined the Hôtel de Bourgogne. French drama might have been poorer by twelve plays; but Racine wrote tragedies and took a keen interest in how his plays were performed. If Racine the actor remains a fascinating potentiality, Racine the director was real.

5

Racine the Director

De mes intentions je pourrais vous instruire
(*Mithridate*)

In everyday life Racine had a sharp eye for interpreting visual signs. One day he spotted Valincour rushing into the gallery at Versailles: 'Ah Monsieur', asked Racine jocularly, 'where is the fire?' Racine was teasing Valincour for his hurried gait, suitable for a man announcing news of a conflagration. Louis Racine tells the story to illustrate his father's wit (*Mémoires*, p. 82). The wit may be feeble, the story may be apocryphal, but it can stand as a symbol for Racine's visual imagination, and it tallies with all the other evidence for Racine the director, his eye alert to the language of bodily movement and facial expression —a keen theatrical eye.

Authors usually chose the cast and attended rehearsals. D'Aubignac reveals that 'our poets usually arrange rehearsals of their plays in their presence, and instruct the actors in everything that needs to be done' (*Pratique*, i. 8, p. 47). Chappuzeau reports that the playwright 'can correct the actor if he falls into any error, such as misunderstanding the text, or adopting unnatural tones or gestures, or putting too little or too much energy into the passions he is required to portray' (pp. 72–3). The playwright in Poisson's *Poète Basque* (1695) gave demonstrations for the actors' benefit: 'I'll emphasize the tones where there are changes, the facial expressions in particular and the actions' (Act I, Scene ix, p. 219). Grimarest spoke of Racine having initiated his actors into 'the subtleties requisite for delivery' (*Traité*, p. 78). The evidence from these sources gives credibility to accounts of Racine the director which are related by his two sons, even though one of them gives this information incidentally for the purpose of safeguarding the moral reputation of his father.

(*a*) La Champmeslé

Louis Racine is concerned to refute the rumour that his father slept with his leading actress La Champmeslé and had an illegitimate son by her. He explains that his father spent long periods with the woman in order to give her lessons in how to deliver her lines. To make this more plausible Louis Racine claims that La Champmeslé 'was not a born actress' and 'anyway she had so little intelligence that she had to be told the meaning of the verses she had to recite and the tone which was required'. He adds the crucial sentence: 'He first explained the meaning of the verses she had to recite, he showed her the gestures, and dictated the tones, which he even noted down for her.' Louis Racine does not attempt to deny his father's 'assiduities' towards La Champmeslé, but he palliates them by attributing to the actress's stupidity the necessity for his father to spend a long time in her company (*Mémoires*, pp. 58–9). The apologetic context casts a shadow over this precious information; but the evidence for incompetent acting arising from ignorance and misunderstanding of the text (see Chapter 4, section *c*) gives a plausible scenario for the account of Racine making sure that La Champmeslé knew what was going on in the play; and the demonstration of the tones of voice, facial expressions, and gestures has a parallel in the practice recorded in the *Poète Basque*. So, Racine's method of instructing La Champmeslé can be accepted as probably true.[1]

But what exactly was the Racinian style of acting? The style which he dictated to La Champmeslé and which according to Louis Racine made his father's pupil 'faithful to his lessons, and, even though an actress by precept, appear on the stage as if inspired by nature; and for this reason she performed much better in the plays of her teacher than in those of others' (*Mémoires*, p. 59). Here the waters get cloudy. Some light is shed by Racine's elder son, Jean-Baptiste, who dictated between 1721 and 1742 to a friend his reminiscences of his father. This text has been published by both Vaunois and Dussane. Jean-Baptiste Racine is reported to have said of the dramatist:

[1] Brossette gives the more common view that Racine was both the lover and the teacher of La Champmeslé in *Mémoires*, p. 518; see also Picard, *Carrière*, pp. 299–300 on La Champmeslé's lovers.

he taught Mlle Champmeslé [...] He did not approve of the excessively uniform manner of reciting in Molière's troupe. He wanted the verses to be given a certain sound which in conjunction with the metre and rhyme distinguished them from prose. But he could not tolerate these extravagant and yelping (*glapissants*) tones which were substituted for natural beauty and which could be noted down like music.

Grimarest provides a useful gloss on *glapir*; it is a kind of falsetto which can arise when expressing surprise in a voice suddenly pitched too high (*Traité*, p. 102). Jean-Baptiste Racine goes on to emphasize his father's aversion to a 'sing-song style', by recounting the anecdote that Racine told the actors they were to be shut down for singing their lines because the musician Lully had the sole right to put singers on stage (Vaunois, pp. 201–2). There is uncertainty about the reading of the key term relating to Molière's diction of which Racine is said to have disapproved. Vaunois prints 'manière trop unie'. Dussane prints 'manière trop vraie' (p. 54). Either *unie* or *vraie* would be consistent with what is known of Molière's diction for tragedy. It was 'truthful' in its naturalness, and 'uniform' in its monotony. Louis Racine is as keen as his elder brother to refute the charge of sing-song diction: 'Those who believe that the declamation which [my father] introduced into the theatre was florid and sing-song, are, I think, in error. They judge of it by Mlle Duclos, pupil of La Champmeslé.' He goes on to say that La Champmeslé changed her style when Racine retired from the theatre, and in her later years delivered her lines in an explosive manner (*grands éclats de voix: Mémoires*, pp. 58–9).

There may be special pleading here by both sons in the account they give of Racine's instructions to La Champmeslé, because of the swing away from 'rhetorical acting' towards a more natural delivery during the eighteenth century (Grear, pp. 412–17). Both sons seem anxious to distance their father from any association with 'rhetorical acting', even though that was the style favoured at the Hôtel de Bourgogne, to which Racine transferred his plays when he broke with Molière. Louis Racine does not assert categorically that his father disapproved of the florid sing-song style associated with the Hôtel de Bourgogne; he only *thinks* people are in error who characterize Racinian acting in this way. According to Louis Racine, people suggested that one of the reasons why Racine surreptitiously switched his *Alexandre* from Molière's troupe to that of the Hôtel de Bourgogne was that he did not like Molière's innovations in the style of tragic acting (*Remarques*, p. 327). It is plausible, and would follow from the statements by Jean-Baptiste Racine, but there is no direct evidence that disapproval of Molière's acting style for tragedy was the cause of Racine's underhand manœuvre. Jean-Baptiste Racine suggests that his father wanted a compromise between Molière's natural style and the Hôtel de Bourgogne's 'rhetorical' style, but with a leaning towards the rhetorical, provided it did not degenerate into a yelping and monotonous sing-song.

Racine's views on acting are especially important because of the general opinion that it was the actors who were essential to his theatrical success. The same was indeed said by Scudéry of Corneille (Picard, *Carrière*, p. 255); but the evidence is much more abundant and varied for Racine. Saint-Evremond thought that *Andromaque* fell flat after the death of Montfleury because 'the play needs great actors to compensate by their delivery for what the play lacks'.[2] Robinet implied that the success of *Britannicus* owed much to the décor, costumes, and actors' performance (iii. 1136–8). Madame de Sévigné thought her daughter reading *Bajazet* might find that without La Champmeslé 'it loses half its attraction' (letter of 16 March 1672). Boileau characterized Racine as one who had the secret of 'moving, astonishing, transporting his audience with the help of an actor' (*Epître*, vii). Pradon took up Boileau's point: 'the works of M. Racine [. . .] owe not a little to the skill of the actors who performed them'. But Pradon turned this to Racine's disadvantage by suggesting that the plays lost their attraction when they were read in published texts.[3] Doubtless there is here an element of the commonplace that 'drama is better on the stage than on the page'. None the less, the evidence is clear that Racine wrote scripts to be exploited by actors, rather than texts for the printed page.

'He showed her the gestures', said Louis Racine, 'and dictated

[2] 'Elle a besoin de grands comédiens, qui remplissent par l'action ce qui lui manque', Letter to Lionne, *c.*Mar. 1668, *Lettres*, ed. R. Ternois, i. 136–7.
[3] Pradon, *Nouvelles remarques sur tous les ouvrages du Sieur* *** (1685), 68–70; NCR 180.

the tones, which he even noted down for her.' No direct evidence for Racine's guidance of La Champmeslé has survived. What would it have been? It seems likely that Racine employed terms such as those used by Bary and Grimarest for the expression of the various passions, since these were in common use: 'voix forte', 'voix douce', 'voix éclatante', 'ton de voix plein', 'ton élevé, vif, fier'. A manuscript with the music of the choruses of *Athalie* has similar annotations: 'gracieusement', 'tendrement', 'rondement', 'lentement', 'vivement'. These indications are written over or under certain words or phrases indicating how they should be sung. The exhortation of the enemies of God, 'let us massacre all his saints', is to be sung briskly (*vivement*) (fol. 12^r). Pitch is also indicated: 'Let us see his anger again' is to be sung loudly (*fort*) (fol. 9^r), and variations of pitch are indicated: 'His divine oracle' is to be sung loudly, followed by 'the tender grass' sung softly (*doux*) (fol. 7^v–8^r). Unfortunately the sung choruses are not the best place to find evidence for the kind of tones of voice relevant to moments of passion or figures of speech in normal dialogue, which Racine may have noted down for La Champmeslé. Nor is it clear that Racine had anything to do with these annotations for *Athalie*, though it is not implausible that they may derive from him.[4]

That variations of pitch and volume may have been a special part of Racine's directions to his actors and actresses is implied by later testimonies relating to the role of Monime. The abbé Dubos reports that for *Mithridate*, Act III, Scene v, Racine instructed La Champmeslé to lower her voice for 'We loved each other', and then jump up an octave at 'My lord, your countenance is changed' to convey her shock at Mithridate's reaction (*Réflexions*, i. 465–6). Brossette describes Boileau reciting these verses and imitating the vehemence with which La Champmeslé was taught by Racine to deliver the final 'My lord your countenance is changed' (*Mémoires*, p. 521). These testimonies are rendered more plausible by what seem to be stage

---

[4] Grear (pp. 239–40) describes this MS as 'Chants de la tragédie d'Athalie de la main de Racine, MS 66, Bibliothèque municipale de Versailles', but the catalogue entry in the Bibliothèque municipale of Versailles dates the whole MS to the 18th century· which would rule out annotations in Racine's hand; I am grateful to Dr Valerie Worth for assistance in this matter.

directions implicit in the text.[5] Racine takes every opportunity
to indicate that Agrippine should speak loudly and stridently.
Burrhus hopes that her resentment will confine itself to 'useless
cries' (*Bri.* III. i. 766) and he warns Agrippine herself that
'threats and cries' will only make Néron more recalcitrant (iii. 3.
831); Albine pleads with her mistress before her interview with
Néron: 'Hide your anger' (III. iv. 875); Néron, who confessed
to fearing her 'flaming eyes' (II. ii. 485), returns to the subject of
his mother's stridency when discussing with her 'the [political]
power which your cries seemed to demand' (IV. ii. 1238). In
Iphigénie Clytemnestre is depicted in similar fashion. Agamemnon hopes to divert his wife from Aulis: 'Spare me the cries of a
furious mother' (I. i. 147); and when Clytemnestre has delivered
her final outburst against her vacillating husband her loud voice
reverberates in Agamemnon's ears: 'I did not expect any less
fury; those were the cries I feared to hear [. . .] yet I'd be happy
if her cries were all I had to fear!' (IV. v. 1317–20). The
insistence with which Racine alludes to the loud voices of
Agrippine and Clytemnestre makes the allusion to 'cries' in their
case more than a metaphor for agitation; he is instructing them
on the pitch and volume of their delivery, just as Dubos said
Racine instructed La Champmeslé. All this points to a quest for
variety, in opposition to the recurrent repetitive climaxes at the
hemistich and the rhyme which seem to have been characteristic
of Montfleury and the Hôtel de Bourgogne. It also suggests a
departure from Molière's style of delivery if it is true that Racine
judged it to be 'too uniform' (Vaunois, pp. 201–2).

(b) The Alexandrine

Such a quest for variety is confirmed by Louis Racine's indications of the varied phrasing of the alexandrine which he illustrates with two examples of his father's verse in his *Traité de la
poésie dramatique* (p. 477). Although Louis Racine is illustrating a
general characteristic of French alexandrines rather than claim-
ing any special merit for his father here, the examples none the
less confirm that Racine's verse lent itself to varied phrasing.

---

[5] Capatti, however, in a detailed discussion of these lines expresses reservations
about Dubos's testimony (pp. 159–60).

'Foreigners', says Louis Racine, 'imagine that in pronouncing two lines, we make four pauses, because there are four half-lines (*hémistiches*). But the meaning and the order of words often run counter to this, especially in verses of passion, where one is obliged to make two or three breaks, and to run on over the line (*enjamber*).' He then quotes four lines spoken by Hermione in *Andromaque* (V. iii. 1561–4) to show how the pauses do not fall regularly at the half line, and he continues: 'Here is how the voice should be governed by the passion depicted in these verses.' Dashes indicate the pauses recommended by Louis Racine:

> Adieu.—Tu peux partir.—Je demeure en Epire:—
> Je renonce—à la Grèce,—à Sparte,—à ton Empire,—
> A toute ma famille;—Et c'est assez pour moi,
> Traistre,—qu'elle ait produit un monstre—comme toi.[6]

The variety Louis Racine is emphasizing is created by having two pauses in the first line and three in the second line of the first couplet so that the groups of syllables run 2, 4, 6/3, 3, 2, 4. Then in the second couplet the enjambment creates phrasing with groups of 6, 8, 7, 3 syllables. This is Louis Racine's scansion based on pauses. Modern scansion would divide the syllables according to stress rather than pauses, so that the final unstressed syllables of *traistre* and *monstre* would belong to the following syllabic group. The break up of the regular rhythm of the alexandrine can be readily appreciated by rearranging the syllable groups as follows:

> A toute ma famille;—
> Et c'est assez pour moi, Traistre,—
> qu'elle ait produit un monstre—
> comme toi.

Louis Racine gives a second example to show that even verses without passion should be recited with irregular syllabic groups. He chooses the opening eight lines of *Athalie*:

> Oui, je viens—dans son temple adorer l'Eternel.—
> Je viens,—selon l'usage antique et solennel,—
> Célébrer avec vous—la fameuse journée

---

[6] Punctuation followed in this quotation and in the following four displayed quotations (which are discussed by Louis Racine or Grimarest) is that of the 1697 edn.

Ou sur le mont Sina la loi nous fut donnée.—
Que les temps sont changés!—Sitôt que de ce jour
La trompette sacrée annonçait le retour,—
Du temple,—orné partout de festons magnifiques,—
Le peuple saint—en foule inondait les portiques—

Here the breaks marked by Louis Racine throw into relief the repetition of 'je viens' in lines 1 and 2, and emphasize the enjambment between lines 3–4 and 5–6. The only surprise is in line 8 where the sense would certainly permit division of the line into two halves: 'Le peuple saint en foule—inondait les portiques', but the recommended break after 'saint' seems a deliberate attempt to divide the line into groups of 4 and 8 syllables and to avoid the regularity of 6 and 6. These examples are not presented by Louis Racine as particular recommendations of his father, but as a corrective to foreigners who thought that French alexandrines were monotonous. However, other evidence suggests that Racine did pay special attention to metrical variety and variety of delivery.

Grimarest advanced the view that Racine was particularly concerned to punctuate his verses so that incompetent actors would not rush through them. This tallies with Gherardi's portrayal of the bad actor 'in a furious hurry to get through his part as if it were some exceedingly tiresome task' ('Avertissement'). Grimarest did not altogether approve of Racine's practice, but in expressing reservations about it, he furnishes some useful insights into Racine's use of punctuation: 'I think M. Racine often used the full stop instead of the colon simply to delay the declamation of the actor who always tends to hurry somewhat' (*Traité*, p. 32). On Grimarest's hypothesis, Racine punctuated Phèdre's opening lines (*Phè*. I. iii. 153–7) with full stops to ensure that they were not rushed:

PHÈDRE N'allons point plus avant. Demeurons, chère Œnone.
Je ne me soutiens plus, ma force m'abandonne.
Mes yeux sont éblouis du jour que je revoi,
Et mes genoux tremblants se dérobent sous moi.
Hélas!

Grimarest is not happy with this because the full stops imply a break in the sense which can confuse the actor or reader, whereas in reality 'Phèdre is telling her confidant of the grievously sad situation in which she finds herself [. . .] and no one can fail to see that all these expressions belong to the same emotion' (*Traité*, p. 33). Consequently Grimarest would prefer that the full stops which Racine uses should be replaced by colons, so that the reader or actor who is reading this passage, knows that it is a sequence of sad laments and that no change of voice is required. Grimarest is equally critical of the full stops which in his view obscure the meaning of Eriphile's speech in *Iphigénie*, II. viii. 761–3:

> J'ai des yeux. Leur bonheur n'est pas encore tranquille.
> On trompe Iphigénie; on se cache d'Achille;
> Agamemnon gémit. Ne désespérons point; [. . .]

Grimarest contends that all these expressions are connected with the last phrase 'let us not despair', and that Eriphile's feelings are revealed in the continuous sequence of clauses, whilst Racine's full stops give the impression that new ideas are being introduced all the time (*Traité*, pp. 33–4).

On the other hand, Grimarest sees the value in pauses after conjunctions to keep the audience in suspense. He suggests a pause after 'mais' in Agrippine's speech to Albine concerning Néron (*Bri.* I. i. 31):

> Non, non, mon intérêt ne me rend point injuste:
> Il commence, il est vrai, par où finit Auguste;
> Mais [*pause*] crains que l'avenir détruisant le passé,
> Il ne finisse ainsi qu'Auguste a commencé.

Such a pause, says Grimarest, would 'keep the listener more attentive' (*Traité*, p. 34). It is an example of using delivery to create suspense in the theatre.

In the important matter of punctuation and delivery, Louis Racine was giving general advice on reading French alexandrines, and Grimarest was discussing Racine's punctuation in the context of his own novel ideas on the subject. Taken together they suggest that Racine was attentive to ensuring that his actors were forced to learn their lines with appropriate pauses and variety of diction. The full stop after Eriphile's 'J'ai des yeux' is a sharp reminder that in this line the main caesura is not at the hemistich but after the first three syllables. The same applies to many other lines. Grimarest's observations are confirmed by a computer-assisted study of Racinian sentences. The statistics tabulated by Flowers (p. 209) show that the median length of sentences in most of Racine's tragedies is just over twelve syllables or a single alexandrine line. By contrast in Corneille's *Tite et Bérénice* the median length is twenty-three syllables, that is just under two alexandrines, whilst in Pradon's *Phèdre et Hippolyte* the median length is thirty syllables, about two and a half lines. Although Flowers offers a comparison with only two plays by other authors, this is a striking indication that Racine differed from his contemporaries in using punctuation to introduce a greater number of pauses in the declamation of his alexandrines.

Yet Racine also exploits the regular formal structure of the alexandrine for theatrical effect.[7] Hemistichs are balanced so that they highlight the conflicts which are the essence of drama:

ŒNONE Ils ne se verront plus.
PHÈDRE   Ils s'aimeront toujours.

(*Phè*. IV. vi. 1252)

Inversion is deliberately employed to force a key word to the end of the hemistich where it can receive emphasis. Thésée reveals to Phèdre that Hippolyte has even accused *her*:

THÉSÉE Sa fureur contre *vous* se répand en injures.

(*Phè*. IV. iv. 1185)

There was nothing to prevent Racine writing 'Sa fureur se répand contre vous en injures' but the thrust of *vous* in the direction of Phèdre would have been less emphatic. Hemistichs often contain the same verb in different morphological forms (paronomasia), creating a sense of balance, whilst avoiding mechanical repetition:

ORESTE Tu *vis* mon désespoir; et *tu m'as vu* depuis
    Traîner de mers en mers ma chaîne et mes ennuis.

(*And*. I. i. 44–5)

NARCISSE Commandez qu'on vous *aime*, et vous serez *aimé*.

(*Bri*. II. ii. 458)

---

[7] See Howarth, 'L'Alexandrin classique comme instrument du dialogue théâtral' and 'Some Thoughts on the Function of Rhyme in French Classical Tragedy'.

ŒNONE Vous l'*osâtes* bannir, vous n'*osez* l'éviter.

(*Phè*. III. i. 764)

This figure of speech 'attracts the ear of the audience and excites their attention by some resemblance, equality, or contrast of words' (Quintilian IX. iii. 66). If it has that effect in prose, the effect is even greater when reinforced by the metrical framework of the alexandrine delivered on stage. Yet the variation of verb form offers the leisured reader scope for deeper reflection on the significance of the tenses employed.[8]

Malherbe, who denounced with puritanical fervour all forms of poetic permissiveness, would have been scandalized by Racine's easygoing enjambments and effort-free rhymes. Instead of the rich and the rare, Racine favoured the simple, the obvious, and the predictable: *père/mère, moi/toi, amitié/pitié*, and a host of similar rhymes abound in his plays. However, whilst these may disappoint the reader in search of novelty, when they are heard on stage their simplicity assists understanding and when repeated they act as a leitmotif. Racine takes every opportunity to place proper names at the rhyme, and he does not flinch from repetition: *Oreste/funeste* occurs eight times in *Andromaque*. The repetition of this rhyme strengthens the association between Oreste and his inescapable fate (Howarth, 'Rhyme', p. 153). When the alexandrine is divided between speakers, predictable rhymes provide simple satisfaction, inviting the audience to participate in the game:

ALEXANDRE   Parlez donc. Dites-moi,
    Comment prétendez-vous que je vous traite?
PORUS   En roi.

(*Ale*. V. iii. 1500)

That audiences were sensitive to rhymes is attested by Scarron's anecdote of the wretched actor who mutilated the only couplet he had to say by rhyming 'vous tombiez' with 'jambes' instead of 'pieds'. 'This bad rhyme surprised everybody' says Scarron, 'and they all fell about laughing.'[9] Although obvious rhymes are preponderant in Racine, he spices the diet with a few excursions

---

[8] See Ratermanis, *Les Formes verbales*, for a comprehensive analysis of such effects.

[9] *Roman comique*, part ii, ch. 3, p. 681.

into the exotic, such as *humectée/Erechthée* (*Phè.* II. i. 426). He also springs surprises on the audience when they are least expecting it. Nothing is more relaxing at the conclusion of a play than a comfortable couplet. Not so in *Bérénice*. Just as the heroine seems to be rounding everything off in her final speech, the last two syllables of the play are given to a different speaker, and Antiochus utters his metrically audacious *Hélas*.[10]

It seems that Racine wanted to get the best of all possible worlds in the performance of his plays: an acting style which was natural enough to make his characters seem real, musical enough to do justice to his poetic talents, dignified enough to suit the elevated status of the tragic genre. Variety seems to have been the key feature—variety of expression, variety of pitch, variety of rhythm.

The external evidence for Racine the director taken from Louis Racine, Grimarest, and other sources is not as certain or as conclusive as one would wish. Fortunately, the external evidence is not the only source for understanding Racine the director. His plays contain stage directions, implicit and explicit, which can guide the performance of the actors if they are alert to them. His manner of directing has already been seen at work in the earlier chapters on the predominantly visual language of décor, bodily posture, and stage properties. Now, in the light of the concept of speech as action and an understanding of the relevance of rhetoric to drama, it remains to examine Racine the director, at work in the areas where verbal and visual languages interact most intimately. The text of the plays will be the chief source. Four areas will be examined: conventional and incongruous delivery of the speeches, the listener's performance, interrogations, and visual focus. These have hitherto received little attention. Those aspects which have been explored have been treated in isolation, rather than as part of a coherent theatrical system. Where appropriate, Racine's directions can be supplemented by material from the treatises on *actio* and particularly from Grimarest's *Traité du récitatif*, which

---

[10] For an attempt to link rhyme and tragic action illustrated from *Mithridate*, see Scott, pp. 149–77. For an examination of the conflicting claims of the theatrical power of the alexandrine and the material aspects of theatricality, see Bernard, 'Esquisse d'une théorie de la théâtralité d'un texte en vers'.

uses examples from Racine to illustrate the vocal and gestural codes associated with the art of persuasion.

(c) Conventional and incongruous *actio*

Actio, the fifth and final part of rhetoric, has special relevance to the way in which Racine's characters deliver their speeches as orators. As explained in Chapter 4, in this theatrical context 'orators' must be interpreted in a wide sense, to embrace characters who engage in any verbal activity involving persuasion. Oratorical skills are not confined to scenes of formal oratory, where characters represent ambassadors or counsellors, whom the audience would recognize as official orators, but also extends to scenes of informal deliberation within a family, or private discussions between protagonists and confidants. The persuasive skills of the orator are even, indeed especially, at work in the intimate circumstances of characters' declarations of love. And the *récits* of tragedy, so often considered to be simply narratives, can have a strong persuasive element which brings them into the orbit of the art of rhetoric in its most active form.

Racine's characters have been described as orators in the wide sense of the word, in order to evoke the picture of characters persuading other characters on stage, that is to say along the character axis. The spectator axis must also be taken into account in assessing the impact of the persuasive delivery which is essential to successful oratory. Persuasion is simultaneously directed by the characters towards each other, and by the dramatist through his actors towards his audience. The significance of the persuasion may work along the two axes in the same way. When Andromaque, a mother pleading for her son's life, falls at Pyrrhus's feet and begs Pyrrhus to relent, her intention as a fictional character is to excite pity in Pyrrhus (*And.* Act III, Scene vi). The delivery of her speech—her *actio*—will also excite pity in the spectator in much the same way. The effect is similar along the two axes. Andromaque has adopted the conventional *actio* for such a situation. It is also possible to speak of incongruous *actio*, when the speaker uses *actio* which is either unbefitting to the character or unsuitable for the situation. When Queen Clytemnestre kneels to the warrior Achille, it is inappropriate to her status (*Iph.* III. vi. 952). Titus's strangled declaration of love to Bérénice is inappropriate to the situation (*Bér.* II. iv. 624). The spectator derives theatrical pleasure from witnessing the incongruity. The incongruous *actio* is sometimes evident only to the audience but may also be evident to other characters on stage and excite their comments, so that the spectator can share in the characters' response to the situation.

Conventional 'Actio'

In more formal speeches, where there are no implicit stage directions, it seems reasonable to assume that, unless Racine gave special instructions in rehearsal, the actors would deliver the speech according to conventional *actio*. This certainly did not rule out individual interpretation, in so far as the actors like Montfleury, Floridor, or Molière had their own styles. Nor were the manuals of rhetoric identical in their recommendations for tone of voice and gesture for the various oratorical situations, though there was much similarity, as can be seen from Grear's tabulation of Cicero, Quintilian, and ten French authors from 1647 to 1722 on tones of voice for figures and passions (appendix 3). Some impression of conventional *actio* may be gained by bringing Racine's text into conjunction with the recommendations on these matters offered by Le Faucheur, *Traité de l'action* (1657), Bary, *Méthode pour bien prononcer un discours* (1679), and Grimarest, *Traité du récitatif* (1707).[11]

For the different divisions of the speech Le Faucheur and Bary are broadly in agreement in the guidance they offer. Le Faucheur says that the *exordium* requires a moderate voice, to indicate esteem for the character addressed (p. 133), whilst the *narratio* requires a clear and distinct voice, so that the facts are clearly understood (p. 139). Le Faucheur gives only general advice for *confirmatio* and *refutatio*: they require varied tones. Bary fills in the details: bold voice for expounding reasons, louder voice to put objections, manly voice to refute them. Le Faucheur recommends the speaker to pause before the *peroratio*

[11] Some extracts from Grimarest's *Traité* are given in France and McGowan, 'Autour du *Traité* de Grimarest'; extracts from Le Faucheur, Bary, and Grimarest in Roy, 'Acteurs et spectateurs'.

and start again on a lower pitch, rising gradually with excitement and ending on a grandiose or triumphant note (pp. 133–41). Bary agrees and recommends a resounding conclusion (Grear, p. 418).

Ephestion's speech as ambassador from Alexandre to the Indian kings might be annotated for conventional *actio* according to Le Faucheur and Bary as follows:

EPHESTION [*exordium: voix modeste*]
 Avant que le combat qui menace vos têtes
 Mette tous vos états au rang de nos conquêtes,
 Alexandre veut bien différer ses exploits,
 Et vous offrir la paix pour la dernière fois.
  [*narratio: voix bien articulée et distincte*]
 Vos peuples, prévenus de l'espoir qui vous flatte,
 Prétendaient arrêter le vainqueur de l'Euphrate;
 Mais l'Hydaspe, malgré tant d'escadrons épars,
 Voit enfin sur ses bords flotter nos étendards.
  [*confirmatio: voix hardie, haussée, masle*]
 Vous les verriez plantés jusque sur vos tranchées,
 Et de sang et de morts vos campagnes jonchées,
 Si ce héros, couvert de tant d'autres lauriers,
 N'eût lui-même arrêté l'ardeur de nos guerriers.
 Il ne vient point ici souillé du sang des princes,
 D'un triomphe barbare effrayer vos provinces,
 Et cherchant à briller d'une triste splendeur,
 Sur le tombeau des rois élever sa grandeur.
 Mais vous-mêmes, trompés d'un vain espoir de gloire,
 N'allez point dans ses bras irriter la victoire;
 Et lorsque son courroux demeure suspendu,
 Princes, contentez-vous de l'avoir attendu,
 Ne différez point tant à lui rendre l'hommage
 Que vos coeurs, malgré vous, rendent à son courage;
 Et recevant l'appui que vous offre son bras,
 D'un si grand défenseur honorez vos états.
  [*peroratio: pause—ton plus bas*]
 Voilà ce qu'un grand roi veut bien vous faire entendre,
  [*voix plus excitée*]
 Prêt à quitter le fer, et prêt à le reprendre.
  [*voix éclatante*]
 Vous savez son dessein: choisissez aujourd'hui,
 Si vous voulez tout perdre ou tenir tout de lui.

         (*Ale.* II. ii. 445–72)

From the point of view of verbal action, Ephestion's speech is that of a skilful orator who employs *mores* as his chief source of persuasion. None the less, it is an arrogant speech in that it dwells almost entirely on the character of Alexandre. Nowhere does Ephestion allude to the character of the Indian kings, although it was normal practice for an ambassador to flatter the ruler to whom he was speaking, as Oreste flatters Pyrrhus (*And.* Act I, Scene ii). So there may be some tension between the probably conventional *actio* of the ambassador's formal speech and its arrogant content. At the end of the scene, however, this tension explodes in a burst of incongruous *actio*, when the ambassador suddenly rises unbidden from his seat and interrupts King Porus. The verbal arrogance is translated into visual terms, and the ambassador's abrupt discourtesy signifies the disruptive pretensions of Alexandre, a subtext to the measured formality of his ambassador's initial speech.[12]

Advice on conventional *actio* for rhetorical figures and for the passions was more abundant than for the divisions of the speech. Here it is worth turning to Grimarest, who in his *Traité du récitatif* (1707) illustrates his recommendations with examples from Racine. In his chapter on declamation he takes his readers through three kinds of love (gentle, joyful, and suffering); through three tones suitable for hatred; through violent, moderate, and feeble desire. Recommendations are more concise for aversion, joy, sadness, hope, despair, boldness, fear, envy, and jealousy. Indignation is variously expressed according to whether it is contemptuous or desirous of preventing evil. Compassion varies according to whether its object is the victim of misfortune or injustice, or whether it is full of tenderness. Anger receives the fullest treatment and Grimarest ends his discussion of the simple passions by acknowledging that the actor often has to register a mixture of passions in such a way that the spectator recognizes and is touched by a mixture of emotions (*Traité*, pp. 81–93). He then proceeds to discuss tones of voice for the figures of speech: interrogation, apostrophe, prosopopeia, antithesis, oath, irony, exclamation, epizeuxis, gradation (*Traité*, pp. 96–105).

---

[12] For a detailed rhetorical analysis of this speech, see Hawcroft, 102–4; for the protocol of seating, see Ch. 3, section *b* above.

For Andromaque's plea to Pyrrhus, Grimarest himself gives specific recommendations for tonal variation according to the various figures of speech and emotions (*And.* III. vi. 901–5).

ANDROMAQUE
   [*Exclamation: ton véhément et voix fort élevée*]
   Ah! Seigneur, arrêtez! Que prétendez-vous faire?
   Si vous livrez le fils, livrez-leur donc la mère.
   Vos sermens m'ont tantôt juré tant d'amitié!
   [*Crainte: voix faible et hésitante*]
   Dieux! Ne pourrai-je au moins toucher votre pitié?
   Sans espoir de pardon m'avez-vous condamnée?[13]

Grimarest warns the actress not to let her voice break into a falsetto for the exclamation 'Ah! Seigneur', even though her exclamation of fear requires the most forceful delivery of all exclamations (*Traité*, pp. 102–3).

The recital of events off-stage has been criticized as an untheatrical feature of French tragedy where words are thought to replace action, though some have welcomed words as a superior form of appeal to the intellect and the imagination (see Fumaroli, p. 232). In fact, these narrations are theatrical for three reasons. There is verbal action in the speeches themselves by virtue of their persuasive function. Secondly, the figure of enargeia often conjures up word-pictures. Thirdly, they require *actio*, that is tone of voice and gesture appropriate to their delivery in the theatre. *Narratio*, it must be remembered, could mean either a formal division of a speech preceding a *confirmatio*, or a whole speech which was primarily intended to relate past events. The manuals of rhetoric laid down guide-lines for the *actio* of both kinds. If the *narratio* is one of the divisions of persuasive discourse, such as the recital of historical events included in Agrippine's speech to Néron, then it is theatrical by virtue of its active function in the speech of persuasion. Failure to recognize this led Lady Morgan astray in condemning Agrippine's speech to Néron as 'simply the history of the early life and reign of Nero, taken from Tacitus' (p. 92). She did not appreciate that this *narratio* formed an active and necessary part

---

[13] Punctuation of 1697 edn. This annotation reconciles Grimarest's slightly inconsistent recommendations on pp. 87 and 102–4 and is based on the suggestions of Grimarest's editor of 1740.

of Agrippine's argument. Such a narration, a subsidiary part of the speech of persuasion, had its special kind of *actio*; it should be delivered in 'a clear and distinct voice' (Le Faucheur, p. 139) and indeed this is exactly how Mademoiselle George, according to Lady Morgan, delivered it: 'with great clearness, elegance of enunciation and graceful calmness of action' (p. 92). But even when the main purpose of a speech is to narrate an event off-stage, such as a death, there is usually an element of persuasion in the structure of such a speech which gives it its theatricality, and this can be reinforced by appropriate *actio*. Ephestion's account of the duel between Porus and Taxile (*Ale.* V. iii. 1427) does not contain any internal stage directions from Racine but the actor might follow Grimarest's advice for this particular narration and make it 'loud and rapid' (*Traité*, p. 57). In the case of death *récits*, Racine the director usually does give some guidance to the actor. Créon in Act V of *La Thébaïde* relates the death of his own son, and that of Polynice and Etéocle in their single combat. The tone of his narrative is set by his opening remark:

> Vous ignorez encor mes pertes et les vôtres,
> Mais, hélas! apprenez les unes et les autres
>
> (*Thé*. V. iii. 1306)

Having introduced the *récit* with such words, Racine does not need to be more explicit about a sad demeanour. It arises naturally from what Créon has said—a sad narration requires a sad tone.

What of the direct speech, which Créon includes in this *récit*, and which is such a common feature in narrations of the death of a character? Créon reports the final words of Polynice exulting in the defeat of his brother, King Etéocle:

> «Et tu meurs, lui dit-il, et moi je vais régner,
> «Regarde dans mes mains l'Empire et la victoire;
> «Va rougir aux Enfers de l'excès de ma gloire;
> «Et pour mourir encore avec plus de regret,
> «Traître, songe en mourant que tu meurs mon sujet»
>
> (*Thé*. V. iii. 1360)

How are these lines to be delivered? Is it plausible that Créon in his grief at his son's death should start imitating the tone of voice in which Polynice uttered these exultant words on the battlefield? Grimarest gives a clear answer. The actor must pronounce the direct speech 'according to the person speaking', and he comments on this very case: 'for the recital by Créon of the result of the combat between Etéocle and Polynice, one must give one's voice a tone appropriate to the character of Polynice, and to the pleasure he feels in seeing his enemy in his death throes' (*Traité*, p. 99). This advice would therefore require Créon's lines just quoted to be spoken with a tone of joyous exultation, contrasting with the sadness of the report of the deaths. The advice that direct speech introduced into a narration must be spoken with a different voice, suitable to the fictional character whose words are reproduced, is echoed by all the writers on *actio* at the time.[14]

This performance-within-performance can be seen in the *récit* of Théramène who brings news of Hippolyte's death to his father. There is a persuasive element here, because the death is being reported to Hippolyte's father by the man who was supposed to be looking after Hippolyte. Racine controls the *récit* through the preliminary accusatory question which Thésée addresses to Théramène: 'What have you done with my son? [. . .] wherefore these tears I see you shedding now?' (*Phè*. V. vi. 1488–90). This question, which precedes the narration, directs Théramène to be weeping ('wherefore these tears') and at the same time requires him to defend himself against an accusation ('what have you done with my son?'). The speech is also a defence of Hippolyte, whom Théramène, the counsel for the defence, so to speak, describes as 'the least guilty of men' in order to rebut the charge of his having seduced Phèdre (*Phè*. V. vi. 1494). The speech is not therefore a funeral oration as it has often been called (e.g. Barrault, p. 181). It is a piece of active judicial oratory, where Théramène and Hippolyte are the accused, and Thésée is the judge. In response to Thésée's accusation, Théramène proceeds to narrate Hippolyte's departure in his chariot, his bold javelin thrust at the sea-monster, and the bolting of his horses at the sight of the wounded monster. When Théramène comes to describe how Hippolyte falls

---

[14] Grear, appendix 3, s.v. Prosopopée. For discussion of Ulysse's imitation of the voices of Calchas and Eriphile (*Iph*. Act. V, Scene vi), see Capatti (pp. 180–1).

entangled in the reins, the theatrical logic of Racine's text requires a dramatic pause to be inserted, as Théramène punctuates his narration thus:

> Dans les rênes lui-même il tombe embarrassé.
> [*Pause*]
> Excusez ma douleur. Cette image cruelle
> Sera pour moi de pleurs une source éternelle.
>
> (*Phè*. V. vi. 1544–6)

After the word *embarrassé* Théramène must stop speaking. Barrault suggests a moment of complete immobility by every-one on stage, until Théramène has recovered sufficiently to explain the pause—'Excusez ma douleur'—and then to continue his narration. The pause and the expression of grief are powerful means of evoking pity for both Théramène and Hippolyte. Racine has given Théramène the orator clear guidance for his delivery. Finally, Théramène reports Hippolyte's last loving words towards Aricie:

> «Le ciel, dit-il, m'arrache une innocente vie.
> «Prends soin après ma mort de la triste Aricie.
> «Cher ami, si mon père un jour désabusé
> «Plaint le malheur d'un fils faussement accusé,
> «Pour apaiser mon sang et mon ombre plaintive,
> «Dis-lui qu'avec douceur il traite sa captive,
> «Qu'il lui rende . . . »
>
> (*Phè*. V. vi. 1561–7)

Hippolyte's reported words break off at *rende*. Here Grimarest suggests: 'Love should be expressed [. . .] in urgent and plaintive tones, as can be felt in the last words of Hippolyte in *Phèdre*' (*Traité*, p. 81). Again Théramène is required to play the part of a skilful actor-orator using all the techniques of *actio* to persuade, to excite emotion, and to delight the spectator.

The concept of conventional *actio* is not confined to tones of voice or gestures recommended in the manuals. It can extend to innovations by actors which, though not strictly justified by any implicit stage directions, none the less conform to the persuasive intentions of the speech. When Baron played Pyrrhus, he uttered the words 'Madam, embrace your son and try to save him', not in the menacing manner to which audiences were accustomed, but cradling his arms as if he were holding out the child to its mother (*And.* I. iv. 384).[15] On the spectator axis this was a new visual sign, a theatrical innovation, but on the character axis it remained consistent with Pyrrhus's desire to bend Andromaque to his will by whatever means he could.

Incongruous 'Actio'

In the examples so far considered conventional *actio* predominates, though always with the possibility of being undermined, as in the case of Ephestion's transition from the conventional *actio* of his formal speech, where Racine has not inserted any directions, to the incongruous *actio* of rising from his seat in the presence of the Indian kings, which Racine takes care to indicate by an explicit stage direction. On the whole, it can be assumed that conventional *actio* is employed when Racine does not write specific directions into his text. This contrasts with incongruous *actio* which necessarily has to be made explicit. Incongruity can take two forms according to whether it relates to the character of the person speaking or to the situation in which characters find themselves, though both these can be combined.

Incongruity of *actio* functions simultaneously on the level of both character and of situation to create comedy in *Les Plaideurs*. This is the only case where Racine gives directions for tone of voice in italicized stage directions. The trial of the dog is an oratorical display in which Racine makes explicit the oratorical substructure implicit in so much of his tragic drama. The trial scene is a straightforward judicial situation. Two servants play the parts of barristers, and deliver speeches which make fun of all the parts of rhetoric. Petit Jean exploits the *loci* of *inventio* with gay abandon, piling up irrelevant examples of inconstancy and vicissitude (*Pla.* III. iii. 674). His speech concludes weakly. In reply, Léandre comments ironically on this aspect of Petit Jean's *dispositio*: 'What a fine conclusion [i.e. *peroratio*] and so worthy of the exordium!' (*Pla.* 715). Comedy of *elocutio* lies in the tangle of popular and learned expressions. In this scene Racine's treatment of oratory is so comprehensive that he even

---

[15] Marmontel, s.v. Déclamation théâtrale.

creates comedy from *memoria*. He introduces the prompter to remind the audience of the humour deriving from failure of memory in public speaking. As for *actio*, the art of correct tone of voice and gesture, Petit Jean is the focus for incongruity of gesture and L'Intimé for comedy of incongruous tonal variation.

Petit Jean starts by removing his hat as a mark of respect, not knowing that barristers addressed the court with their hats on. He finds himself at odds with the irritated judge and Racine finally directs that he speaks 'putting his hat on' (sd, *Pla*. III. iii. 673). The spectator then sees Petit Jean speaking with his arms hanging at his side and his feet planted rigidly like a statue. Léandre encourages him to use the proper *actio*: 'You are doing well. But what are your arms doing hanging at your side? Look at your feet, straight as a statue. Shake yourself up! Come on! Get your act together!' (*Pla*. 696). To continue in this farcical vein, Racine directs Petit Jean to speak with incongruously comic gesture, 'waving his arms' (sd, *Pla*. 697).

From Petit Jean's incongruous gestures, Racine proceeds to L'Intimé's incongruous tones of voice. In turn the audience hear L'Intimé speak in falsetto, in the grand manner, in a vehement tone, and in a ponderous tone (sds, *Pla*. 727, 735, 769, 792). And for the *narratio* Racine makes L'Intimé speak 'quickly' (sd, *Pla*. 754), which is comically at odds with Le Faucheur's advice that the *narratio* must be clearly articulated so that the magistrates understand exactly what is at issue. Dandin spells out the incongruity: 'What a marvellous way to set out the affair! He takes his time over what doesn't matter, and gallops along when he gets to the facts [. . .] What barrister ever employed such a method?' (*Pla*. 763–7).

The trial scene in *Les Plaideurs* is invaluable because it provides a sample of the misapplication of all five oratorical skills, and is especially rich in Racine's explicit stage directions for *actio*. The *actio* of the comic characters is incongruous to the situation when they do the wrong thing, and to their own characters when they act parts for which they are not trained, and so make fools of themselves. This judicial scene in *Les Plaideurs* can serve as a starting-point for interpreting the theatrical effects of incongruous *actio* in the tragedies.

Racine gives directions for Titus to pronounce the speech which he has long prepared and which he could not bring himself to deliver earlier to Bérénice (*Bér.* II. ii. 473; II. iv. 624). The speech is delivered with tears: 'Help me if possible [. . .] to check my ceaseless flow of tears' (*Bér.* IV. v. 1055–6). Bérénice confirms that Titus is weeping: 'You are emperor, my lord, and yet you weep' (*Bér.* IV. v. 1154). Tears were incongruous to the character of the emperor. More frequently, the *actio* specified by Racine is incongruous to the situation, and has particular significance for the audience. Of special importance are cases of incongruous *actio* in declarations of love. Titus declares his love to Bérénice in an unpersuasive way. She comments: 'You swear your love with such coldness' (*Bér.* II. iv. 590). Bajazet deliberately employs similar coldness and excites Roxane's suspicions at his 'icy words and sombre demeanour' (*Baj.* III. vi. 1026–36). These incongruities provoke inquisitions, which play an important part in the structure of the tragedy and furnish opportunities for further combinations of speech and action which will be considered later.

Racine exploits incongruity of *actio* to sharpen the focus of the dénouement of *Britannicus.* Junie's behaviour is inconsistent with the joyful prospect of the reconciliation between Britannicus and Néron. She pleads with her lover not to enter the fatal room, and sheds tears saying: 'Suppose I were to be speaking to you for the last time. Ah, Prince!' Britannicus replies in astonishment: 'You are weeping!' (*Bri.* V. i. 1544). The incongruity of Junie's tears is further emphasized when Agrippine draws attention to them (*Bri.* V. iii. 1574). For Britannicus and Agrippine it is inappropriate that Junie should be weeping on the joyous occasion of his reconciliation with Néron. The spectator knows better. Britannicus and Agrippine are united in their surprised reaction to Junie's tears as they are united in their downfall. Their joint reaction gives visual expression to the fact that the tragedy, according to Racine, is equally the death of Britannicus and the disgrace of Agrippine. They are both shown to be credulous victims of Néron.

In *Bajazet* Racine directs Roxane's performance in such a way that she continually tries to persuade Bajazet to marry her by inappropriate means of persuasion which involve both verbal and visual effects. She tries to persuade Bajazet of her devotion to him by offering him proof of her affection—she will put him on the throne to replace his brother as sultan. Bajazet hesitates to accept the offer of marriage before becoming sultan. Roxane then threatens him with death. Bajazet blunts Roxane's persuasion by consenting to be killed. Roxane has now exhausted her verbal strategies, and resorts to visual means to reinforce her threat. She starts to leave the stage: 'Your death will suffice to justify me. Doubt it not, I hasten to carry it out, this very instant' (*Baj.* II. i. 536). Bajazet is unmoved by the threat. Roxane tries again by delivering her plea in incongruously direct language and with an attempted exit: 'Bajazet, listen; I feel that I love you; you are destroying yourself. Do not allow me to leave' (*Baj.* II. i. 538). One way of visualizing this scene is to picture Roxane hovering at the door, hoping that Bajazet, threatened by her imminent departure, will relent. But instead of persuading Bajazet that she is attractive and worthy of love, the contrast between her direct confession of love and her actions in threatening to leave Bajazet make her pathetic to the spectator. Even more full of pathos is the final meeting between Roxane and Bajazet. There is grotesque incongruity in her final ultimatum to Bajazet. To prove his love for her, she invites him to come and watch Atalide being killed: 'My rival is here! follow me at once, and see her expire in the hands of the mutes' (*Baj.* V. iv. 1543). Courville visualizes this as 'Without looking at him, she indicates her apartment' (p. 135). This seems to fit Racine's text. A single gesture here would suffice to give immediacy to the planned fate of Atalide whom the spectator has seen taken to the adjacent room. Of course the gesture and the order merely produce horror in Bajazet, and presumably horror in the spectator. Roxane's persuasion misfires. She craved love; she generates disgust. In this same scene and as a prelude to Bajazet's dramatic exit to his death, the spectator sees Bajazet switch rapidly from incongruous *actio* to conventional *actio*. His response to Roxane's ultimatum is one of fury and an implicit threat to kill her. Suddenly, however, he realizes that she holds all the cards and that such anger on his part is inappropriate to the situation if he is to save Atalide. So he corrects his *actio* and pleads for Atalide's life in more suitable tones. Here one could insert Courville's stage directions to make explicit the change of *actio* which is certainly implicit in Racine's text. The moment of change is emphasized by the typographical indentation:

BAJAZET [*allowing his resentment to burst out he advances upon Roxane*]
Je ne l'accepterais que pour vous en punir,
Que pour faire éclater aux yeux de tout l'Empire
L'horreur et le mépris que cette offre m'inspire.
  [*Roxane faces up to him. Bajazet recoils, suddenly
  terrified by the danger to Atalide: he speaks quietly*]
      Mais à quelle fureur me laissant emporter,
Contre ses tristes jours vais-je vous irriter?
  [*He returns to centre, thinking only of defending Atalide*]
De mes emportements elle n'est point complice,
Ni de mon amour même et de mon injustice.

(Baj. V. iv. 1548–54)

It is a measure of Bajazet's predicament that neither his inappropriate display of anger nor a conventional plea for mercy on behalf of Atalide is of any avail. The spectator sees Bajazet the orator exhaust all resources of *actio*; all the languages of persuasion collapse before a higher power.

Just as actors can innovate within conventional *actio*, so too within incongruous *actio*. When Agrippine sits before Néron and commands the emperor to take his place, it is a clear case of incongruous *actio*, because social codes are infringed and Agrippine betrays her inopportune assertiveness (*Bri.* Act IV, Scene ii). In the early nineteenth century Talma, playing Néron, exploited the infringement of social codes by playing with his cloak during his mother's long speech to signal his indifference and boredom (Descotes, p. 77). Courtin's handbook of etiquette, dating from Racine's time, condemned fiddling with anything while seated in discussion (p. 52). The infringement of social codes is clearly indicated by Racine for Agrippine in her speaking role; Talma simply extended this to Néron's listening role. It is a measure of the vitality of Racine's theatrical text that it provides stimulus for visual innovation.

(*d*) The Listener's Performance

Grimarest says that listening is important:

An actor must not only be fully attentive to what he is expressing, but in addition, when he is not alone on stage, he must pay the same attention to what the actor is saying who is speaking to him. This is a strict requirement of the action. The listener must follow the speaker, to adapt to his expression, his gestures, his demeanour and his posture [. . .]. The spectator will be scrutinizing the listener, in order to watch the effect which the words of the speaking character have on him; if the listener appears impassive, the performance is absolutely spoiled and the audience derives little satisfaction. (*Traité*, p. 76.)

Racine the director does not forget the listener. He guides his listeners as much as his speakers by reminding them to keep up their performance with their expressions, their reactions, or even by requiring them to remain silent when they are expected to speak.

The most elementary manner of ensuring that the listener did not fall into the errors criticized by Grimarest was to ensure that speeches contained references to the listening character by name. Atalide in a speech of sixty-one lines addresses Zaïre by name four times (*Baj*. I. iv. 345–406). The naming of the listener may be reinforced by direct address and with such phrases as 'you know'. Ismène listens to a speech of forty-seven lines from Aricie. The confidant is addressed twice by name. In addition, Aricie engages with her at intervals of about ten lines with 'you know' (*tu sais*) or its equivalent (*Phè*. II. i. 415–62). Obviously, on stage this guidance must be interpreted with discretion. Barrault suggests playing down these repetitions: 'Do not emphasize the *tu sais*. Aricie should *feel* the presence of Ismène more than she addresses her' (p. 105 n. 17). Barrault directs Aricie to engage with Ismène towards the end of her speech, in a manner which gives visual expression to the naming of the confidant and the use of the vocative. His directions, if inserted into the text, would read as follows:

ARICIE [*moving towards Ismène, centre*]
  Mais, chère Ismène, hélas, quelle est mon imprudence!
  On ne m'opposera que trop de résistance.
    [*Aricie takes Ismène's arm again and goes with her to half centre left*]
  Tu m'entendras peut-être, humble dans mon ennui
  Gémir du même orgueil que j'admire aujourd'hui.
                                        (*Phè*. II. i. 457–60)

In this way the naming of interlocutors and direct address to them can secure attention from the listening actor or actress. Racine develops this simple procedure further when he puts into his longer speeches implicit stage directions which require the listener to register particular emotions and responses. These non-verbal reactions range from surprise, grief, tears, attempted interruption, or silence. Many of Racine's longer speeches contain indications of this sort.

The listener's emotions

In *Bérénice* Antiochus has to relate his love to Bérénice in such a way that he will not offend her on the day which they both think she is to be formally acknowledged as Titus's wife-to-be. Antiochus's speech in effect runs to seventy-three lines, punctuated only by a half-line of intervention from Bérénice: 'Ah, what are you telling me', when he actually mentions being in love with her (*Bér.* I. iv. 209). This intervention terminates the first section of this long narration. In the second section, Racine gives guidance for non-verbal acting to the actress playing Bérénice. He devotes four lines to directing the listening actress's performance. Antiochus says: 'I see that your heart secretly applauds me; I see that I am listened to with less regret, and that, greatly attentive to this fateful story, you will forgive me the rest for Titus's sake' (*Bér.* I. iv. 225). In this way, Bérénice's mute performance is controlled during the forty-eight lines of the second section of Antiochus's speech. She must register keen interest in Antiochus's story and show some pleasure in it. Racine's implicit stage direction for Bérénice the listener produces a theatrical contrast when she actually makes her reply. The pleasure displayed by the listening Bérénice suddenly vanishes when she actually speaks, rebuking Antiochus in a haughty manner for his temerity.

Néron listens to forty-eight lines of Burrhus's pleading. Racine gives no specific guidance for Néron until near the end, when Burrhus says: 'But I see that my tears touch my emperor' (*Bri.* IV. iii. 1381). Néron must mutely convey assent to Burrhus's plea. The opposite occurs when Abner, the emissary of Athalie, begs the high priest Joad to save the temple from Athalie's army by handing over the child. Abner's final plea contains directions for Joad to remain absolutely unmoved: 'But I see that my tears, and my vain arguments are but a feeble help in persuading you' (*Ath.* V. ii. 1641). In fact, Joad's impassivity is actually controlling Abner; he is forcing Abner to talk himself into the position where he will co-operate in the stratagem to lure Athalie into an ambush (Le Roy, 235).

One of the greatest tests for the listener is Mithridate's exposition of his plans to conquer Rome. The speech runs to 107 lines and is the longest in Racinian tragedy. It taxes the two sons, Pharnace and Xipharès, who listen, as much as Mithridate, who delivers it. Racine is sparing in directions for performance. The three men sit for the deliberation. At the moment Mithridate formulates his enterprise, his words indicate that the two sons are taken aback: 'It is to Rome, my sons, that I intend to march. This plan surprises you' (*Mit.* III. i. 787). This is the signal that they must have expressed mute surprise. For another seventy-five lines Mithridate outlines his plan. Only once does he refer to his listeners, 'Princes' (*Mit.* 817), to ensure their attention. However, Pharnace has a more complex listening role to perform than merely remaining attentive. The first words of Pharnace's reply are: 'My lord, I cannot disguise my surprise. I listen with excitement (*transport*) to this great enterprise; I admire it' (*Mit.* 863). Pharnace's excitement could plausibly manifest itself during Mithridate's speech, as the father invites his sons to join him on his journey of conquest with a sequence of imperatives: 'Let us march . . . let us attack . . . let us burn the Capitol . . . let us destroy its trophies' (*Mit.* 831–9). But Pharnace is actually opposed to the expedition against Rome, so whilst these exhortations will genuinely excite Xipharès, Pharnace can only register feigned excitement and even this evaporates when he learns that he must depart to Parthia to marry a princess there. At the end of Mithridate's long speech Pharnace the listener is forced into a situation where feigned excitement must be mingled with anxiety.

Racine prepares a more active listening role when the listener is on the verge of interrupting a long speech. Esther establishes that Aman is likely to interrupt her plea to save the Jews: 'I beg [. . .] that Aman especially does not dare to trouble my speech' (*Est.* III. iv. 1043). For forty lines Aman hears Esther sing the praises of the Jewish god. His mounting impatience explodes in a long awaited interruption which gives Esther the opportunity to accuse him to Assuérus: 'Our enemy has declared himself before you' (*Est.* 1091). Aman's listening role seems just the kind of theatrical experience which Grimarest envisaged when he wrote 'the spectator will be scrutinizing the listener, in order to watch the effect which the words of the speaking character have on him' (*Traité*, p. 76). In like manner Josabet anxiously follows the interrogation of the young Joas by Athalie. She tries to reply for the child but is silenced by Athalie:

ATHALIE Jeune enfant, répondez.
JOSABET [*interrupting*] Le ciel jusqu'aujourd' hui . . .
ATHALIE Pourquoi vous pressez-vous de répondre pour lui?
   C'est à lui de parler.

(Ath. II. vii. 625–7)

This gives Josabet the cue to be on the verge of interruption during the rest of the interrogation, and creates an atmosphere of tense anxiety.

All these directions for the listener which can be observed in the longer speeches can be found in plenty among shorter exchanges. Expressions of surprise kindle the interest of the spectator in the action. This is a valuable technique for the dramatist when he needs to contrive a means of holding the attention of the audience in the exposition of the background to the play, which typically in Racine takes place between a confidant and a protagonist in Act I. The first scene of a Racinian tragedy usually abounds in expressions of surprise: 'Quoi!' or implicit directions to the same effect. The same technique is employed in the ritual scenes of revelations of love to confidants:

ORESTE L'amour me fait ici chercher une inhamaine [. . .]
PYLADE Quoi? votre âme à l'amour en esclave asservie

(And. I. i. 26–9)

NÉRON J'aime (que dis-je aimer?) j'idolâtre Junie.
NARCISSE Vous l'aimez?

(Bri. II. ii. 384–5)

Doris responds to Eriphile's revelation of love with 'Ah! what are you saying?' (*Iph.* II. i. 477) and Œnone with even more surprise and horror at Phèdre's revelation (*Phè.* I. iii. 265). The listener's performance here has the theatrical function of engaging the spectator in the drama.[16]

---

[16] Lapp has discussed the role of the listener in scenes of exposition (pp. 97–9). According to Ekstein 77% of Racine's *récits* have an address to the listener (p. 63).

Pause and silence

One aspect of the listener's performance requires special consideration. Racine's plays are studded with pauses and silences. It was a commonplace that silence could signify great emotions. Seneca's phrase 'Curae leves loquuntur, ingentes stupent' (Light cares can speak, but heavy ones are dumb) was current in English drama of the late sixteenth and early seventeenth century. It was exploited on stage as a theatrical technique by Shakespeare, and echoes down the centuries in poems and novels. 'Great sorrow cannot speak', wrote Donne; 'She was always more inclined to silence when feeling most strongly', wrote Jane Austen (Slater, pp. 121–36). Racine shows ample awareness of this and spells out in narrative form the variety of emotions which can be signified by silence. It may betray repressed love as Oreste confesses (*And.* II. ii. 575). Néron wanted to declare his love to Junie and he tells Narcisse: 'I wished to speak to her, but my voice was lost' (*Bri.* II. i. 396). Agamemnon found that grief strangled his speech when he heard that his daughter had to be sacrificed: 'I remained mute, and sounds only returned when countless sobs burst forth' (*Iph.* I. i. 65). These quotations are all narrative: Oreste, Néron, Agamemnon are describing past experiences to their confidants.

The spectator sees this behaviour put into practice again and again in Racine's drama. Silences and pauses may be signalled by such phrases 'you do not reply', 'you are silent', 'speak', or ellipsis stops when a character's speech tails off. Taxile's silence signifies a complexity of emotions. Axiane is upbraiding him for not joining Porus in the fight against Alexandre:

AXIANE De mon trône et du tien deviens le défenseur;
  Cours, et donne à Porus un digne successeur.
  [*pause—Taxile is silent*]
  Tu ne me réponds rien. Je vois sur ton visage
  Qu'un si noble dessein étonne ton courage.
                              (*Ale.* IV. iii. 1199–1202)

In these lines Taxile is on the verge of erupting into anger against Axiane, and reminding her that she is his prisoner. His facial expression during his pause signals barely controlled fury which Axiane interprets as a sign of cowardice. In many ways Axiane is Racine's rehearsal for Hermione in his next tragedy.

Pyrrhus's silence in Hermione's farewell speech is as eloquent as Taxile's was in the face of Axiane's reproaches. Hermione begs Pyrrhus to delay his marriage to Andromaque for a day, so that she may not be humiliated by witnessing the triumph of her rival. Pyrrhus does not reply. A barely perceptible movement hints at his impatience to be done with Hermione. The written text suggests the following performance, one of the most poignant moments in Racinian drama:

HERMIONE

    Achevez votre hymen, j'y consens. Mais du moins
    Ne forcez pas mes yeux d'en être les témoins.
    Différez-le d'un jour, demain vous serez maître.
     [*Pause. Pyrrhus is silent*]
    Vous ne répondez point.
     [*Pyrrhus makes a slight movement*]
                 Perfide, je le voi,
    Tu comptes les moments que tu perds avec moi.
                    (*And*. IV. v. 1374–8)

Pyrrhus's cruel impatience is further indicated by his wandering eyes. Hermione's suspicious scrutiny sees this and she accuses him of wishing to catch sight of Andromaque.

A longer period of silence is indicated for Hermione herself when she reappears with her confidant Cléone, who opens this short scene with the words: 'Non, je ne puis assez admirer ce silence. Vous vous taisez, Madame' (*And*. IV. ii. 1131). Hermione listens to Cléone speak for twenty lines. Cléone's words are uttered for the sole purpose of allowing the spectator to watch Hermione's lethal silence, which is made the more intense by her brusque articulation of a single phrase 'Will you send for Oreste', which is her sole response to Cléone's anxiety (*And*. 1142; Parish, pp. 397–9).

These examples show how the listener must perform during speeches when the interlocutor who has the major share of speaking temporarily stops in the expectation of a reply which does not come. Obviously the prompters had to be able to distinguish a dramatic pause from a lapse of memory, otherwise, says Chappuzeau, they might trouble the actor with needless assistance. He records seeing actors who had to tell over-enthusiastic prompters to shut up (pp. 145–6). The risk of this was perhaps diminished when the pause occurred in a quicker exchange of dialogue. Whenever one character says 'Speak' there is always the potential for a pause before the reply is delivered by the other character. Approximately fifteen occurrences of the imperative 'parlez' throughout the plays of Racine suggest tense pauses between exchanges of words. Such a theatrical reading finds confirmatory evidence in *Alexandre*. Porus bids farewell to Axiane before going to battle with Alexandre. He begs her give some sign to indicate whether she returns his love, before he goes off to a likely death. She can only reply by a mute look:

PORUS Voulez-vous qu'en mourant un prince infortuné
    Ignore à quelle gloire il était destiné? [*pause*] Parlez.
AXIANE [*pause*] Que vous dirais-je?

(*Ale.* II. v. 669–71)

The theatrical effect of Porus's insistent questioning during this scene lies more in his facial expression, particularly his eyes, than in the words he utters. This can be deduced from Axiane's later description of this scene which provides guidance on how to perform it. Axiane describes Porus's eyes doing the questioning during their farewell: 'When your eyes revealed to me your languor, and asked me what place you held in my heart' (*Ale.* IV. i. 972). In these retrospective stage directions Axiane also reveals her own hesitations: 'How often your eyes, breaking down my resistance, nearly made my heart break its silence' (*Ale.* 978). This suggests that in performance Axiane should make as if to speak and then remain silent. It is a strong cue for playing the situation rather than the words.

This example from *Alexandre*, where the stage directions are clearly contained in a later scene, can serve as a pattern for a theatrical reading of similar exchanges where Racine gives less explicit guidance. This can occur where the emotional climate is relatively subdued. Paulin may pause before telling Titus what Rome thinks of Bérénice:

TITUS Parlez; qu'entendez-vous?
PAULIN [*pause*]   J'entends de tous côtés
    Publier vos vertus, Seigneur, et ses beautés.

(*Bér.* II. ii. 345–6)

Paulin's pause allows the cautious orator to draw upon *mores* in order to lighten his message of doom: the result is his exquisite flattery of both the emperor and his mistress. Later in *Bérénice*, at one of the most highly charged moments, there is scope for Titus to pause before delivering to Bérénice his separation speech:

BÉRÉNICE Dites, parlez.
TITUS [*pause*]   Hélas! que vous me déchirez!

(Bér. IV. v. 1153)

Silences and pauses in drama are like those in music. This was Grimarest's opinion. His remarks suggest that he was sensitive to the variety of tempo which the Racinian text required, and equally alert to the way in which acting styles in the last two decades of the century obscured Racine's intentions: 'It is a great source of pleasure to contrive appropriate silences and sighs in the agitations of emotion, as is customary in music. The whole scene of Phèdre with her confidant [*Phè.* Act I, Scene iii] should be adorned in its delivery with these sighs and silences.' Grimarest objects to the excessively emphatic delivery of most of those who declaim this scene as not being appropriate to 'a woman on the verge of dying because of the passion which devours her'. He recommends that Phèdre should deliver her lines in 'a plaintive and weak voice, interrupted by silences and sighs'. This, he says, 'is a much better way of demonstrating to the spectator all the painful movements of this scene' (*Traité*, pp. 105–6). Silence and pause may seem to be the very negation of drama based on words, but Racine the director constantly orchestrates his characters' performance so that words alternate with silence to express the deepest human feelings.

As well as providing moments of theatrical tension, failure to speak is frequently part of the overall structure of Racinian drama. Many of Racine's plays are structured around a secret, which some characters try to conceal while others pursue the truth. This pattern starts with *Bérénice*, where the heroine gradually discovers that Titus requires her to leave him. This unwelcome news is hidden from her in Act I, hinted at in Act II, disbelieved by her in Act III, formally declared in Act IV, accepted in Act V. In *Bajazet* Roxane does not discover that she is the victim of a conspiracy of concealment until Act III; then she is remorseless in her quest for the truth. The plots of *Mithridate, Iphigénie*, and *Phèdre* all depend upon guilty secrets. Queen Athalie also investigates a mystery. In this way Racine makes suspense integral to his drama and engineers some extremely dramatic silences which signal a mystery to be solved.

Bérénice begs Titus to indicate if she is unwelcome to her:

TITUS Non, Madame. Jamais, puisqu'il faut vous parler,
　　Mon cœur de plus de feux ne se sentit brûler.
　　Mais . . . [*pause*]
BÉRÉNICE　　　　　Achevez.
TITUS　　　　　　　　Hélas! [*pause*]
BÉRÉNICE　　　　　　　Parlez.
TITUS　　　　　　　　　　　Rome . . . L'Empire . . .
　　[*long pause: Titus tongue-tied*]
BÉRÉNICE Hé bien?
TITUS　　　　Sortons, Paulin: je ne lui puis rien dire.
　　　　　　　　　　　　(*Bér.* II. iv. 624–7)

Iphigénie suffers the same anguish in the face of her father's silence:

IPHIGÉNIE Verra-t-on à l'autel votre heureuse famille?
AGAMEMNON Hélas! [*pause*]
IPHIGÉNIE　　　　Vous vous taisez?
AGAMEMNON [*pause*]　　　　　Vous y serez ma fille.
　　　　　　　　　　　　(*Iph.* II. ii. 577–8)

Racine combines intense emotion, mysterious silence, and dramatic exit in these exchanges. The attempts at concealment lead to interrogation.

(*e*) Interrogations

Interrogation has a powerful role in Racinian drama. It embraces a range of theatrical effects from a single question to a complete scene devoted to eliciting information; and, in its widest form, to the structure of a whole play when some secret is hidden and there is a mystery to be solved. Even a simple question intensifies the interaction between characters and focuses the attention of the audience on what is being said.

Interrogation in all its forms generates suspense. It stands between mystery and revelation, ignorance and knowledge. On stage it engages the spectator in the quest for truth.

Interrogation also has a triple rhetorical dimension for which one might use the terms simple interrogation, persuasive interrogation, and inquisition. Classical rhetoric treated interrogation as no more than a figure of speech under *elocutio*; this is simple interrogation. The normal arts of persuasion can be used to elicit information which is being withheld, as in the case of Bérénice's relentless interrogation of Antiochus. This might be called persuasive interrogation. There was also a specialized technique in judicial oratory, where interrogation involves the questioning of witnesses; this can be described as an inquisition. It is in the interrogation of witnesses that rhetoric offers advice which is particularly appropriate to those dramatic situations favoured by Racine, where there is an attempt to trick a witness into revealing what they wish to conceal. This can be seen when Roxane interrogates Atalide, Mithridate interrogates Monime, or Athalie interrogates the mysterious Eliacin.

Simple Interrogation

A small figure of rhetoric is the question. D'Aubignac says 'it is good for the theatre because it is the mark of an agitated mind' (*Pratique*, iv. 7, p. 318). Grimarest in his discussion of punctuation as a guide to correct reading says 'the question mark indicates that one must pronounce the expression with an elevated or raised tone; it is impolite to interrogate a great nobleman, without adding some corrective to one's expression [. . .] Both the exclamation mark and the question mark indicate not only the pause which they require, but also the emotion inherent in these terms' (*Traité*, p. 30).

Grimarest distinguishes several tones for simple interrogation. He envisages a quiet voice for Oreste questioning Pylade about Pyrrhus and Hermione: 'You, who know Pyrrhus, what do you think he might do?' (*And.* I. i. 101). For Agamemnon's response to Achille's offensive proposal to save Iphigénie from sacrifice, the tone should be loud, fierce, and haughty: 'Who has told you to look after my family? Can I not dispose of my daughter without you? Am I not her father? Are you her husband?' (*Iph.*

IV. vi. 1349). Grimarest gives examples from plays by other dramatists of mournful questioning in a tender and plaintive voice, reproachful questioning in a firm and plaintive voice, boastful questioning in a loud, proud, and scornful voice (*Traité*, pp. 96–8). In some of these examples Grimarest is talking of questions which are not intended to elicit replies, but which verge upon exclamations, that is to say, rhetorical questions. The ambiguous status of the rhetorical question accounts for modern editors often substituting exclamation marks for the question marks which appear in the original printed texts.

Simple interrogation is frequent in the exposition scenes of Racinian drama. It creates a plausible framework in which to give the audience the information necessary for the understanding of the background and future action. Gentle questions between confidant and protagonist elicit information. Suspense is generated when the answer is incomplete. In scenes of exposition an excited tone of voice or display of passion focuses the spectators' attention upon important pieces of information. The exposition of *Bérénice* is rich in questions. *Iphigénie en Tauride* shows how Racine, even in drafting a play, gave priority to interrogation and passion in the exposition. Iphigénie appears in a state of sadness. She is questioned by her companion. The background to the play is revealed in active dialogue enhanced by visible displays of emotion (Act I, Scene i).

Persuasive Interrogation

Persuasive interrogation is more theatrical. It is stimulated by some visual sign of concealment such as averted eyes, tears, silence, or frosty demeanour. The visual effect is the stimulus for the verbal action. Junie's silence and averted eyes worry Britannicus into his questions: 'You say nothing? What greeting is this? What coldness! [. . .] What do I see? You fear to meet my gaze?' (*Bri*. II. vi. 707–37). Titus's demeanour excites Bérénice's anxiety and she says: 'What! you do not reply and turn your eyes away' (*Bér*. II. iv. 597). Roxane sees Bajazet's troubled expression: 'You are sighing and seem to be troubled' (*Baj*. II. i. 559). Agamemnon's grief-stricken attempt to conceal his anguish provokes Iphigénie's questions: 'My lord, you seem to sigh, and scarcely look upon me' (*Iph*. II. ii. 552). The list of

averted eyes, silences, tears, and sighs which provoke questioning is long in Racine. Not only are questions directed at the
character whose demeanour is the source of mystery, but the
questioning continues afterwards in a vain attempt to interpret
the mysterious signs. Bérénice questions Titus on his visible
discomfiture (*Bér.* Act II, Scene iv). Then she discusses possible
explanations with her confidant Phénice in Act II, Scene v, and
reaches an erroneous conclusion about the cause of Titus's
behaviour.

Persuasive interrogation implies that the character employs all
the arts of persuasion in order to force the concealing character
to say something which will shed light on the mystery. Such a
scene has a deliberative function, summed up as 'to speak or not
to speak'. Bérénice meets Antiochus by chance just after the
latter has been told by Titus that he must give Bérénice the fatal
news that she must leave Rome. Antiochus does not wish to
impart the bad tidings. He constructs arguments to prove that it
is better he should not tell Bérénice what he and Titus were
talking about: 'I prefer to displease you and fear your grief more
than your anger.' Bérénice sees his troubled expression. She
then deploys different passions in her successive attempts at
persuasion. First an angry order to prevent Antiochus leaving,
followed by an appeal to pity. The two emotions can be seen in
the following lines, very clearly marked by Racine with implicit
stage directions:

BÉRÉNICE [*angrily stopping Antiochus*]
    O ciel! quel discours! Demeurez.
        [*changing to a quieter, pleading tone*]
    Prince, c'est trop cacher mon trouble à votre vue.
        [*offering herself to him as an object of pity*]
    Vous voyez devant vous une reine éperdue

                            (*Bér.* III. iii. 871–3)

When Bérénice's appeal to pity fails, she quickly resorts to
anger again, the stage direction being contained in Antiochus's
reply:

ANTIOCHUS Je n'ai qu'à vous parler pour me faire haïr.
BÉRÉNICE [*with violent anger*]
    Je veux que vous parliez.
ANTIOCHUS   Dieux! quelle violence!

                            (*Bér.* III. iii. 883–4)

Bérénice goes on to achieve her objectives by exploiting the *loci* of cause and effect delivered in menacing tones. She says that if Antiochus does not speak she will hate him for ever. This forces Antiochus to reveal that Titus has ordered Bérénice to depart from Rome. She refuses to believe him, and sends him from her sight. Bérénice's relentless interrogation to extract Titus's message from Antiochus is the central scene of the play. It illustrates how the character deploys all the arts of persuasion, especially the use of passion, in order to grip the audience's attention. In addition, Bérénice's persuasive technique with its abrupt changes of emotions, provides her with her character, her ethos. Racine the director obliges Bérénice to appear excitable, changeable, and manipulative. The actress, Julia Bartet, picked on this when she wrote that *Bérénice* was a tragedy in which human passions *sharpen* the suffering caused by fate.[17] Far from being a monotonous elegy, *Bérénice* shows how characters enmeshed in an irretrievable situation torture themselves with every variety of human passion.

Equally revealing of character are Iphigénie's persuasive strategies when she finds that her father will not embrace her or respond to her smiling welcome. Agamemnon is burdened with the knowledge that he must sacrifice his daughter. His attempts to elude her embrace cause Iphigénie to question him insistently. She relies on a submissive approach, appropriate to her status. All her attempts to persuade her father to explain his anxiety emphasize her daughterly love and accentuate the pathos of the scene (*Iph*. Act II, Scene ii).

Inquisitions

The preceding scenes of persuasive interrogation come about when the characters make it clear that they are seeking information. The interrogation takes on a different guise when the interrogator does not reveal his or her purpose directly to the victim. Here the techniques of judicial interrogation come into play. One can describe such scenes as inquisitions. Advice from the rhetoricians on inquisitions is applicable both to the lawcourts and to the theatre. According to the *Rhetorica ad*

---

[17] 'La tragédie des passions humaines, *aiguisant* les douleurs de la destinée' (her emphasis), letter to Paul Gaulot, 4 Feb. 1912, quoted in Chancerel, p. 19.

Alexandrum, attributed to Anaximenes, the orator should conduct his inquiry 'not in a bitter but in a gentle spirit' since this will appear more persuasive (§ 37). Quintilian evokes the spectacle of witnesses being led into a trap. The orator should start with apparently innocent questions to lead the victim on so that in spite of himself he reveals the information sought (v. vii. 11 and 27). Such a spectacle can produce a powerful theatrical effect.[18]

There is an inquisitorial flavour to Néron's spying on Junie. From behind his curtain, he watches her face for signs of love for Britannicus. This is certainly a trap but it is not an inquisition in the rhetorical sense. The first time Racine exploits inquisitorial techniques analogous to those recommended by the rhetoricians is in *Bajazet* when Roxane has decided at the end of Act III to investigate whether Atalide and Bajazet are in love. She confronts Atalide with a letter; Atalide faints. Roxane, the inquisitor, has the proof she needs: 'My rival has revealed herself to my very eyes' (*Baj.* IV. iv. 1209). Roxane plays a similar deception upon Bajazet to induce him to reveal his love for Atalide (*Baj.* Act V, Scene iv). Having found this theatrical device to his taste Racine exploited it to the full in his next play. Mithridate is the arch-inquisitor. From the moment he enters he is probing his confidant Arbate in a suspicious manner. Why are his two sons in Nymphaeum? It is a harsh interrogation. Mithridate could hardly employ more brutal questions: 'What happened? What have you seen? What do you know?' (*Mit.* II. iv. 481). It is measure of Arbate's composure that he reveals only what he wishes, and manages to throw suspicion on Pharnace, whilst protecting Xipharès. Arbate performs well in the witness box, even with Mithridate as interrogator.

Monime is not so successful. What she says is innocent enough, but her tone, her looks, betray her. Ironically it is Mithridate's attempt to be gentle and gallant which provokes the most evident signs of Monime's irritating submissiveness. Mithridate asks indignantly:

> Tout mon empressement ne sert qu'à vous confondre.
> [*Pause. Monime tries to control her tears.*]

[18] For rhetorical analysis of the scenes discussed in this section, see Hawcroft, pp. 186–94.

Vous demeurez muette; et loin de me parler,
Je vois, malgré vos soins, vos pleurs prêts à couler.

(*Mit.* II. v. 580–2)

On the evidence of silence and tears Mithridate reaches the erroneous conclusion that Monime loves Pharnace. So he tests Pharnace. Mithridate summons his sons for the great deliberation on his plan to conquer Rome (Act III, Scene i). He ends his long speech by requiring Pharnace to marry a Parthian princess. Pharnace is ordered to leave at once to demonstrate his obedience. His hesitation gives Mithridate the chance to pounce upon Pharnace's guilty secret. As Pharnace leaves under arrest he accuses Xipharès.

Mithridate now has new suspicions to follow up. As he debates what course of action to take, his words are those of the lawcourts: 'Let me examine [. . .] who will enlighten me? what witnesses? what clues?' He decides to summon Monime, his choice of witness (III. iv. 1026). Mithridate talks of a trap, of deception, and his concluding line sums up the essence of judicial inquisition: 'By clever deceit, let us extract the truth' (III. iv. 1034). The inquisition of Monime in *Mithridate*, Act III, Scene v, depends greatly on the interraction of the verbal and the visual. Mithridate's trap is to pretend to Monime that she must marry Xipharès in the hope that her joy will force her to reveal her love for Xipharès. Monime's task is to control her feelings, to protest her desire to marry Mithridate, and above all to give no hint that her love is really for Xipharès. The inquisition is given strong visual focus by two suggested exits which show Monime pulled in opposite directions. Monime endeavours to emphasize her fidelity to Mithridate by offering to complete their marriage ceremony:

MONIME [*urging Mithridate to accompany her off stage*]
  Je sais qu'en ce moment, pour ce nœud solennel,
  La victime, Seigneur, nous attend à l'autel.
  Venez.   [*Mithridate refuses to move.*]

(*Mit.* III. v. 1077–9)

Monime's movement is then imitated by Mithridate, as he adds urgency to his proposal that Monime should marry Pharnace instead of Xipharès:

MITHRIDATE [*urging Monime to accompany him off stage*]
  Venez. Je ne saurais mieux punir vos dédains,
  Qu'en vous mettant moi-même en ses serviles mains;
  Et sans plus me charger du soin de votre gloire,
  Je veux laisser de vous jusqu'à votre mémoire.
  Allons, Madame, allons. Je m'en vais vous unir.
MONIME [*refusing to move*]
  Plutôt de mille morts dussiez-vous me punir!

(*Mit.* III. v. 1090)

The spectator sees the two protagonists urge each other to leave in opposite directions for opposite purposes: Monime to convince Mithridate of her obedience, Mithridate to trick Monime. Peyron's illustration portrays this visual dimension (Pl. 27).

In addition to these movements, Racine has written into the text further theatrical effects of silences, facial expression, and tone of voice. These directions are given partly concurrently and partly retrospectively. Important guidance for this scene comes later in the play, when Monime recalls her behaviour during this inquisition: 'If only you knew with what cruel cunning he came to uncover my love [. . .] The gods inspired me with secret promptings, but I did not follow them well. Three times they made me keep silent. I ought to have continued thus' (*Mit.* IV. ii. 1231–9). Mademoiselle Clairon, when studying the text to play the part of Monime, found only two clear silences on the part of Monime in the inquisition of Act III, Scene v. She supplied the third silence at the point she judged most appropriate. The first of the silences is when Mithridate offers to place Monime in Xipharès's hands. Monime nearly gives herself away but stops just in time: 'What are you saying? O heaven! Could you really approve . . . [*Pause. Monime realizes the danger.*] But why, my lord, why do you wish to test me?' (III. v. 1074). Mithridate then suggests that Monime in reality despises Xipharès. Monime again nearly reveals the truth: 'I despise him!', but for the second time she goes no further and maintains her silence. The third silence was conveyed by Mademoiselle Clairon with facial expression alone. When Mithridate accuses Monime of loving Pharnace instead of Xipharès (*Mit.* 1087), Clairon decided to play this by coming forward with the expression of a woman who is about to tell all, then changing to an expression of fear and retreating

without speaking, thus conveying the third silence mentioned
by Monime when she recalls this scene. Clairon's acting worked.
'The spectators,' she recalled, 'who had never seen this *jeu de
scène* before, rewarded me for all my careful preparation with
their applause' (*Mémoires*, pp. 58–9). The inquisition ends with
Monime's celebrated octave jump which Racine is reported to
have taught La Champmeslé (Dubos, i. 465–6):

MONIME
    Avant que votre amour m'eût envoyé ce gage,
      [*She points to the diadem, the sign of her betrothal to
      Mithridate. She lowers her voice.*]
    Nous nous aimions . . . [*She breaks off in horror at Mithridate's
    expression. Her voice rises an octave.*]
                  Seigneur, vous changez de visage.
                        (*Mit.* III. v. 1111–12)

Racine's last major scene of inquisition is in *Athalie*. Encour-
aged by Mathan, Athalie summons the child Joas for interrogation. Athalie starts with incongruous *actio*. Instead of the gentle
approach recommended by the rhetoricians, she scrutinizes the
child closely in an unfriendly manner: 'The more I look closely
at him . . . It is he! I feel horror again all over' (*Ath.* II. vii.
620–1). Athalie's hostility makes her questions sharp and
peremptory: 'What is your name [. . .] Your father's name?
[. . .] You have no parents?' (*Ath.* II. vii. 633–7). The child's
answers are truthful but miraculously they do not incriminate
him. Indeed, he turns the tables on his inquisitor by changing
Athalie's hostility into confused compassion. The directions for
this change of attitude are conveyed by Athalie's own words,
which describe the effect the young boy has on her: 'his voice,
his childishness, his gracefulness, are gradually changing my
hostility into . . . [*She pauses and speaks aside*] Am I succumbing
to compassion?' (*Ath.* 651–4).

    Each of Racine's three major inquisitorial scenes has similar-
ities and differences. Each witness is in danger of incriminating
not only a third party but also themselves. Atalide and Monime
succumb to superior interrogators. Only the child Joas manages
to resist, but even in his case the seeds of suspicion are sown
in Athalie's mind. The visual effects of each scene are quite
different. When Roxane thrusts a letter into Atalide's hand,

Atalide betrays herself by fainting and is carried off stage. Mithridate breaks through Monime's hesitations by urging her off stage for marriage to the hated Pharnace, which brings Monime's fatal admission. In *Athalie* a queen enthroned leans over a young child, while a crowd of anxious onlookers, Josabet, Abner, Zacharie, Salomith, Levites, and chorus of young girls watch the contest (Pl. 30). As with embraces, headbands, arrests, and curtains, so also with inquisitions; Racine in his last play exploited theatrical devices which he had found successful in his earlier plays (see Chapter 3, sections *b* and *c*).

(*f*) Visual Focus

Oratorical techniques of persuasion provide a framework for understanding the nature of verbal action, which is an essential ingredient of the theatricality of Racinian drama. They also extend to the physical delivery of speeches. Within this framework it is possible to establish various relationships between verbal and non-verbal means of communication. One can say that the verbal action predominates and physical effects are subordinate, when tone of voice and gesture simply support the delivery of the speech in a conventional manner. But when, for theatrical purposes, Racine exploits an inappropriate delivery (incongruous *actio*), then the physical dimension becomes more important because it signifies something extra to the spectator. In the case where an actor is not speaking but listening, then visual communication is the only possible method of performance. Racine the director provides guidance for all these varieties of theatrical language, and these have been considered in the preceding sections. There are, however, further aspects of the relationship between the verbal and visual. There are moments in the play when all eyes will be turned upon a character. At such moments the words play a subordinate role.

Static Focus

At its simplest, visual focus can consist in characters drawing attention to themselves. Andromaque entreats Pyrrhus, and thereby the spectator: 'My Lord, see the state to which you have reduced me' (*And*. III. vi. 927). Bérénice implores Antiochus: 'You see before you a tormented queen' (*Bér*. III. iii. 872). Hippolyte appeals to Aricie: 'You see before you a most wretched prince' (*Phè*. II. ii. 529). The spectator is also invited to contemplate and savour the visual expression of personal misery, or, in the case of Mithridate, to contemplate a heroic delusion, when he focuses attention upon himself to indicate his grandiose isolation as the opponent of Rome: 'I alone resist them' (*Mit*. III. i. 781).

Characters may point to others in a dramatic way. Racine uses this device to highlight a turning point in the play and to emphasize a moment of truth. This was Racine's first idea for the dénouement of *Andromaque*. Oreste returns from the killing of Pyrrhus, bringing with him Andromaque under arrest as tangible proof to Hermione that he has carried out her orders and saved her from disgrace. Oreste points to his prisoner in the text of 1668 only: 'See this captive. She can tell you, better than I, that Oreste fulfilled his promise' (*And*. V. iii. 1492*a*). As part of Oreste's persuasion, Andromaque is a *probatio inartificialis*, concrete proof of his obedience to Hermione. At the same time the spectator is invited to contemplate the spectacle of Andromaque's disgrace. *Britannicus* ends with two such moments as Agrippine designates first Néron and then Narcisse in their true colours. After the murder of Britannicus Agrippine halts Néron's progress across the stage:

AGRIPPINE Arrêtez, Néron. J'ai deux mots à vous dire.
  Britannicus est mort, je reconnais les coups;
  Je connais l'assassin.
  NÉRON   Et qui, Madame?
  AGRIPPINE   Vous.
                (*Bri*. V. vi. 1651–3)

Gravelot's illustration catches this moment, at which Agrippine at last sees the truth and accuses Néron (Pl. 18). Agrippine's head is held high, her outstretched finger pointing at Néron. He hangs his head slightly, and one arm is raised across his chest as if for protection against Agrippine. Narcisse skulks behind his master. His turn for the spotlight comes when he tries to defend Néron's action. Agrippine cuts him short:

'Continue, Néron, with such counsellors' (*Bri.* 1673). Here again a pause would be appropriate to allow the spectator to contemplate Narcisse, while Agrippine's contempt engulfs the evil confidant. Such a moment might qualify for Thody's vibrant evocation of the shock of recognition: 'One of the highest aesthetic values that the theatre can attain is the "moment of truth" when the audience becomes collectively conscious of the nature and significance of the drama being enacted before it; when the emotions of the public enable it to share the feelings simulated by the actor' (p. 35).

There are obviously close links between dramatic pauses, when characters and audience wait for a character to speak, and this kind of static visual focus. This can be seen in *Les Plaideurs*, when, in the only solemn moment of the comedy, all eyes are focused upon Isabelle, watching for her to indicate whether she consents to the marriage with Léandre, who is also waiting eagerly for an answer: 'I will abide by the decision of the charming Isabelle' (*Pla.* III. iv. 867). Jean Fabre, in his edition of *Les Plaideurs*, suggests that, after Léandre has spoken this line, 'it is appropriate that the actors pause for an anxious silence: Isabelle has become the focus for all eyes' (p. 101 n. 12). Isabelle's father breaks the spell with: 'Are you dumb? Come, it is up to you to speak' (*Pla.* 868). The gap between the lines spoken by Léandre and by Isabelle's father is the moment of visual focus, emphasized by the presence on stage of all the characters for the final scene of the play.

An instructive passage in *Alexandre* shows Racine in his later years replacing verbal with visual communication, and indicating by visual focus the turning point of the drama. It is puzzling to read in the later editions of *Alexandre* how Porus, at the very moment that Axiane declares her love for him, seems to ignore her and addresses Alexandre instead. Axiane makes her declaration to Porus as follows:

> Oui, oui, Porus, mon cœur n'aime point à demi;
> Alexandre le sait, Taxile en a gémi.
> Vous seul l'ignoriez; mais ma joie est extrême
> De pouvoir en mourant vous le dire à vous-même.

Porus replies:

> Alexandre, il est temps que tu sois satisfait.
> Tout vaincu que j'étais, tu vois ce que j'ai fait.
>
> (*Ale.* V. iii. 1479–84)[19]

One would expect Porus to acknowledge Axiane's loving remarks, rather than turn to Alexandre; but such a break in the logical sequence of verbal communication is usually Racine's signal for a visual effect. The scene only makes sense if Porus, before turning to Alexandre, acknowledges Axiane's declaration of love by eye contact, focusing the spectator's attention on this long-awaited union of the two lovers. Such a theatrical reading of the text derives support from considering the earlier versions of this scene when Porus did indeed reply to Axiane:

> PORUS Ah! Madame, sur moi laissez tomber leurs coups.
> Ne troublez point un sort que vous rendez si doux.
> Vous m'allez regretter. Quelle plus grande gloire
> Pouvait à mes soupirs accorder la victoire?
>
> (*Ale.* Act V, Scene iii)[20]

These lines came between Axiane's declaration and Porus's address to Alexandre just quoted, but Racine deleted this verbal exchange between Porus and Axiane, and in his later versions relied on an exchange of looks between Axiane and Porus to focus the spectators' eyes upon the lovers before Porus turns to Alexandre and receives the reward for his haughty defiance of the conqueror.

Focus on Action

It is characteristic of such moments of static focus to be fleeting though memorable. In other cases the spectator may watch a character intently to see if a physical action will be performed on stage in response to persuasion by another character. Here verbal and physical action combine. Jocaste urges her two sons to greet each other, but they move further apart (*Thé.* IV. iii. 985). She then urges Polynice: 'Start by embracing your brother'. Will Polynice perform the physical action? No. His

[19] Text of 1687–97 only.
[20] Text of 1666–76 only.

response is: 'What use all this mystery? These embraces are hardly appropriate' (*Thé.* 1001). In *Mithridate* all eyes will be on Pharnace as Mithridate tests him by ordering him to marry the Parthian princess and demanding an embrace before he leaves to do so. The text suggests the following sequence of tense physical movements. The ellipsis stops are Racine's:

MITHRIDATE Allez; et soutenant l'honneur de vos aïeux,
   Dans cet embrassement recevez mes adieux.
      [*Mithridate offers Pharnace an embrace. Pause. Pharnace stands immobile or steps back.*]
PHARNACE Seigneur . . .
MITHRIDATE [*advances towards Pharnace*]
                         Ma volonté, Prince, vous doit suffire.
   Obéissez.
      [*Mithridate again offers an embrace*]
            C'est trop vous le faire redire.
PHARNACE [*refusing the embrace but confronting his father*]
   Seigneur, si pour vous plaire il ne faut que périr,
   Plus ardent qu'aucun autre on m'y verra courir.
   Combattant à vos yeux permettez que je meure.
MITHRIDATE Je vous ai commandé de partir tout à l'heure.
   Mais après ce moment . . . [*repeats the offer of embrace*]
                         Prince, vous m'entendez,
   Et vous êtes perdu si vous me répondez.
      [*Long, tense pause*]
PHARNACE Dussiez-vous présenter mille morts à ma vue,
   Je ne saurais chercher une fille inconnue.
      [*with a gesture of proud submission*]
   Ma vie est entre vos mains.
MITHRIDATE [*exultant*]   Ah! c'est où je t'attends
                         (*Mit.* III. i. 957–69)

   In *Les Plaideurs* Racine focuses visual attention on physical violence when L'Intimé disguised as a *sergent* invites Chicanneau to hit him again so that he can sue him for it (*Pla.* II. iv. 441). There is a theatrical analogy when a character in the tragedies begs to be killed. Racine focuses attention on the physical movement which such an offer involves. Jocaste offers her breast to her sons (*Thé.* IV. iii. 1077); Burrhus begs death from Néron, doubtless proffering his sword (*Bri.* IV. iv. 1378); Phèdre urges Hippolyte to strike her with his sword (*Phè.* II. v. 711).

Focus on Leaving or Staying

Poised athletically on one foot, Mithridate points off stage with his left hand, while his right hand urges Monime to accompany him. Less assertive but equally determined, Monime gestures forcefully in the opposite direction. Thus Peyron focuses on the movements of the two characters each urging the other to leave the stage (Pl. 27). This linking of verbal and visual action is a constant feature of Racine's drama. Characters deploy the art of persuasion to detain on stage a character who is impatient to leave, or to urge a character away who is reluctant to depart. This exploits the characteristic feature of seventeenth-century French drama, the frequency with which characters enter or leave the stage.

The physical action of detaining a character is found in *La Thébaïde*. Créon is offering Antigone marriage and the throne of Thebes, now that all other members of the royal family are dead. Antigone is impatient to escape his unwelcome attentions, and makes to exit. Racine's explicit stage direction is the key point here:

ANTIGONE Adieu: nous ne faisons tous deux que nous gêner.
　Je veux pleurer, Créon, et vous voulez régner.
CRÉON *arrêtant Antigone*
　Ah! Madame, regnez, et montez sur le trône:
　Ce haut rang n'appartient qu'à l'illustre Antigone.
(*Thé.* V. iii. 1405–8)

The stage direction, 'stopping Antigone', strongly suggests that Créon lays a restraining hand on Antigone to detain her. This is followed by attempts at verbal persuasion. Then Racine intensifies the visual effects with more stage directions:

CRÉON [. . .] Ordonnez seulement ce qu'il faut que je fasse:
　Je suis prêt . . .
ANTIGONE *en s'en allant* Nous verrons.
CRÉON *la suivant*　　　　J'attends vos lois ici.
ANTIGONE *en s'en allant* Attendez.
(*Thé.* V. iii. 1418–20)

Racine has clearly visualized Antigone's impatience to leave, represented by her movement towards the exit. Créon follows

her and then obeys her orders to stay on stage when Antigone
actually makes her exit after 'Attendez.'

The same kind of visual focus within a persuasive framework
is offered to the spectator in *Phèdre*. Edmunds's account of
rehearsing the first scene stresses Hippolyte's restless shifting
of position as he evades Théramène's attacking moves. The
movements implicit in the text (e.g. 'I am leaving . . . I shall
escape . . . I must escape', ll. 1, 28, 50) can be seen in part as
a response to 'Théramène's dangerous probing of the most
sensitive areas of the prince's psyche' (p. 44). Hubert also
emphasizes the way in which Hippolyte sketches movements of
flight throughout this scene (pp. 84–9). This continues in the
rest of the play where it is signalled by implicit stage directions,
both preparatory and retrospective. Phèdre is humiliated by
having to make her declaration of love to a man who is
impatient to leave her presence. Hippolyte is visibly anxious to
leave Phèdre, because she has interrupted Hippolyte's own
declaration of love to Aricie in the previous scene. As Phèdre
enters he tells Théramène to deliver him from 'this unpleasant
interview' with Phèdre as soon as possible:

HIPPOLYTE Fais donner le signal, cours, ordonne, et revien
Me délivrer bientôt d'un fâcheux entretien.

(Phè. II. iv. 579–80)

Naturally Hippolyte's courtesy disguises his impatience; but
while Phèdre speaks to him, his agitation must be signalled
beneath the surface. There are no overt indications of this
during the exchanges between Phèdre and Hippolyte, but the
retrospective stage direction makes Hippolyte's demeanour
very clear. Phèdre recalls this scene in the next act: 'How he
listened to me! [. . .] How he longed for a quick escape!' (*Phè*.
III. i. 743–5). Taken on its own this could be interpreted as
a delusion on Phèdre's part, and might not qualify as a retrospective stage direction. But taken in conjunction with Hippolyte's description of his meeting with Phèdre as an 'unpleasant interview' Phèdre's words surely must be interpreted as
Racine's guidance for Hippolyte's demeanour during this scene,
a theatrical effect which is of Racine's invention and not in his
sources.

The same humiliation of having to plead with an interlocutor who is impatient to leave adds pathos to Andromaque's plight when Hermione makes clear how unwelcome Andromaque's arrival is:

HERMIONE Dieux! ne puis-je à ma joie abandonner mon âme?
Sortons: que lui dirais-je?
[*Hermione makes to leave. Andromaque stops her by kneeling at her feet.*]
ANDROMAQUE   Où fuyez-vous, Madame?
N'est-ce pas à vos yeux un spectacle assez doux
Que la veuve d'Hector pleurante à vos genoux?

                                    (*And.* III. iii. 857–60)

Andromaque's anguish is intensified not only by having to persuade Hermione to intercede for her son, but by having to persuade an impatient Hermione to listen to her at all. Hermione is later punished by having to endure the same from Pyrrhus (*And.* Act IV, Scene v). In almost every play Racine uses this technique. Hémon tries to restrain an impatient Antigone (*Thé.* Act II, Scene i); Axiane an eager Porus (*Ale.* Act II, Scene v); Léandre an obsessive Dandin (*Pla.* II. xiii. 594); Bérénice a reticent Antiochus (*Bér.* III. iii. 851); Phœdime a desperate Monime (*Mit.* V. i. 1453); Iphigénie a mortified Agamemnon (*Iph.* II. ii. 535).

In *Britannicus* arguments for staying or leaving are deployed to give visual focus to a dilemma. Britannicus is intent on leaving the stage by the door which leads to Néron's apartment in order that he may enjoy the supposed reconciliation. Junie restrains him, first by visual means when her looks turn towards heaven, and then by expressing her anxious doubts about Néron's sincerity. She produces a stream of arguments to delay Britannicus who all the while is impatient to leave, yet unwilling to disobey the woman he loves. The text suggests a sequence of movements for Britannicus, towards Néron's door and then back to Junie (*Bri.* V. i. 1543). Then Agrippine arrives to reinforce the visual focus of Britannicus's dilemma. Whereas Junie had been employing every means of persuasion to delay Britannicus's exit, Agrippine employs persuasion to hurry him through the door (*Bri.* V. ii. 1555–64). Finally Britannicus makes his fatal exit. Agrippine has unwittingly urged him to his death.

In *Bérénice* the same visual representation of dilemma is seen both in monologues, where a character is divided in himself, and in persuasive exchanges between two or more characters. In each case the doors serve as visual focus for the actions of leaving or staying (see Chapter 1, section *d*).

The argument may also be visually focused by one character urging another to accompany him off stage. This has added force when the stage represents a particular place. Porus urges a reluctant Axiane to leave the camp of the submissive Taxile: 'Let us leave a camp where, incense in hand, the faithful Taxile awaits his sovereign' (*Ale*. I. iii. 263). After the murder of Pyrrhus, Oreste urges Hermione to come with him: 'Come to my ships' (*And*. V. iii. 1494; text of 1668 only); these are the ships which are depicted in the scenic backdrop at the Hôtel de Bourgogne. Albine invites the wakeful Agrippine to desist from prowling outside the door to Néron's apartment: 'Madam, return to your apartment' (*Bri*. I. i. 5). A whole sequence of arguments are deployed by different characters to persuade Athalie to leave the vestibule of the temple. Agar: 'Abandon this temple [. . .] and come and restore your troubled mind in your palace' (*Ath*. II. iii. 432–4). But in response to this, Athalie, by sitting down, signals her unwillingness to be persuaded (SD, *Ath*. 438). Then Abner urges her to come away, by reminding her that her presence in the temple is contrary to Jewish law: 'Are you ignorant of our laws?' (*Ath*. III. iv. 449). Mathan also urges Athalie to leave: 'Great queen, is this your place? [. . .] Do you make bold to approach this profane temple?' (*Ath*. II. v. 459–62). Athalie's recital of her dream is an active part of the visual drama, being her reply to these attempts to persuade her to come away from the temple.

Muratore rightly points out that although Racine appears 'to imbue his characters with movement as they bolt about', much of the movement is abortive (p. 113). This underlying stasis creates an atmosphere of frustration, powerlessness, and futility. However, the evidence does not seem to support Muratore's contention that 'in Racinian drama communication does not move the action forward' (p. 117). Ekstein is closer to the truth in concluding that 'Racine's characters often do not attain the performative ends of their *récits*' (p. 26). For, alongside the many failures of persuasion, there must be counted many successes. Jocaste may fail to persuade her sons to embrace, but Polynice succeeds in rushing his brother off to fight a duel (*Thé.* Act IV, Scene iii). Porus may fail to persuade Taxile to come and fight against Alexandre (*Ale.* Act I, Scene ii), but he succeeds in obtaining Axiane's blessing for the battle, and he exits to combat (Act II, Scene v). There are analogous examples of the progress of the action in each play. Joad in *Athalie* is particularly successful in achieving his aims.

The last act of Corneille's *Horace* was performed as a ballet with mime at Sceaux in 1714 and the ballet-master Jean-Georges Noverre produced a balletic version of the whole story (Goodden, p. 6). Racine's drama is just as suggestive of mime and movement. By making speeches of persuasion focus on performing physical actions, on leaving, or on staying, Racine gives the verbal action a physical dimension. The arguments of his characters gain in intensity and clarity. In the context of the rowdy conditions in the Parisian theatres, the shaping of a scene by visual focus may also have helped the spectators to overcome the many distractions. When Thésée condemns Hippolyte with repeated commands to leave his presence, the father's menacing movements and gestures can be seen driving Hippolyte off stage (*Phè.* IV. ii. 1053, 1059, and 1063). So even if audience missed some of the words they would be in no doubt about the development of the action. This theatrical dimension is frequent in Racine and distinguishes him from those of his contemporaries for whom verbal subtlety alone was either the limit or the pinnacle of their achievement. Racine succeeded in making the arguments relevant to movement in stage space, and in linking discourse and spectacle.

6

Across Verbal Frontiers

Ce langage, Seigneur, est facile à comprendre
(*Britannicus*)

Where did Racine learn his theatrical language? Where in particular did he learn to manipulate the visual effects which form
such an important part of that language, which contribute to its
intelligibility and add to its significance? The first possibility is
that it was the stock-in-trade of any dramatist. Perhaps we
should be no more surprised that Racine exploits décor, entrances and exits, facial expression, eyes, kneeling, and sitting
than that he uses the words *cœur*, *amour*, *vivre*, and *mourir*, part
of the verbal vocabulary which he undoubtedly shares with his
contemporaries. Some comparisons will quickly dispose of the
notion that such effects were automatic.

(*a*) Comparisons

Corneille and Racine both composed plays on the story of Titus
and Berenice in 1670. Both dramatists chose to engineer the
exposition through conversation between a protagonist and a
confidant. Racine gives the scene a strong visual dimension.
It is focused on the door to Bérénice's apartment. Antiochus
sends his confidant through the door to seek an interview with
Bérénice. Left alone Antiochus debates whether he should enter
to talk to Bérénice. When the confidant rejoins his master there
is real verbal conflict between them while they wait on stage for
Bérénice to emerge from her apartment: Arsace has to work
hard to persuade Antiochus to divulge the reasons why he
wishes to leave Rome (*Bér.* Act I, Scenes i–iii). On the other
hand, Corneille's first scene is completely static and scenery
plays no part. The private discussion between Domitie and her
confidant requires the audience to presume that it takes place in

Domitie's apartment. As the same set will later represent Titus's apartment, the precise place cannot have the significance it has in Racine. Domitie tells of her love for the emperor, just as Antiochus tells of his love for Bérénice, but Corneille's Domitie makes only too evident the implausibility of revealing things which her confidant must already know. She tells of her claims to the throne and then remembers: 'But you know this'. Later she says: 'Let me remind you of my life: you know me well enough to know my story, but you cannot have known what were my feelings of illustrious pride on each separate occasion' (*Tite et Bérénice*, I. i. 41 and 75).

This theatrical comparison can be extended to a later scene in the two Bérénice plays. Both dramatists show the first occasion on which Titus tells Bérénice to her face that he cannot marry her (Act IV, Scene v, in Racine, Act III, Scene v, in Corneille). Racine directs his Bérénice to appear with dishevelled hair (IV. ii. 968–78). Racine's Titus prepares for this scene in a long dilemma monologue outside Bérénice's door. Finally Bérénice erupts onto the stage, snatching herself away from her attendants with whom she expostulates through her door (*Bér*. IV. ii. 1040). Above all, Racine's Titus weeps, and this forms a significant part of the verbal battle (*Bér*. IV. v. 1154 and 1175). In Corneille's play, it is Tite who enters upon Bérénice in a calm and undramatic manner. No dishevelled hair, no bursting through doors, no tears. Just a slight hint of movement when he says joyfully 'Let us go to your kingdom', and a moment of drama when he exclaims to the retreating Bérénice: 'No, madam, if it cost me throne and life, I will not marry Domitie' (*Tite et Bérénice*, III. v. 1029–47). But compared to the vigorous exit which Racine contrived for his Bérénice, hurling imprecations at a tearful Titus, Corneille's end of scene climax is theatrically pallid. As for verbal action, Corneille's protagonists do not seem to know what they want, whilst in Racine's play the conflict is sharply defined. Perhaps Corneille was illustrating Racine's maxim: 'How poorly a lover knows his own desires' (*Bér*. II. ii. 435), and perhaps the aimless discussion between Corneille's Tite and Bérénice succeeded in conveying this on stage. Racine himself, however, took care not to portray the vacillations of lovers in anything but the most vivid theatrical language.

A second comparison will show how, even where there is a visual element common to Racine and another dramatist, Racine's scene is enriched with more varied visual effects. The central scene of *Andromaque* resembles a scene in Quinault's tragicomedy *Stratonice* (1660). Quinault's two protagonists meet by chance. They say they wish to avoid each other, but actually they stay on stage. They are urged by their confidants to leave. Quinault conveys all this in a series of mechanical exchanges. Each character speaks exactly half a line:

ANTIOCHUS Mais je vois Stratonice.
STRATONICE   O dieux ! le Prince sort.
ANTIOCHUS Evitons sa rencontre.
STRATONICE   Evitons son abord.
ANTIOCHUS Montrons que je la hais.
STRATONICE   Montrons que je l'abhorre.
TIMANTE *à Antiochus* Vous avancez toujours.
ZENONE *à Stratonice*   Vous demeurez encore.
ANTIOCHUS Allons, retirons-nous.
STRATONICE   Allons, sortons d'ici.
ANTIOCHUS *à Stratonice* Hé quoy, vous me fuyez?
STRATONICE   Vous me fuyez aussi.
ANTIOCHUS Si je vous fuis, au moins j'apprends de votre fuite
    Que ce ne doit pas être un soin qui vous irrite.

(Stratonice, II. vi. 627–34)

Certainly the movements of the actors on stage do convey the conflicting emotions of the two protagonists. Even as their words signify that they wish to avoid each other, their actions contradict this. But the lines above represent the entire extent of the visual dimension in Quinault's scene, which then continues with purely verbal exchanges slightly enhanced by pauses.

In *Andromaque* the equivalent scene is much more varied and the movements carry a much greater charge of significance. It involves Pyrrhus misinterpreting Andromaque's averted eyes as a sign of pride, whereas they are really a sign of despair. When Andromaque makes to leave, believing that all hope is lost, Pyrrhus responds with his threat to hand over Hector's son to the Greeks. This elicits Andromaque's cry of maternal anguish and her appeal to Pyrrhus: 'Ah stop! my lord. What do you mean to do?' Andromaque, on the verge of leaving the stage, is brought back and probably falls to her knees. This is all conveyed in the following lines:

PYRRHUS Que dit-elle Phœnix?
ANDROMAQUE   Hélas! tout m'abandonne.
PHŒNIX Allons, Seigneur, marchons sur les pas d'Hermione.
CÉPHISE Qu'attendez-vous? Forcez ce silence obstiné.
ANDROMAQUE Il a promis mon fils.
CÉPHISE   Il ne l'a pas donné.
ANDROMAQUE Non, non, j'ai beau pleurer, sa mort est résolue.
PYRRHUS Daigne-t-elle sur nous tourner au moins la vue?
   Quel orgueil!
ANDROMAQUE Je ne fais que l'irriter encor.
   Sortons.
PYRRHUS Allons aux Grecs livrer le fils d'Hector.
ANDROMAQUE Ah, Seigneur, arrêtez. Que prétendez-vous faire?

(And. III. vi. 893–902)*

Chauveau's illustration shows Andromaque kneeling to Pyrrhus which adds to the visual variety (Pl. 6). Quinault in *Stratonice* certainly visualized a theatrical situation, but the mechanical symmetry of the verbal patterns is contrived, and the visual effects do no more than convey a momentary *dépit amoureux*. Racine, on the other hand, strongly differentiated his protagonists, and made their various movements a matter of life and death.

Above all, Racine took a further theatrical step by giving visual significance to the verbal cliché of the power of a woman's eyes. Hermione committed the fatal mistake of sending Andromaque back to Pyrrhus with the taunt that her eyes have power over him (*And.* III. iv. 885). Céphise reassures Andromaque that one look at Pyrrhus would confound Hermione (III. v. 889). Racine shows this in action, by introducing into the chance meeting between Andromaque and Pyrrhus the spectacle of the heroine averting her eyes, as she assumes that all is lost, then turning her gaze upon Pyrrhus. From that moment Andromaque is in the ascendant, and Pyrrhus, by provoking that fatal gaze both here (III. vi. 900) and when he is alone with Andromaque (III. vii. 952), marches towards his death.

The originality of Racine's investing the verbal cliché with visual significance can be appreciated by comparisons with scenes in other plays. Rotrou's *Hercule mourant* (Act II, Scene iii) and Corneille's *Pertharite* (Act III, Scene ii) both show captive women taunted by jealous rivals, but neither delivers the taunt with reference to the power of the eyes in the way that Racine's

Hermione does to Andromaque. Corneille's Cléopâtre does boast of the power of her eyes over César, but when César meets Cléopâtre, her eyes play only a verbal part (*Pompée*, II. i. 395; IV. iii. 1276 and 1319). Racine's visual effects in the central scene of *Andromaque* are not mere convention but innovation.

Mouflette published a long comparison between the testing of Monime in Racine's *Mithridate* (1673) and the testing of Cléante in Molière's *L'Avare* (1669).[1] One would expect that in this scene Racine, writer of tragedy, would be more restrained in visual effects than Molière, writer of comedy. The reverse is true.

In both plays the inquisitor (Harpagon, Mithridate) seeks to discover whether the victim really loves a rival. The inquisitor deceitfully proposes a marriage to provoke the victim into a confession of true feelings. Harpagon tells Cléante he will marry Mariane himself (*L'Avare*, Act IV, Scene iii); Mithridate offers Monime marriage with Xipharès (*Mit.* Act III, Scene v). There are no stage directions either explicit or implicit in Molière's scene, whilst Racine's is full of them. There are movements to leave the stage as Monime urges Mithridate to take her to the altar in order to demonstrate her fidelity to him and to cover up her real love for Xipharès. Mithridate urges Monime in the opposite direction to make more immediate his offer of marriage to his son. Three times Monime is on the point of declaring her true love; three times she stops just in time, according to the retrospective stage directions which provide the visual cues (see Chapter 5, section *e*, for detailed analysis). Molière's text is purely verbal with no hints of physical movement or facial expression. The contrast is especially striking at the moment when the victim is finally tricked into confession. Molière's Cléante, prompted by six questions from Harpagon, gives a full verbal account of his affair with Mariane. Harpagon then reveals that he has tricked his son and forbids him to have further dealings with Mariane. Racine relies mainly on facial expression, gesture, and tone of voice. Monime confesses that before she was betrothed to Mithridate—and here she points to her diadem—she did indeed love Xipharès. Her confession is economically related in a single line. She then sees

---

[1] Mouflette, *De la prévention de l'esprit et du cœur* (Paris, 1689), 55–6; *NCR* 227–8.

a terrifying expression flit over Mithridate's face, and conveys her anguish in her change of voice. The response of each inquisitor is quite different. Harpagon has a lengthy speech:

I am very pleased to have learned such a secret. That is exactly what I was after. Come my son, do you know what? You must now resolve, if you please, to rid yourself of your love, and cease from all courtship of a person whom I intend to marry myself. You are shortly to marry the lady to whom you are destined. (*L'Avare*, Act IV, Scene iii, p. 564.)

Mithridate's response to hearing the truth from Monime is laconic and menacing. To Monime's distraught 'Your expression has changed', he replies in staccato fashion—six full stops in two lines: 'No, madam. That's enough. I will send him to you. Go. Time presses. It must be well employed. I see you mean to obey me. I am well pleased' (*Mit.* III. v. 1113).

The absence of stage directions in Molière's text did not of course preclude the actors from embellishing it with appropriate stage business. Given that Molière was directing the performance and playing Harpagon himself, he perhaps chose not to write stage directions into this particular scene, though that did not prevent him from including numerous stage directions elsewhere in his plays. The point of the comparison is not to suggest that Molière was in any way less a man of the theatre than Racine. It is simply to show that the theatricality of Racine's written text was not automatic. There is therefore a prima-facie case for exploring further how far Racine's theatrical language, especially its visual dimension, differed from that of his contemporaries. Such a question obviously cannot be answered on a strict statistical basis. It is no good counting the teardrops, enumerating the genuflections, or measuring the distances walked on stage. It would be hard to quantify the number of visual effects, let alone their significance. But some tendencies can be discerned.

(b) French Tragedies 1659–1664

One way to test the theatricality of Racine is to measure him against the group of French tragedies which were first performed between 1659 and 1664, that is, in the five years before

his own first tragedy *La Thébaïde* (1664). The date 1659 is
not arbitrary. It marks Racine's first arrival in Paris and his
opportunity to visit the theatres there (Picard, *Carrière*, p. 28).
The year 1659 saw Corneille's return to the theatre after a silence
of eight years. This group of tragedies includes three by Pierre
Corneille: *Œdipe* (1659), *Sertorius* (1662), *Sophonisbe* (1663), and
four by his younger brother Thomas Corneille: *Stilicon* (1660),
Camma (1661), *Maximian* (February 1662), and *Persée et Démétrius*
(December 1662). Leaving aside for the moment Racine's relationship with other genres, these tragedies form the immediate
theatrical context in which he made his début in the genre of
tragedy.

Racine himself invited comparison with Corneille in the
choice of subject for his first play. Corneille had given a version
of the Oedipus story in his *Œdipe*. Five years later Racine
challenged Corneille with *La Thébaïde*, drawn from the same
Greek legend. Whilst Corneille had shown Oedipus discovering
his frightful crime, Racine showed the effects of this crime on
the warring brothers, Eteocles and Polyneices, who were the
offspring of the monstrous union of Oedipus with his mother,
Jocasta.

The two tragedies have been compared on a thematic basis by
Cave (pp. 327–33), but not for their theatricality. *La Thébaïde*
has all the familiar features of Racine's visual language. Tension
is created when one character tries to prevent the exit of another
by force of argument: Hémon and Antigone (II. i. 343); Polynice
and Jocaste (Act II, Scene iii); Antigone, Etéocle, and Polynice
(end of Act IV, Scene iii); Antigone and Créon (Act V, Scene
iii). Entrances are dramatic or symbolic: the soldier 'all agitated'
(Act II, Scene iv), Polynice's odious proximity to Etéocle (Act
IV, Scene iii), Olympe 'all in tears' (Act V, Scene v). Etéocle
enters with blood-stained clothes (Act I, Scene iii); he alludes to
his sword, and to the crown he wears (IV. iii. 1076). The
brothers recoil from each other when Jocaste urges them to
embrace (IV. iii. 990). They turn their heads away, and the only
time they are seen to agree is when both leave the stage to go to
their duel and death (Act IV, Scene iii). Jocaste points to her
womb, the source of incest, and invites her sons to plunge their
swords into it—a heavily charged visual metaphor which goes
to the heart of the Oedipus legend (IV. iii. 1082).

Corneille in *Œdipe* does not shrink from mentioning incest. Admittedly the word 'inceste' only occurs five times, but that does not justify the claim that he does not mention it at all.[2] However, Corneille never reinforces the references to incest with a visual metaphor such as Jocaste's pointing to her womb in Racine's play. The text of Corneille's *Œdipe* does imply some visual effects and there are some explicit stage directions; but compared with Racine the harvest is meagre. Dircé urges Thésée to leave plague-stricken Thebes (Act I, Scene i) but with little urgency and no obvious movement. Thésée makes a feeble effort to prevent Dircé going off stage to die (Act II, Scene iv), as does Jocaste (Act III, Scene ii); there is none of the vigour with which Racine's characters try to frustrate an exit. There is a more striking visual effect implicit in the last act of Corneille's play. Iphicrate, the messenger from Corinth, probably embraces the Theban Phorbas, described as 'old and broken' (l. 1005), when they are reunited (V. iii. 1744). Such an embrace would highlight the joy of their reunion and throw into tragic relief the appalling revelations which are to emerge from it. Furthermore Iphicrate, believing that his news from Corinth will cause joy, cheerfully keeps Phorbas guessing as to the identity of the child that they exchanged. Although there are no stage directions in Corneille's text, the following exchanges strongly suggest that Phorbas recoils in horror when Iphicrate points to the king. Phorbas believes the child referred to is Thésée, but,

IPHICRATE Ce n'est point lui, mais il vit en ces lieux.
PHORBAS Nommez-le donc de grâce.
IPHICRATE   Il est devant tes yeux.
PHORBAS Je ne vois que le Roi.
IPHICRATE   C'est lui-même.
PHORBAS   Lui-même!

(*Œdipe*, V. iii. 1751–3)

In the next lines, Iphicrate's cheerfulness continues to contrast with the horror registered on the faces of Phorbas and Œdipe. It is the only occasion in Corneille's *Œdipe* where implicit visual effects are theatrically related to the main action, namely to the

---

[2] 'Dans *Œdipe* Corneille évite de faire allusion à l'inceste entre Jocaste et Œdipe' (Scherer, p. 395); the word *inceste* occurs in ll. 378, 990, 1547, 1821, 1917.

recognition of Oedipus. The three explicit stage directions are nugatory. Mégare is directed to interrupt Dircé's conversation with Thésée by whispering in her mistress's ear (SD, 116). The secrecy is of no import since Dircé immediately reveals the message, namely that she has been summoned to speak with the queen. Later Iphicrate asks Œdipe to dismiss his retinue so that they can talk privately: 'Œdipe nods to his retinue to oblige them to withdraw' (SD, 1674). Finally when Cléante and Dymas report the end of the plague, 'Cléante enters from one side and Dymas from the other about four lines after Cléante' (SD, 1953). Corneille is at pains to explain that no single person could have given a full account of all that happened in Thebes as it recovered from the plague, so the two separate entrances represent Cléante bringing news from the town and Dymas from the palace (*Examen*, p. 156). The fact that Corneille had to explain suggests that the visual effect had missed its mark. Nor does a possible reference to décor amount to much. Jocaste says that Phorbas lives at the foot of a rock, 'which we can see closest to these dreary walls' (III. iv. 1006). But no rock is mentioned in the *Mémoire de Mahelot* as a necessary part of the décor, and, according to D'Aubignac, Jocaste merely caused laughter when she gave the order 'Get my chariot ready', in order to travel there and back in an hour (III. iv. 1008–1111; *Dissertation sur Œdipe*, p. 57).

This rapid survey of those visual effects in *Œdipe* and *La Thébaïde* which can be ascertained from reading the text does suggest that they were more numerous and more effectively deployed by Racine than by Corneille. This is not to imply that the visual dimension is the sole criterion of theatrical success nor that its absence is a defect. *Œdipe* won applause. Even the hostile D'Aubignac admitted this, though he attributed it to cabal and favour at court. What D'Aubignac deplored was the time wasted exchanging epigrams when tragic circumstances required tears (*Dissertation sur Œdipe*, pp. 16, 46). Corneille in his 'Au lecteur' boasted that *Œdipe* was considered to be the summit of his dramatic art by most of his audience—he uses the word 'auditeurs' (listeners). *La Thébaïde* also had an honourable success on stage: significantly, Racine dedicated the published text to the duc de Saint-Aignan with words that stress the theatrical rather than the verbal: 'I hope that you will still look favourably upon it, even without the ornaments of the theatre' (*Œuvres*, i. 131).

There are two scenes in Thomas Corneille's *Camma* (1661) which are directly comparable to scenes in Racine's *Andromaque* (1669). In the first act of each play, both dramatists use implicit visual means to show the aversion of the heroine for the man who is blackmailing her. Camma wishes to hurry away to her apartment (*Camma*, I. ii. 109). Andromaque is anxious to rejoin her captive son (*And.* I. iv. 260). But Racine also embellishes the scene with suggestions of further physical movement. Both women urge their tormentor to marry someone else and leave them in peace. Andromaque's language contains the implication of a reinforcing gesture: 'Go back, go back to the daughter of Helen [Hermione]' (*And.* I. iv. 342). Camma is more abstract: 'Marry the princess [Hésione] to merit the throne; respond to the love that she pours out for you, and thereby justly gain what you usurp' (*Camma*, I. ii. 178). To close the scene Racine has Pyrrhus brusquely hasten Andromaque on her way with words that signify physical actions: 'Go, madam, go and see your son [. . .] and as you embrace him think how you can save him' (*And.* I. iv. 380). Sinorix, however, is more abstract and more oblique: 'I can tyrannize others besides you. I leave you to think on this, madam' (*Camma*, I. ii. 227). In each case Racine uses words implying physical movement where Thomas Corneille has none.

The second point of comparison is the scene when Andromaque pleads with Pyrrhus for her son's life (*And.* Act III, Scene vi). The equivalent scene in *Camma* is when the heroine appeals to King Sinorix to save the life of her lover Sostrate (Act IV, Scene ii). Thomas Corneille's scene is quite lacking in any visual effect, whilst Racine's contains abortive exits, kneeling, and averted eyes (shown above in the comparison with Quinault).

Certainly *Camma* does include a spectacular attempt at murder on stage, when Camma tries to stab Sinorix and has the dagger dashed from her hand by Sostrate (Act III, Scene iii). It ends with Camma dying on stage whilst attendants try to restrain Sostrate from drawing his sword to kill himself (Act V, Scene vi). However, such physical action is exceptional among the tragedies of the early 1660s, though Racine was to use such effects consistently: attendants restrain Créon from killing himself, Atalide stabs herself on stage, Arcas dashes poison from

Monime's hand (*Thé.* Act V, Scene vi; *Baj.* Act V, Scene xii; *Mit.* Act V, Scene iii). It would be wrong to deny Thomas Corneille's capacity for generating suspense. In his four tragedies of this period his protagonists—Sinorix, Honorius, Maximian, and Philippe—play the part of detectives in their search for conspirators and criminals. From this point of view, his tragedies still make good reading. But there is another side. Thomas Corneille's versification is remarkable for the sequences of quatrains which predominate throughout his plays. He has especial fondness for couplets joined by 'and' or 'but'. The monotony is varied from time to time, especially in the rare moments of intense passion, after which the characters resume their relentless quatrains with grim determination. He also relies heavily on verbal ingenuity, antithesis, paradox, and equivocation. *Stilicon* (1660) offers a good example of his peculiar style of psychological analysis and of the use of quatrains:

> De l'éclat de son choix l'âme préoccupée
> S'offre sans cesse aux traits qui d'abord l'ont frappée,
> *Et* par sa complaisance à nourrir son erreur
> Ouvre aux sens une voie à séduire le cœur.
> Comme par la raison leur rapport s'autorise
> D'une aimable imposture il aime la surprise
> *Et* d'un trouble inquiet goûtant le faux appas,
> Cède à mille transports qu'il n'examine pas.
>
> (*Stilicon*, I. i. 48)

Peter France comments on such lines: 'When this metonymic heart becomes involved in metaphorical battles with reason or virtue, as so often in Thomas Corneille's psychological passages, the result is frequently a tedious *galimatias*' (pp. 77 and 80). Such charges were also levelled at the elder Corneille. The anonymous wit who penned the parodic comparison between Corneille and Racine, *Tite et Titus ou les Bérénices* (1673), was severe on Corneille's *galimatias* and wondered who would have the patience to pierce its obscurity (pp. 316–19).

Although convoluted verbalizing is untheatrical in that it lacks either a visual dimension or persuasive force, it apparently enjoyed some success on the Parisian stage in the 1660s. D'Aubignac's dissertation on Pierre Corneille's *Sertorius* deplored the perversity of the audience: 'The first lines in which

Perpenna tries to explain his uncertainty of mind, are merely grandiloquent nonsense [. . .] and yet the *parterre* does not fail to applaud when it catches some antithesis or metaphor [. . .]; these are the pretentious passages which deceive the *parterre*' (pp. 271, 278). The *parterre* apparently applauded anything that they could not understand. When the actor Baron complained that he couldn't make out his lines in *Tite et Bérénice*, Corneille said: 'I don't really understand them myself, but say them all the same; those who can't understand them will admire them.'[3] Racine himself was not entirely exempt from some criticism on this score. A few expressions in *Andromaque* were wittily ridiculed by Subligny in *La Folle Querelle*. Unintelligibility, however, is not characteristic of Racine. He presents arguments clearly and his visual language is easy to understand.

Another form of verbal drama can be seen in the deliberation scene of Corneille's *Sertorius*. The two protagonists discuss affairs of state for over two hundred lines (Act III, Scene i). Once again the lack of physical action did not preclude theatrical success. People of the time relished the art of conversation (Magendie, pp. 860–4). Corneille in offering *Sertorius* to the reader claimed that this single scene was prized as much as a whole play by highly placed people at court. Saint-Evremond, admittedly a Corneille admirer, says this scene 'engrossed our minds'.[4] Even the hostile D'Aubignac admitted its success and conceded 'the beauty and force of the middle part, where they discuss politics'. But D'Aubignac criticized the meeting place as implausible, disliked the superfluous exchange of compliments with which the scene begins, and feared that the deliberations were so inconclusive that they might have rambled on for ever but for the entrance of Pompée's wife.[5] Comparison of this deliberation scene in *Sertorius* with Racine is revealing. 'We need to know who is speaking, who is listening and what each is trying to persuade the other of,' said Marmontel in his article on 'Eloquence poétique'. Racine does just that. The deliberations in *Alexandre*, Act II, Scene ii, *Britannicus*, Act IV, Scene ii, or

---

[3] 18th-cent. anecdote quoted without source by Chevalley, p. 94; Baron was complaining of Domitian's first speech in the play.

[4] 'remplit nos esprits', *Diss. Alexandre*, p. 77.

[5] D'Aubignac, *Diss. Sertorius*, pp. 265–6; see Kibédi-Varga for a rhetorical and dramatic analysis of *Sertorius*: 'Analyse d'une tragédie'.

Mithridate, Act III, Scene i, are all clearly focused on an issue made known to the audience, and in addition are enhanced by visual effects. This is not the case in *Sertorius*.

In *Sophonisbe* Corneille did attempt more striking visual effects than in his two preceding tragedies. Syphax is seen in chains; Sophonisbe toys with a letter and phial of poison (Act III, Scene vi; Act V, Scene ii). These experiments misfired badly. According to D'Aubignac spectators found it repellent that Sophonisbe should heap reproaches upon her former husband when he appeared in chains (*Dissertation sur Sophonisbe*, p. 151). Corneille had to defend himself against this criticism in his preface to the play (in *Writings*, ed. Barnwell, p. 165). Moreover the play suffered from verbal inaction in many ways: important speeches were given to female confidants in whom no one was interested; Lélius wasted time on useless disquisitions while Sophonisbe was committing suicide; the hapless Syphax appeared far too docile in captivity. D'Aubignac claimed that at the performance he attended, the audience were roused from their torpor to applaud only four or five times—'an infallible proof that the affairs on stage were languishing'.[6] Donneau de Visé also complained that the issues were far from clear, and that the spectacle of Syphax in chains was a puerile device worthy only of a school play (*Critique*, pp. 119–20, 124). The fickle De Visé later retracted his censure, largely, it seems, for the pleasure of defending Corneille against D'Aubignac's strictures (*Défense*, p. 194); an anonymous refutation of D'Aubignac explained the lack of applause and the profound silence of the spectators as a sign of 'admiration and interior joy'.[7] But posterity has sided with D'Aubignac: *Sophonisbe* has languished as Corneille's least performed play.

The French tragedies of the Corneille brothers between 1659 and 1664 are not totally devoid of visual effects, but the visual dimension lacks coherence and the verbal action lacks vigour. None the less, elusive equivocations had their devotees. The taste of Parisian theatre-goers was catholic; they paid for,

---

[6] D'Aubignac, *Diss. Sophonisbe*, pp. 135 (little applause), 141 (female confidants), 145 (Lélius), 151 (Syphax).
[7] Anon., *Lettre sur les 'Remarques'*, p. 196.

enjoyed, or tolerated a degree of verbalizing which later genera-
tions have rewarded with indifference or oblivion. 'Tragedy
becomes a purely psychological drama [. . .] drama becomes
detached from time and place [. . .] the décor is abolished.'[8]
These phrases have been used to characterize Racinian tragedy.
They do not. They would be much better applied to the predominantly verbal dramas which preceded Racine in the early
1660s, and in contrast to which Racine based his stagecraft on
precise time and place, forging a dynamic relationship between
words and visual effects. Racine dared to be simple, straightforward, even crude. He generally painted in broad strokes.
The spectator is told what the objectives of the characters are.
Not for Racine the teasing enigma that proves to be sterile, nor
obscurity that masquerades as profundity. His characters seldom
merely talk about their emotions and feelings: they embody
them in action, often in physical action. Racine crossed the
verbal frontier into true theatrical territory.

(c) The Visual Tradition

If Racine's stagecraft did not derive from the tragedies of the
early 1660s where did he learn it? He covered his tracks well. He
admits to reading only one French dramatist, Jean Rotrou,
whose *Antigone* (1638) provided the structure of Racine's *La
Thébaïde*. However, Racine acknowledged no debt to Rotrou;
he merely criticized his predecessor's *Antigone* for containing
two separate plots, and claimed credit for simplifying them
(preface to *La Thébaïde*, p. 133).[9]

A theatrical reading of these two plays immediately reveals a
far greater affinity in visual language between Racine and Rotrou
than between Racine and his immediate predecessors who composed tragedies in the 1660s—such as Pierre or Thomas Corneille. The affinities arise from Racine imitating certain visual
effects, but the extent to which he also modifies them indicates
constructive inspiration. We do not know if Racine ever saw
Rotrou's *Antigone* on stage; probably not, since it is not listed
amongst Rotrou's plays performed in the latter part of the
century.

---

[8] Picard, 'Racine and Chauveau', p. 262.
[9] Detailed comparison of the two plays in Knight, pp. 251–4.

The closest parallels are in the confrontation scene between the brothers. Both dramatists use visual focus when Jocaste urges the brothers to lay down their weapons and to embrace her. In Rotrou hostility is represented by the angry look Polynice gives to Eteocles: 'What is this greeting? How ungracious it is! Why do you gaze upon your brother so?' (*Antigone*, Act II, Scene iv). Racine represents hostility by the alternative means of the brothers turning away from each other (*Thé*. IV. iii. 1030). Rotrou's Polynice uses his sword to hint at his character. A single line and a single gesture paint the man: 'The right I seek is on the end of this sword' (Act II, Scene iv). Racine rewrote the gesture, applied it to Etéocle instead of Polynice and embellished the visual effect with a reference to the crown worn by Etéocle, which the king contemptuously offers to his brother 'on the end of this sword' (*Thé*. IV. iii. 1076). Both dramatists conclude the scene with virtually the same words. The two brothers exit to their final duel. One says 'Let us choose a place', the other agrees 'Let us go quickly'. At the very end of the scene, Racine improves on Rotrou by omitting Créon's intervention, and by having Antigone, who is absent from Rotrou's scene, try to restrain the brothers from departing. All this suggests sensitive adaptation of Rotrou by a young dramatist who knew his own mind.

Rotrou's *Antigone* was composed for multiple décor. Many of his theatrical effects could not be imitated on the single set convention of the 1660s, but to a theatrical eye they could be adapted. Antigone appears on the ramparts and addresses her brother on the ground below. The high wall prevents physical contact between them. Antigone's lines are manifestly written by a dramatist who had visualized the scene: 'We are not allowed a single embrace; we speak apart like two enemies' (Act II, Scene ii, p. 98). In Rotrou the wall becomes a symbol of separation. Here was a potential lesson in imaginative utilization of décor, which Racine exploited throughout his career—sea and ships in *Andromaque*, doors in *Britannicus*, entwined initials in *Bérénice* (see Chapter 1, section *d*). Obviously there is a gulf between the theatrical impact of multiple décor and that of the single set; but multiple décor was precise, and this is a link between Racine and the earlier scenic tradition.

Racine seems to have been a willing and sensitive pupil of

Rotrou. Although he only admits to reading *Antigone*, it would be surprising if Racine had not read a wider selection of Rotrou's plays. Both dramatists wrote tragedies on Iphigeneia in Aulis. In addition Racine may have seen *Venceslas* (1647), the only one of Rotrou's tragedies for which there is evidence of performance later in the century—thirteen performances by Molière's troupe in June 1659. It also remained in the repertoire of the Hôtel de Bourgogne in 1678.[10] It is easy to give examples of visual effects in *Venceslas* which have parallels in Racine. Prince Ladislas staggers on stage and collapses on a chair like Phèdre; Cassandre enters throwing angry words back at characters off-stage, just as Bérénice throws words back as she emerges from her apartment.[11] *Venceslas* makes significant use of embraces, kneeling, weeping, dagger, and crown. The affinities are not confined to Rotrou's tragedies. Tragicomedies made their contribution. The spying scene in *Britannicus* (Act II, Scenes iv–vi) echoes a similar scene in Rotrou's *Bélissaire* (1643). Morel's detailed study of Rotrou's stagecraft concludes: 'For him dramatic invention constitutes a complex but coherent whole, whose parts—recited text, scenery, actors' movements—are closely controlled by each other' (p. 281). Racine has strong affinities with the cohesive theatricality which characterizes Rotrou.[12]

It is inconceivable that Racine did not also read and watch the plays of Pierre Corneille. We have seen above how Racine diverged from the prevailing verbalizing of Corneille's later tragedies, such as *Œdipe* or *Sertorius*, but from a theatrical standpoint the later plays of Corneille are significantly different from his earlier ones. Corneille's tragicomedies *Clitandre* (1630) and *Le Cid* (1637), written for multiple décor, do have the theatrical coherence that Rotrou displays. Visual effects also form part of Corneille's theatrical language in his pre-1659

---

[10] Howarth, *Molière*, p. 313; *Mémoire de Mahelot*, p. 115.

[11] *Venceslas*, Act IV, Scene ii, *Phè*. Act I, Scene iii; *Venceslas*, Act III, Scene ii, *Bér*. Act IV, Scene v.

[12] Morel's study of Rotrou provides all the material for comparison with Racine with regard to scenery, entrances and exits, stage properties and visual effects. However, Morel implies that Racine did not visualize stage and gesture as Rotrou does (p. 281 n.). Affinities between Racine and Rotrou are explored by Moravcevich in relation to the supernatural, violent passion and some verbal echoes, but not stagecraft except for mirror scenes.

tragedies, though on a more modest scale than in his tragicomedies. Some examples: Horace refuses to cross a threshold to see
the body of the sister he has just killed, and so conveys his
inflexible self-righteousness (*Horace*, IV. vii. 1336); in *Polyeucte*
Sévère waits for Pauline in circumstances which make her
entrance exceptionally poignant (Act II, Scene ii); Cornélie has
to converse with César who is reluctant to listen and impatient
to be off (*Pompée*, Act III, Scene iv). Corneille displayed a keen
sense of theatre in his early career. He produced one machine
play, *Andromède* (1650) 'purely for the eyes' ('Argument') and a
second machine play, *La Toison d'or*, in 1661. It is therefore very
puzzling that the exploitation of décor, entrances, exits, gesture,
and visual focus which can be found in his earlier tragedies of
the 1640s, is so lacking in the later ones. This decline in theatricality may help to explain Corneille's theatrical decline.

 We can never know the full range of Racine's knowledge
of French drama. Like the indefatigable Henry Carrington
Lancaster he may have read every French play composed in the
seventeenth century. Certainly he could have learnt theatrical
tricks from any genre—tragicomedy, pastoral, comedy. Theatrical language crosses genre boundaries. It need therefore
cause no surprise to consider Racine's relationship to his great
comic contemporary, Molière. Herzel has shown how the illustrations to Molière's comedies by Chauveau and Brissart come
much closer to depicting what the spectators saw on stage than
was customary in illustrations to tragedies. Using this evidence
Herzel traces the development of Molière's handling of stage
space. Molière's early plays use the traditional outdoor settings
of comedy showing a street flanked by houses with doors;
but with *Les Précieuses ridicules* (1659), *La Critique de l'École
des Femmes* (1663), *Tartuffe* (1664), and *Le Misanthrope* (1666),
Molière experimented with sets depicting the closed interior of
individual houses. Doors becomes significant in *Les Précieuses*:
Mascarille makes a boisterous entrance with his porter complaining that the door is too narrow for the sedan chair (Scene
vii, p. 271); *Le Misanthrope*, set in Célimène's house, depicts a
territorial dispute as Célimène's suitors jostle for access to her.
Alceste's objective is to gain exclusive privacy with Célimène.
Many entrances and exits mark stages in this territorial dispute
and have a significant bearing on Alceste's relationship with

Célimène. Herzel argues that this use of single precise décor 'serves to focus and concentrate the comedy' (p. 950).

The affinities with Racine are obvious. In *Andromaque* (1668) the scenic backdrop of sea and ships focuses and concentrates the tragedy. The constricted interior settings of *Britannicus* (1669) and *Bérénice* (1670) carry this process even further. How far Molière influenced Racine is a matter for conjecture. That Racine's first two tragedies were performed by Molière's troupe in 1664 and 1666 at least establishes personal theatrical contact between the two dramatists. If Grimarest is to be believed, Molière gave Racine the plan for *La Thébaïde* and rebuked him for filling it in with speeches lifted from Rotrou.[13] It is easier to find visual analogies between Racine and Molière than between Racine and the tragedies of 1659 to 1664. For example, Alceste makes as if to leave Célimène, hoping to be restrained by her. Roxane makes to leave Bajazet with similar intent (*Misanthrope*, Act II, Scene iii; *Baj.* Act II, Scene i). Of course the attempted exits are contextualized differently so that Roxane's movement is menacing and Alceste's is comic, but in Roxane's threat 'Take care you do not let me leave' (l. 539) is implicit the stage direction which is spelt out by Molière for Alceste: 'He makes as if to depart' (l. 552). Molière's *Dom Juan* (1665) exploits the act of sitting and the hierarchy of seats. Dom Juan flatters Monsieur Dimanche by offering him a better seat than his social rank merits (Act IV, Scene iii); Dom Juan scorns his father's reproaches with the insolent 'If you were seated you could talk better' (Act IV, Scene iv), and then shows his courage by inviting the Statue to sit at his table (Act IV, Scene viii). In 1670 Le Boulanger de Chalussay satirized Molière in *Elomire hypocondre*. Here, too, the social hierarchy of seating arrangements provided visual variety and theatrical significance. At the start of Act I, Scene iii, Bary, Orviétan, and Elomire 'all refuse the armchair and the high-backed chair, and offer to sit on the stool out of politeness, whilst making great reverences to each other' (p. 1236). The tragedies of 1659 to 1664 do not make significant use of seats. The deliberation scene in Pierre Corneille's *Sertorius*, Act III, Scene i, has no mention of seating. Thomas Corneille's

---

[13] Grimarest, *Vie de Molière*, p. 55 and n. 3 for the accounts of La Grange Chancel, abbé Dubos, Louis Racine, and the Frères Parfait on relations between Molière and Racine.

Persée et Démétrius shows King Philippe ordering his two sons to sit, but there is no attempt to exploit this theatrically (Act II, Scene iv). Racine, however, resembles Molière in the significant use of sitting and rising in *Alexandre* (1666), *Britannicus* (1668), and later tragedies (see Chapter 3, Section *b*). Chronology is important here. Molière developed his use of precisely defined stage space between 1659 and 1666. Racine developed his from 1664 onwards, after Molière's company had performed Racine's first two tragedies in 1664 and 1666.

Racine's extreme reticence on his relationship with the French drama of his century makes it hard to determine where he learnt the visual language of the theatre. The evidence suggests that he certainly learnt from Rotrou, probably from Corneille's earlier plays, perhaps from Molière, and that he had a keen eye for visual effects in whatever play came his way. It also suggests that Racine's place in the evolution of French seventeenth-century drama must be reconsidered. Far from representing the apogee of pure and abstract tragedy Racine retheatricalized the genre of tragedy, by seeking inspiration in the visual tradition of the 1630s and 1640s, whereas it was his immediate predecessors who were drifting towards an excessively verbal tragedy. If one abandons the notion of Racinian tragedy being predominantly verbal and abstract, this disposes of the apparent anomaly that 'Racine abandoned most of the essential characteristics of his dramatic technique' when he created the spectacular effects of his last two plays, *Esther* and *Athalie*.[14] As opera grew in popularity in the later seventeenth century with its strong scenic and spectacular effects, especially its use of precise place (Voltz, pp. 54, 74), Racine's affinities with the earlier visualizing tradition of drama made it quite natural for him to exploit the visual aspects of opera in his two choral tragedies. This was a logical development of the theatricality evident from his very first plays.[15]

[14] Picard, 'Racine and Chauveau', p. 266. Voltaire's *Disc. de la tragédie* is perhaps the original culprit, with its partially true but wholly misleading formulation: 'La seule pièce où M. Racine ait mis du spectacle, c'est son chef d'œuvre d'*Athalie*' (p. 83). Voltaire's general survey of French classical tragedy in this *Discours*, with his emphasis on the constraints of rhyme, the prohibition of enjambment, and lack of action, is particularly misleading as a guide to Racine.

[15] See McGowan, 'Racine, Menestrier and Sublime Effects' for the links between Racine's conception of tragedy and Menestrier's views on opera; she demonstrates the continuity of theatrical technique in Racine's last four plays.

Racine disguised his debt to French dramatic traditions but he proclaimed from the roof-tops his debt to ancient Greek tragedy. This was a legitimate claim, but not in the way that has sometimes been suggested.

(*d*) Greek Tragedy

'Ancient Greek tragedy hardly contains any dramatic action.' This comment has been offered to elucidate Racine's *Athalie* in Salomon's edition of the play (p. 36). Such a view of Greek tragedy has been successfully challenged. T. S. Eliot, a sensitive theatrical reader, wrote: 'Behind the dialogue of Greek drama we are always conscious of a concrete visual actuality [. . .]. Behind the drama of words is the drama of actions.' This is the theme of Taplin's *Greek Tragedy in Action*.

Racine was also a theatrical reader of Greek drama and noted the action in it. Pen in hand he read the plays of Aeschylus, Sophocles, and Euripides. In the margins he noted theatrical devices, entrances and exits, movements on stage. In particular he noted how Sophocles establishes the precise place for the action. He is constantly alert to the effects on the spectator, and 'spectator' is the word he uses, not 'reader'. Knight, who gives the best critical survey of these annotations, paradoxically undervalues their importance for understanding Racine as a man of the theatre, and dismisses them as the lowly mechanics of dramatic craft—'la basse cuisine du métier théâtral' (p. 219). The annotations are more significant than that. They confirm that when Racine read drama he was alert to all that is involved in theatrical reading; in addition they demonstrate the links between his stagecraft and that of Greek tragedy.[16]

Of special interest are Racine's annotations to Euripides' *Phoenissae*, for he claims that he based his first tragedy *La Thébaïde* on the *Phoenissae*.[17] Racine is concerned with entrances and exits: 'The pedagogue justifies his exit' (l. 88); 'Reason for Antigone's departing' (l. 193). He notes costume at line 324: 'She is dressed in mourning.' Several notes identify the emo-

---

[16] See also Knight, 'Sophocle et Euripide ont-ils "formé" Racine?' and Stewart, 'Racine's Response to the Stagecraft of Attic Tragedy'.

[17] Preface to *La Thébaïde*; text of the annotations to *Phoenissae* in *Œuvres*, ii. 876–9; discussion in Knight, pp. 221–2; there is no means of knowing whether the annotations came before or after the composition of *La Thébaïde*.

tional climate on stage: 'This is very tender' (l. 615); 'This is very lively' (l. 596); 'This is full of pathos' (l. 1428).

The main scene common to Euripides and Racine is the meeting between the warring brothers which is supposed to lead to reconciliation but which does not. In Euripides there are plenty of significant visual effects but they were not slavishly copied by Racine when he composed *La Thébaïde*. For example, the Greek stage represents a space outside the royal palace of Thebes. When Polyneices enters he is very anxious about the danger of falling into a trap. His jumpiness is represented visually when he draws his sword at a noise and then sheathes it (ll. 261–76). Racine comments on this line: 'Polyneices himself confesses his imprudence in coming amongst his enemies'. Racine does not include this incident in *La Thébaïde* because he handles place differently. *La Thébaïde* is set *inside* the royal palace, but one of his annotations to Euripides gives a clue to the way Racine made his royal palace significant: 'Tenderness for the place where one is born' (l. 366). Racine's Jocaste mistakenly hopes that her appeal to the place where her sons were born may excite tenderness in their hearts. She invites them to contemplate the walls of their birth-place. Her appeal fails (*Thé.* IV. iii. 1023). However, Polyneices' 'imprudence in coming among his enemies', which Racine noted in connection with Euripides' theatrical space, does have an analogy in Racine's *Britannicus*. When Britannicus rushes to Néron's very door, Agrippine uses very similar words: 'What restless zeal propels you blindly amongst your enemies?' (*Bri.* I. iii. 288).

In his annotations to line 455 of *Phoenissae* Racine noted how Euripides' visual language conveys the brothers' mutual hatred: 'The aversion of Eteocles against his brother is well marked; they do not wish to look at each other'. Racine uses the same gesture in a different context, the failure of the sons to respond to their mother. Jocaste laments: 'Alas, they turn their heads away, and do not listen to me' (*Thé.* IV. iii. 1030). This gaze aversion from their mother is rich in significance, since it concerns the scandal of the brothers' birth (Cave, pp. 327–33). Euripides' Eteocles arrives at the interview anxious to depart as soon as possible, because he has broken off his military preparations to come (ll. 446–51). So Eteocles' attitude during the interview is one of impatience. Racine does not use this device in his version of this scene, but there are several examples of similar impatience elsewhere in *La Thébaïde* and in later plays, where one character is forced to deploy arguments to detain another character on stage.

The similarities with Euripides are not the accidental result of servile imitation, because Racine's recontextualizations show that a creative theatrical hand was at work. It seems that Euripides' *Phoenissae* offered inspiration to an apprentice dramatist eager to create from the Theban legend a tragedy with more visual impact than was to be found in Corneille's *Œdipe* of 1659 or most of the French tragedies written shortly before Racine's *La Thébaïde* of 1664. But might one explain the relative paucity of visual effects in Corneille's play by the nature of his source, the *Oedipus Tyrannus* of Sophocles? Is the difference between Corneille's *Œdipe* and Racine's *La Thébaïde* a reflection of the differences between the stagecraft of Sophocles and Euripides? No. Sophocles' stagecraft does differ from that of Euripides, but both use visual effects to highlight the chief points of the action. By a lucky accident we have Racine's annotations on the first half of Sophocles' play. Racine saw the visual effects and noted them. Corneille apparently passed them over. Racine's attention was caught by the theatrical implications of Teiresias' exit, and his comment anticipates that of a modern critic. He translated the following lines from Sophocles' text:

OEDIPUS Will you not leave as quickly as you can?
TEIRESIAS I'd not have come had you not summoned me.
OEDIPUS I did not foresee that you would speak such folly.
TEIRESIAS I may seen foolish to you; but your parents found me wise.
OEDIPUS What parents? Stay!

(*Oedipus Tyrannus*, ll. 430–7)

These lines show how the departing Teiresias is called back by Oedipus with the dramatic 'Stay!' Racine's comment shows his sensitivity to the emotion generated by the verbal and visual action on stage: 'This anxiety of Oedipus is admirable' (*Œuvres*, ii. 856). Seale also brings out the theatricality of this moment, especially the gesture which depicts Oedipus' anxiety:

Teiresias is ready to go, but before he does he refers to the reputation for wisdom which he enjoyed with Oedipus' parents. It is quite clear from what follows that, with this said, Teiresias has turned to leave.

But the mention of parents with its echoing words of birth stirs something deeply in Oedipus: 'What parents? Stay! Who of mortals is my begetter?' This important moment is well dramatized by the piece of stage business which has Teiresias turn round in his tracks to face Oedipus again. (*Vision and Stagecraft in Sophocles*, p. 226.)

Racine only annotated the first half of *Oedipus Tyrannus*, but modern commentators give further examples of significant visual language in this play—entrances and exits, actions and gestures—all of which find parallels in Racine's visual vocabulary. Sophocles contrives a meaningful exit by breaking the convention which normally required protagonists to speak before they left the stage. Oedipus exits in silence at line 462. He cannot understand Teiresias' riddling speech: Oedipus the riddle-solver is defeated (Taplin, pp. 43–4; Seale, p. 227). Gestures and action are used to illustrate the search for truth. Line 728 suggests 'that Oedipus physically turned away from her [Jocasta] for a moment—away from the truth' (Taplin, p. 65). The Theban herdsman 'will not look his master in the face', and the final piece of truth has to be wrung from him by the threat of violence: 'the physical seizure of the herdsman is the theatrical culmination of a development, the tangible grasping of an elusive truth' (Seale, pp. 243–4). None of these effects inspired Corneille to incorporate similar ones into his *Œdipe*, but the visual language of Sophocles bears a marked resemblance to that of Racine, who invested his entrances and exits with significance, wrote averted eyes into his text, and occasionally used the threat of violence to extract the truth, as when Atalide and Acomat threaten Zatime to discover Bajazet's fate (*Baj.* Act V, Scenes viii–ix).

These comments on *Oedipus Tyrannus* show that the relationship between Corneille and Sophocles is thematic, whilst that between Racine and Greek tragedy is theatrical. Armed with a knowledge of Greek enabling him to read Greek tragedies in the original language, Racine crossed another verbal frontier into theatrical territory. The emphasis on the visual allows Racine's relationships with dramatists in any language to be viewed in a new light. The visual dimension has all the characteristics of an international language.

7

Seeing the Tragedy

Regardez d'un autre œil une excusable erreur

(Phèdre)

Designating a play a *tragédie* in seventeenth-century France did not commit the author to very much. The audience would expect to see characters of noble rank—kings, queens, princes. They would expect to witness some weighty peril—a conspiracy, a war, or a dilemma involving life or death.[1] Whilst Racine shared with his contemporaries this elastic notion of tragedy, he had some ideas of his own which set him apart from his rivals and which, in some measure, gave his tragedies a distinctive air. In his prefaces Racine fostered the notion that he was following in the footsteps of the Greek tragedians and that his tragedies conformed to the rules of the genre to be found in Aristotle's *Poetics*. By making these claims he concealed what he owed to his predecessors in seventeenth-century France, and in this respect his statements can be misleading. There has been a tendency to allow Aristotelian concepts of tragedy to eclipse the importance of French dramatic art in Racinian tragedy. None the less, in this chapter Aristotelian concepts will be used initially as the framework for an inquiry into what it meant to *see* a Racinian tragedy. Barnwell has recently investigated how tragic quality arises out of the ordering of plot, surprise, alternations of fear and hope, and fatal miscalculations: 'In all these factors, which coexist, it is possible to see that the audience experiences complex emotions, the so-called dramatic and tragic, simultaneously and indeed inseparably' (p. 222). The particular focus of the first part of this chapter will be the reciprocal relationship between Aristotelian concepts of tragedy and Racine's visual effects.

During Racine's lifetime all collected editions of his tragedies

---

[1] See Knight, 'A Minimal Definition of Seventeenth-Century Tragedy'.

carried the Greek words *Phobos kai Eleos*, meaning Fear and Pity, beneath the engraved frontispiece (Pl. 4). It was a way of expressing allegiance to Aristotle. The motto summarizes the emotions Racine was seeking to engender in the spectators of his tragedies. In the frontispiece Fear is a figure with hair standing on end; Pity wipes tears from her eyes.

Fear implies apprehension that something unpleasant will happen. Spectators see characters facing perils—confronting a powerful adversary, enmeshed in dangerous situations, or led away under arrest. Fear can be communicated to the spectator by a character visibly in the grip of fear. Racine indicates fear and horror in Andromaque when Céphise warns her that her son will die if she does not marry Pyrrhus: 'You shudder, madam?' (*And.* III. viii. 1012). Andromaque admits she is frightened and the actress must convey by some visual means the fear that she feels. The handbooks of rhetoric gave advice. Bary's account of how to express horror and trepidation evokes one possibility: 'One should open the eyes and mouth very wide, turn the body a little towards the left, whilst stretching out both hands as if in defence' (Grear, p. 424). One can also consult Le Brun's handbook for artists: 'When fear is excessive it is shown by the eyebrows being raised in the middle; [. . .] eyes must be wide open, the upper eyelid hidden beneath the eyebrow, [. . .] the muscles of the nose and hands swollen up, the muscles of the cheeks extremely prominent and rising to a point each side of the nostrils; the mouth open' (pp. 10–11). Plate 15 shows Le Brun's own visual representation of extreme fear corresponding to his verbal description. It resembles the expression on Athalie's face in Jean-Baptiste Corneille's illustration which shows Athalie confronted with Joas on the throne (Pl. 14). When enacted on stage, such visual expressions of fear could communicate a *frisson* to the spectator.

Pity was easily generated by the sight of princely personages in distress, and hardly a scene in Racine does not furnish an example of such anguish. Tears in the audience were a good sign that pity had been generated. Racine's pride in the tears produced by *Iphigénie* suggests that he considered this an important objective of tragedy: 'My spectators were moved by the same things which in former times moved to tears the best informed people in Greece, and which gave Euripides the reputation of being the most tragic of poets, in the sense that he had a marvellous skill in exciting compassion and terror, which are the true effects of tragedy' (preface to *Iphigénie*, p. 689). Racine's boast is supported by contemporary evidence. Both the inter-locutors in Villiers's *Entretien* (1675) confessed they could not help weeping at *Iphigénie* (pp. 1–2). Barbier d'Aucour, jesting at Racine's expense, tagged *Iphigénie* with the reputation of provoking a deluge of tears which caused the price of hand-kerchiefs to rise.[2] The tears provoked by *Iphigénie* were partly aroused by a frontal attack on the audience's sensibilities. Tears in characters can generate tears in the audience. So when Racine made his characters weep, he gave the spectator something to see which was relevant to the aims of tragedy. Few could remain dry-eyed when Agamemnon finds not only his daughter weeping, but everyone weeping—'tout pleure' (*Iph.* IV. iv. 1173)—for he evokes the spectacle of communal weeping at-tested by contemporary sources. In 1675, the year of *Iphigénie*, Madame de Sévigné's account of reactions to the death of General Turenne illustrates the ritual of tears. She describes her visit to Madame d'Elbeuf, who was Turenne's niece, in a letter of 28 August:

Madame d'Elbeuf, who is staying a few days with the cardinal de Bouillon, invited me to dinner with the two of them to speak of their affliction. Madame de La Fayette was there. We did exactly what we had resolved upon—our eyes were never dry. Madame d'Elbeuf had a most divine portrait of the hero [Turenne]. All his household had arrived at eleven o'clock. All his people were overcome by tears, and already dressed in mourning. Three gentlemen came, who practically died at the sight of this portrait [. . .]. His valets, lackeys, pages and buglers all dissolved in tears and made everyone else do the same.

This shows how communal weeping was deliberate, infectious, and extensive. Exactly the same as in the theatre.

Characters confronting perils or showing distress or shedding tears which generate tears: these are only the most obvious visual effects linked to the aims of tragedy. The analysis can be refined by considering the dramatic mechanisms which Aristotle specifically recommended for arousing pity and fear. His

---

[2] *Apollon vendeur de Mithridate ou Apollon charlatan* (Paris, 1675); *NCR* 87.

analysis of Greek tragedy led him to the conclusion that successful tragedy should depict the downfall of characters who were
neither extremely virtuous nor extremely wicked but somewhere in between, and that the tragic character should fall into
misfortune through *hamartia* (*Poetics*, ch. 13). There are two
concepts here. One is the concept of the morally ambiguous or
mixed character, who is neither wholly good nor wholly bad.
Racine's prefaces explicitly or implicitly emphasize the extent to
which he exploited this concept in his tragedies. The second
concept is *hamartia*, which brings about the downfall of the
tragic hero. The literal sense of *hamartia* in ancient Greek is 'bad
shot'; other connotations are offence, sin, moral flaw, depravity,
error of judgement, mistake based on ignorance.[3] Racine himself paraphrased Aristotle on *hamartia* using the French word
faute, which can mean fault, defect, or error (*Œuvres*, ii. 925). It
can be also associated with *faiblesse*, meaning weakness or flaw,
as when Racine describes Hippolyte's 'imperfection', namely
his illicit love for Aricie, as a 'faiblesse' (preface to *Phèdre*, p.
764). In a theatrical reading there are good grounds for investi-
gating *hamartia* as error, since error lends itself well to dramatic
representation. The error may be connected with a specific flaw
in character, in which case there is artistic satisfaction in a clever
linking of the two concepts of moral ambiguity and error. But
not necessarily so. *Hamartia* can designate an error of judgement,
a mistake which anyone can make, regardless of their own
individual characteristics. Barnwell makes dramatic considerations the touchstone of interpreting *hamartia*: 'Dramatically,
however, *hamartia* is not a flaw in the character but the error
which precipitates the catastrophe' (p. 243). How then did
Racine communicate this tragic vision in theatrical language?
And to what extent could the spectators actually *see* the tragic
mechanism at work?

(*a*) Moral Ambiguity

There is no shortage of morally ambiguous or mixed characters
in Racine. His prefaces explicitly or implicitly draw attention to
one after another: Pyrrhus is far from being perfect; Britannicus

---

[3] For a discussion of *harmartia*, see Gossip, pp. 156–8; Cave, pp. 67–72.

is a young man of 17, full of courage, love, candour, and credulity—most capable of exciting compassion; Néron is an incipient monster but not yet wholly vicious; Bajazet is not the most delicate of lovers, he remains rather ferocious; Mithridate displays a mixture of violent hatred against Rome, great courage, subtlety, dissimulation, and jealousy; Eriphile to some extent deserves to die, yet is not entirely undeserving of pity; Phèdre is neither wholly guilty nor wholly innocent; Hippolyte is not exempt from imperfection, since he disobeys his father in his love for Aricie, member of a rival family; Joas, whose intellectual gifts were surpassed only by those of Louis XIV's 8-year-old grandson, murdered Zacharie after thirty years of pious rule. This catalogue attests Racine's enthusiasm for moral ambiguity.[4] In some characters good and evil qualities go hand in hand; in others good and evil emerge in sequence. Two examples, Néron and Phèdre, will serve to illustrate moral ambiguity in action.

Néron is a mixed character, a good man turning into a monster, a *monstre naissant*. He is initially portrayed as good. His first words express tolerance of the mother he fears: 'Despite her injustice she is my mother and I will ignore her whims' (*Bri*. II. i. 359). He attributes his problems to the evil counsel of his mother's adviser, Pallas. So he gives visual expression to his tolerance of his mother by sending Burrhus with the order for Pallas's exile. But this simple action is not without ambiguities, since Agrippine in due course interprets the exile of Pallas as a hostile act (*Bri*. IV. ii. 1216). However, for the moment Néron, at least in his own eyes, is a dutiful son. Then in sequence we see Néron spy on Junie, catch Britannicus at Junie's feet, and arrest the young lovers. In Act iv he sits dutifully before his mother, though in feigned submission only. To bring him back to duty Burrhus falls on his knees and asks to be killed rather than witness his master commit a crime. Each of these visual events marks a clear movement towards good or evil, or, significantly for Racine's purpose, the physical action is morally ambiguous.[5]

[4] First preface to *Andromaque*, p. 260; first preface to *Britannicus*, p. 404; second preface to *Bajazet*, p. 549; preface to *Mithridate*, p. 619; preface to *Iphigénie*, p. 688; preface to *Phèdre*, pp. 763, 764; preface to *Athalie*, pp. 891, 893.

[5] Venesoen sees Néron indicating his profound verbal impotence by *gestes*—banishing Pallas by the intermediary of Burrhus, forcing Britannicus to separate from Junie without speaking to him ('Le Néron de Racine').

Phèdre is particularly marked out by Racine as a character who is neither wholly innocent nor wholly guilty. As in the first preface to *Andromaque*, so in the preface to *Phèdre*, Racine is explicit about the link between tragedy, moral ambiguity, pity, and fear: 'The character of Phèdre [. . .] has all the qualities which Aristotle requires in the hero of a tragedy and which are likely to excite compassion and terror. Phèdre, indeed, is neither wholly guilty nor wholly innocent' (preface to *Phèdre*, p. 763). The passage continues with a detailed account of Phèdre's actions which illustrate her mixed character. Racine's own words will be the guide here. This is the dramatic blueprint for Phèdre's moral ambiguity. How does it work on stage?

Racine's account starts by stressing Phèdre's horror, her death-wish, and repressed feelings: 'Phèdre is horrified by her god-given illicit passion; she does all she can to overcome it and would prefer to let herself die rather than reveal it.' These emotions are represented visually by her very first steps on to the stage. Precise stage directions are given for Phèdre's entrance, indicating how close she is to death. She staggers: 'I can support myself no longer [. . .] my trembling knees collapse beneath me' (*Phè.* I. iii. 156). She averts her eyes from the sun: 'My eyes are dazzled by the light of day, which now I see again' (l. 155). Continuing the effect of nervous collapse: 'She sits down' (SD, *Phè.* 157). Her costume itself, jewels and veils, become part of the visual picture of stifled passion, as she fidgets with them: 'How these vain adornments, how these veils, weigh down upon me!' (l. 158). Racine has ensured that even her hair is brought into play. She touches it nervously, perhaps even unties it to let it fall: 'What meddling hand has plaited up my hair and neatly ordered it upon my brow?' (l. 159). Barrault suggests: 'Veils and diadem are taken off. Hair—very little, only a lock— is untied' (p. 83). The language of hair is potentially rich in implications; a covered head implied married state, falling hair could often illustrate degeneracy, loose hair could suggest lunacy (Slater, pp. 137–8, 143). All through the first part of the scene Phèdre's physical distress is glossed by words signifying death, so that the visual signs are reinforced by the words of the dialogue: 'preparing for death . . . to end your days . . . each moment is killing you . . . I am dying . . . then die . . . the horror of seeing you expire before my eyes'.[6] Everything combines theatrically to confirm Racine's indications in his preface that Phèdre is not wholly to blame for her illicit passion, since 'she prefers to let herself die rather than reveal it'.

Racine speaks in his preface of force being required to make Phèdre reveal her secret. On stage he engineers this extorted disclosure partly through verbal, partly through visual means. Œnone after exhausting the resources of purely verbal persuasion, no doubt reinforced by conventional *actio*, appeals to the physical reality of her arms which have nursed Phèdre through her infancy: 'Have you no thought for these, my arms, which cradled you in birth?' (I. iii. 234). This line must surely be accompanied by a gesture drawing attention to these nursing arms. Œnone's persuasion culminates in her falling at Phèdre's feet and grasping the queen's knees. Phèdre is at last *forced* to speak. The moment of disclosure is marked by her raising Œnone to a standing position: 'You want to hear. Then rise' (l. 246).

The preface draws attention to the 'confusion' of Phèdre's speech as a sign that her crime is a punishment of the gods rather than an act of her own will. The French word *confusion* can mean shame or lack of clarity. Certainly Phèdre feels ashamed, but shame alone hardly signifies an uncontrollable force. However, disordered and unclear speech would be a potent theatrical sign that Phèdre was the victim of divine retribution. And so it is that in this scene Phèdre has a number of speeches which do not follow logically from those which Œnone addresses to her: 'If only I were seated in the forest shade!' is one of the most striking of Phèdre's deranged non-sequiturs, as Œnone's puzzled 'What, madam?' indicates (*Phè.* 176). The same confusion is evident in the mysteriously oblique couplets she exchanges with Œnone as her confession begins to unfold (*Phè.* 249–57). That much of Phèdre's speech was unintelligible to Œnone and to French audiences of the time is suggested by the hostile sonnet of 1677 which starts: 'In a gilded armchair Phèdre, trembling and pale, utters verses whose sense is at first quite obscure' (*NCR* 96). Sharp, hostile criticism, often more revelatory than vague praise,

---

[6] *Phè.* 175, 188, 213, 226, 227, and 240.

furnishes evidence for Racine pressing at the frontiers of theatrical language, and baffling those of his audience who were ill-
disposed to innovation. The key to each of the mysterious
couplets lies in the allusions to death, which link them with
Phèdre's physical state. The combination of the verbal and
visual provides the logic lacking in the words alone. Each
couplet contains a word indicative of death: 'O fatal anger . . .
Ariane, you died . . . I perish' (Phè. 249–58), and Phèdre's
physical appearance has signified the approach of her death all
through this scene.[7]

'Phèdre does not directly bring the false accusation against
Hippolyte', explains the preface. To make Phèdre less odious,
Racine in the play establishes Œnone as the persuasive coun-
sellor who urges Phèdre to accuse Hippolyte and to use Hippolyte's abandoned sword as evidence against him (Phè. III.
iii. 889). The power of Œnone's arguments in these scenes, the
theatricality of this verbal action, shifts the burden of guilt away
from Phèdre. To diminish Phèdre's moral responsibility still
further, Racine says in his preface 'that she only consents to
the false accusation against Hippolyte because her mind is
unhinged'. What does the spectator see? Phèdre's overheated
imagination is already perceiving the consequences of her crime
everywhere. First, she imagines the arrival of Thésée in the
company of Hippolyte. Hippolyte, she assumes, will observe in
what manner the faithless wife greets her husband. He will
be bound to accuse her to his father (Phè. III. iii. 839–49).
So Racine establishes that Phèdre's imagination is anticipating
future events and creating an atmosphere of self-accusation. In
this context the celebrated reference to the décor of Phèdre takes
on its full value:

PHÈDRE Il me semble déjà que ces murs, que ces voûtes
    Vont prendre la parole, et prêts à m'accuser,
    Attendent mon époux pour le désabuser.

(Phè. III. iii. 855–7)

Doubtless a gesture by Phèdre to the walls and vaults of the
palace draws the spectator's attention to them, and conveys the
implicit message that Phèdre's mind is so deranged that she can

---

[7] For an analysis of Phèdre's mental distress in terms of monologue-within-
dialogue, see Hawcroft, pp. 303–5.

even invest inanimate walls and vaults with the power of speech.[8] By this reference to the décor, Racine has invented an unusual theatrical device to represent the troubled state of mind which diminishes Phèdre's moral responsibility. Nor, if she can attribute accusatory powers to the inanimate walls, is it surprising that she will read into Hippolyte's expression the evidence that he has already accused her when he makes his entrance at his father's side: 'Ah! I see Hippolyte; and in his haughty eyes, I see my condemnation written plain' (*Phè*. 909). It is a striking moment of visual contact between the protagonists. In her agitation Phèdre has jumped to the wrong conclusion about Hippolyte's demeanour, and immediately she assents to Œnone's criminal plan: 'Do what you will, I leave myself to you; in my confusion I am powerless' (*Phè*. 911). This is the moment Phèdre is seen to commit her worst crime. Yet the audience has also seen Œnone's obstinate persuasion and Phèdre's own derangement, which together absolve her of some responsibility.

In the preface Racine says that after Phèdre has consented to the crime of accusing Hippolyte, 'she comes a moment later with the intention of protecting Hippolyte's innocence by declaring the truth'. Speedy repentance is marked visually by her haste to speak to Thésée when she hears him quarrelling with Hippolyte. She rushes on stage in Act IV, Scene iv. Her plea to Thésée is urgent and indicative of haste. This is confirmed by the retrospective stage direction: 'I rushed (*je volais*) to save his son' (*Phè*. 1196). But her effort to save Hippolyte is cut short by the casually revealed information that Hippolyte is in love with Aricie (ll. 1201–2). The final stage of Phèdre's tortured oscillation between crime and repentance is given visual focus by her dismissal of Œnone: 'Go, cursed monster, go and leave me now to see to my own death' (*Phè*. IV. vi. 1317).

This completes a theatrical commentary on those aspects of Phèdre's conduct which Racine mentions in his preface as contributing to her moral ambiguity. But it is not an exhaustive account of Phèdre's actions in the play. Conspicuously absent

---

[8] Racine was perhaps prompted by Euripides, whose Hippolytos wishes the palace walls could speak to testify to his innocence (*Hippolytos Stephanephoros*, 1074). Racine's Phèdre fears that the walls and vaults may proclaim her guilt.

from Racine's preface is mention of Phèdre's declaration of love to Hippolyte in Act II, Scene v, after which she tries to punish herself by inviting Hippolyte to stab her with his sword. Nor does the preface mention her lingering self-inflicted death which finally purges the scene of her polluting presence in Act V, Scene vii. Both of these scenes have a powerful visual dimension which, added to those evoked in the preface, contributes to the moral ambiguity of the heroine. To sum up then: in each act—chair in Act I, sword in Act II, walls in Act III, hasty entrance in Act IV, lingering death in Act V—an arresting visual image encapsulates the key stages of Phèdre's moral evolution.

(b) Errors of Judgement

The preceding account of how Phèdre's moral ambiguity is depicted in theatrical and especially in visual terms contains one moment of special significance for the tragic mechanism. It is when she misinterprets Hippolyte's expression and immediately allows Oenone to accuse him falsely. Phèdre is actually seen on stage committing the error on which the action depends. The juxtaposition of misinterpretation and assent is so swift that the two kinds of error—mistake and offence—are seen as one, clouded and mitigated by that disturbance of Phèdre's mind which Racine has portrayed through theatrical language. Placed in the very centre of the play, heightened by Thésée's long delayed entrance, Phèdre's *hamartia* is a theatrical climax. It is no isolated example of 'seeing the tragedy'. Other Racinian trage-dies offer the spectacle of *hamartia* placed centrally, often in Act III of the tragedy.

Hermione makes a fatal mistake when she tells the kneeling Andromaque to try her charms on Pyrrhus. Céphise repeats Hermione's recommendation, thus emphasizing Hermione's re-sponsibility for what follows. Andromaque first averts her eyes from Pyrrhus, then is persuaded to throw herself at his feet. Hermione's contemptuous rejection of Andromaque therefore initiates the sequence of events which leads to Andromaque marrying Pyrrhus and to Hermione's death. Central to Her-mione's tragic status, and reinforced by the visual effects which accompany it, is her tragic error in Act III, Scene iv.

Catastrophic errors in *Britannicus* are also seen at the centre of the play, interwoven in more complex fashion than in *Andromaque*, and illustrating visually how it comes about that this play is the tragedy of both Britannicus and Agrippine. Britannicus's error is clearly visible. Oblivious to the dangers of Néron's door, standing his ground despite efforts to persuade him to depart, crowning his recklessness by falling at Junie's knees, unluckily caught in that posture by Néron—Britannicus's fatal error is vividly delineated in visual terms during Scenes vi to viii of Act III. Both lovers pay the price of this error when, after an altercation between the two brothers, guards escort Britannicus and Junie away under arrest. All this takes place on stage. It is interwoven with less conspicuous, but no less momentous action off-stage—a carefully calculated exploitation of stage space by Racine to depict the fatal misunderstanding between the emperor and his mother. Agrippine exits in search of Néron (Act III, Scene v) and catches up with him off-stage, as Junie's comment reveals (III. vii. 959). Right at the end of the act all these threads are drawn together in Néron's monologue:

NÉRON   Ainsi leurs feux sont redoublés.
  Je reconnais la main qui les a rassemblés.
  Agrippine ne s'est présentée à ma vue,
  Ne s'est dans ses discours si longtemps étendue,
  Que pour faire jouer ce ressort odieux.

(Bri. III. ix. 1085–9)

Thus the two main physical actions of Act III, Agrippine's departure in search of Néron in Scene v and Junie's meeting with Britannicus on stage in Scene vii, are inextricably combined, to produce in Néron the mistaken belief that Agrippine contrived the meeting between Britannicus and Junie for the benefit of the two lovers. This aggravates Néron's jealousy of his rival and increases his resentment against his mother. In due course this leads to the death of his brother and the disgrace of his mother. The physical actions in Act III are a visual portrayal of Racine's conception of his subject and they aid the spectator to see that this tragedy 'is no less the disgrace of Agrippine than the death of Britannicus' (second preface to *Britannicus* p. 409). Such theatrical craftsmanship did not come easily: 'This tragedy is the one at which I can say I worked hardest' he wrote in the same preface (p. 407).

Bajazet pivots on weapons—the symbol of war—and on tears—the symbol of unrequited love. In Act II Bajazet was seen as a prisoner. In Act III he has bought his freedom at the price of pretended reconciliation with Roxane. The change is signalled visually by the weapons he now carries, 'At last I see myself with weapons in hand. I am free' (*Baj.* III. iv. 947). The most probable interpretation of these lines is that Bajazet now wears dagger and sword to prove his freedom. They are the starting-point for the tragic error that derives from Bajazet's first speech in this scene. The physical reality of his dagger and sword feeds his imagination with thought of real battles, of noble danger in the struggle against his brother. In his excitement he forgets about Atalide on stage with him (*Baj.* III. iv. 951) and displays fierce insensitivity towards her by evoking his journey to distant climes in order to fight his brother with the eyes of the world upon them. These lines (947–54) exactly illustrate Racine's description of Bajazet in his second preface, where he insists on the distinguishing character of the Turkish male as opposed to the Turkish female: 'I have taken great care to differentiate between Bajazet's passion and the tenderness of his lovers. He maintains the ferocity of his nation amidst his love' (p. 549). But in spite of his bellicose enthusiasm Bajazet scents something amiss in Atalide's reaction. Her tears bring him back to earth. The newly released prisoner, exulting in the weapons at his side, suddenly sees that Atalide fails to join in his dreams. He abruptly questions her: 'What do I see? What's wrong with you? Are you weeping?' (*Baj.* III. iv. 955). It is the turning point in the play. From Atalide's tears and Bajazet's questions flow the sequence of speeches and actions by which the precarious alliance between Roxane and Bajazet is first cracked and finally destroyed. The remoter cause is Atalide's jealousy, carefully presented in the preceding scenes (Act III, Scenes i–iii). But the decisive moment is Bajazet's question 'Are you weeping?' If Bajazet were not carried away by his weapons into insensitive declamations, if Atalide, less overwrought, had restrained her tears, the tragic mechanism would not be set in motion. The juxtaposition of the two visual elements, sword and tears, generates the fatal misunderstanding. Bajazet tries to retrieve the situation and punctuates his next speech (ll. 975–1011) with opportunities for Atalide to succumb to his persuasion, to dry her tears, and to rejoice with him. Courville suggests appropriate stage directions: 'Atalide remains sombre, and turns away, distressed to be brought into the argument' (l. 997); 'Bajazet rises and leans over to see on Atalide's face the effect of his justification' (l. 1002). How does Atalide finally respond? Not with words, but through visual signs:

BAJAZET
Je vois enfin, je vois qu'en ce même moment
Tout ce que je vous dis vous touche faiblement.
    Madame, finissons et mon trouble et le vôtre

(Baj. III. iv. 1003–5)

Racine has clearly indicated Atalide's impassivity with the implicit stage direction: 'I see that all my words touch you feebly', and the indentation after these words signals an abrupt change of mood as Bajazet continues: 'Madam, let us finish'. So it is Atalide's unrelenting demeanour, not any words she utters, which provokes the rupture. Bajazet *sees* that his speech has failed to move her: now he will resort to action.

Roxane arrives unexpectedly. Bajazet demonstrates that he has no love for her (Act III, Scene v). He greets her in a sombre manner and his speech is glacial (*sombre accueil, discours glacé*: III. vi. 1035). When he exits it is in sullen mood (*chagrin*, l. 1048). Roxane's suspicions are aroused. She learns she has been betrayed. The plot leads inexorably to her revenge. Everything stems from the misunderstandings which arose when Bajazet was carried away by his weapons and when Atalide shed her tears.

In *Mithridate* Monime's fatal revelation that she is indeed in love with Xipharès is emphasized visually by standing her ground in the face of Mithridate's vehement command that she accompany him off stage to marry Pharnace; and, if Mithridate does indeed 'change his countenance' at Monime's explicit confession, this would signal to the spectator as well as to Monime that she has made a terrible mistake: 'Oh heaven! have I betrayed myself?' is her own comment at the end of this scene (*Mit.* III. v. 1117).

The ubiquity of these visual depictions of tragic error is

confirmed in the biblical plays. Aman's final downfall is brought about in a strongly visual manner. Exposed by Esther as the instigator of the massacre of the Jews, Aman throws himself upon Esther's mercy, clasping her knees in supplication. King Assuérus catches him in this position, and misinterprets it as an assault upon his wife: 'What's this, the traitor dares lay reckless hands on you?' (*Est.* III. vi. 1168). There are two errors here. Assuérus is misled by his dream into thinking that Aman is the 'fierce ravisher' of his wife (*Est.* II. i. 389). Aman is undone by the very action he hoped would save him; for just as Néron caught Britannicus at Junie's feet, so Assuérus catches Aman, and the fates of both victims are sealed.

In *Athalie* Racine shows error in action when first Athalie, then Mathan, in Act II, Scene iii, and Act III, Scene i, respectively, transgress the temple limits. Racine keeps the fatal error to the last act. Lured into the sacred precinct without guards, failing to see through Joad's deception, Athalie is suddenly surrounded by armed men, and pays the price for her mistake (Act V, Scene v). It is the most spectacular example of an error of judgement in Racine's tragedies.

The investigation of *hamartia* yields a rich harvest of visual effects. The visual focus sharpens perception of the tragic mechanism at work and facilitates analysis of varieties of tragic error in Racine. The errors of Britannicus, Agrippine, and Bajazet spring from defects of character, which are alluded to in the prefaces and confirmed in the plays—Britannicus's reckless courage, Agrippine's obstinate pursuit of power, Bajazet's ferocity. Racine does not comment on Hermione in his preface, but her spurning of Andromaque is consistent with her earlier disdain for the suffering of Oreste. Néron's case is different. He jumps to the wrong conclusion about Agrippine's role in engineering a meeting between Britannicus and Junie, less from a defect of character than from a judgement clouded by his twin obsessions of the moment: suspicion of his mother and desire to possess Junie. Monime is the trusting victim of Mithridate's ruses, whilst Phèdre is shown to be the victim of the forces beyond her control which engender her fatal delusions. Aman's errors, on the other hand, do not spring from character traits but are responses to external stimuli, whilst Athalie falls into a trap devised by Joad exploiting her desire for treasure (*Ath.* V. ii. 1649). Racine consistently portrays errors of judgement in theatrical terms as a key part of the tragic mechanism.

(*c*) Endings

It was a peculiarity of dramatic theory and practice in seventeenth-century France that a tragedy could end happily. Or, to be more precise, plays in which the hero escaped from some peril could be labelled *tragédie*. For tragedy was discussed by the dramatists of the time as a theatrical genre, not in terms of tragic essence.[9] From 1640, when Corneille established with *Cinna* the concept of tragedy with a 'happy ending', the term *tragédie* could be applied to plays to which some modern critics would deny tragic quality. It is often suggested that *Alexandre, Mithridate, Iphigénie, Esther,* and *Athalie* are not real tragedies because they end with deliverance rather than disaster. 'Of Racine's eleven tragedies, five, then, either are not tragic or cannot be considered tragic without reservations. This does not necessarily mean that they are negligible or inferior' (Yarrow, p. 94). In addition, the tragic quality of *Bérénice* has been doubted. Yarrow's comment makes the important point that typological distinctions should not circumscribe theatrical pleasure. For Racine and his spectators these plays were all *tragédies* and broadly in line with contemporary expectations. It was what went on during the play rather than its final moments which justified the designation *tragédie*. Endings are not therefore the decisive factor in determining the genre of the play, and the notion of a tragic ending is a flexible concept in the context of seventeenth-century French tragedy. Yet the final moments of a drama do have a special significance in the theatre. What does the spectator actually see at the end of Racine's tragedies? There is considerable variety.

There are two bouts of madness. In *La Thébaïde* (Act V, Scene vi) Créon tries to stab himself but is restrained and collapses into the arms of his guards. Whether Créon is actually dying is left uncertain, as is shown by the divergent perceptions

---

[9] Detailed discussion of this, and of Racine's use of the word 'tragique' in Barnwell, pp. 214–19.

of different readers.[10] In *Andromaque* Oreste faints after his hal-
lucination of stabbing at Pyrrhus. Two characters, driven out of
their minds by love, are seen to lose their wits in a literal sense.

Three characters—Atalide, Mithridate, and Phèdre—are seen
to be at death's door rather than actually dead (*Baj.* Act V,
Scene xii; *Mit.* Act V, Scene v; *Phè.* Act V, Scene vii). Corpses
on stage were neither plausible nor decent. The verb *expirer* was
used to indicate the character's physical condition. It meant to
breathe one's last.[11] It was a convenient way of fudging the issue
of whether the person was actually dead. Like fainting or losing
consciousness, 'breathing one's last' had all the theatrical impact
of death, whilst preserving decorum and plausibility. Atalide is
seen to stab herself, Mithridate is covered with blood and dust,
Phèdre's poison is seen working on her. The words 'il expire'
or 'elle expire', applied to these characters, are almost the last
words uttered in the tragedy. These 'deaths' raise the problem
of when the final curtain was closed. Sometimes the end of the
play was signalled by the exit of all the characters, a convention
which arose before the use of a stage curtain. In comedy the exit
is to complete a marriage; in tragedy it is the first step towards
the funeral rites. Racine's *Les Plaideurs* and some of his tragedies
imply an ending based on 'Let us go'.[12] But a communal exit
would hardly be suitable for the tragedies which ended with a
character breathing his last on stage, and in these cases Racine's
text seems to imply that the curtain closed on a static tableau.[13]
Phèdre, however, offers a curious mixture of a static tableau
combined with active words. The heroine breathes her last on
stage, but Thésée says 'Let us go [. . .]. Let us go and embrace
the remains of my dear son' (*Phè.* V. vii. 1647). According to
Emelina, Thésée's 'exceptional double "let us go" is not a

[10] Yarrow (p. 29) assumes he goes mad; Cave (p. 327) and Picard in *Œuvres*, i.
126, say he dies; Emelina (p. 176) sees only a symbolic death.
[11] Burrhus distinguishes *mourir* and *expirer*; Agrippine asks 'Il expire?', Burrhus
replies 'Ou plutôt il est mort' (*Bri.* V. iv. 1613); Mithridate uses the verb in the first
person 'J'expire' (*Mit.* V. v. 1664).
[12] 'Allons nous délasser . . .' (*Pla.* Act III, Scene iv); 'Allons voir . . .' (*Bri.* Act
V, Scene viii); 'Venez . . .' (*Iph.* Act V, Scene vi).
[13] The notion of the final curtain closing the play is attested by D'Aubignac:
'C'est un grand défaut quand on entend les spectateurs après que la toile est tirée, se
demander les uns aux autres qu'est devenue une intrigue de la scène' (*Diss. Sertorius*,
p. 241); the stage curtain has been much debated: see Scherer, pp. 171–5; Lawrenson,
pp. 205–11.

movement towards the future, but despondency [. . .]. There is
nowhere to "go"' (p. 173). Perhaps there is a deliberate discrepancy between word and deed. Barrault has Thésée make to
exit, but then stop to offer reconciliation with Aricie (p. 189).
Such a sequence of movements might signify that Aricie wipes
out the unhappy memories of Phèdre and Hippolyte. A happy
ending can be discerned in *Phèdre*.

In three other plays death is evoked by more oblique means.
The protagonist makes an exit which signifies death. Britannicus
is seen to enter Néron's appartment, Aman and Athalie are both
led off under arrest (*Bri.* Act V, Scene ii; *Est.* Act III, Scene vi;
Ath. Act V, Scene vi). There follows a narration recounting the
death. In these tragedies the theatricality of the ending lies in the
death *récit* itself and in the reactions of the characters to it. The
narration of the death can be a potent source of verbal action,
particularly in *Britannicus*, Act V, Scene v. 'In the hands of
Burrhus, the death *récit* becomes a piece of judicial oratory'
(Hawcroft, 'Death *Récit*', p. 35).

Of special interest are the tragedies where the impact of the
death is more remote and the predominant note is deliverance. In
these circumstances Racine relies on a variety of means to
convey the atmosphere of majestic melancholy, which according to the preface of *Bérénice*, was the mark of tragic action.

The atmosphere of rejoicing as Alexandre pardons Porus,
restores his kingdom to him, and unites him with Axiane has
been considered to lend an untragic air to the ending of *Alexandre*
(Act V, Scene iii). It is part of Alexandre's triumph that both
Porus and Axiane submit to his generosity. But theatrically the
triumph is clouded by Cléofile's reactions to the death of her
brother Taxile in combat which is narrated by Ephestion.
Cléofile's tears are important. They contribute to the majestic
melancholy of her final exchange of speeches with Alexandre,
who has offered her marriage. A tearful Cléofile appears behind
Alexandre in Chauveau's illustration in the same attitude as Pity
in the frontispiece to Racine's theatre (Pls. 4 and 5). The mention
of a tomb in the penultimate line is a strong suggestion that the
protagonists exit to prepare for Taxile's funeral rites. This is a
straightforward case of clouding joy with grief. This contrasts
with the ending of Boyer's *Porus* (1648) on the same subject,
which ends with unclouded joy.

Racine employs a quite different technique in two other endings. *Iphigénie* presented a particular challenge because the whole action revolves around the fear that Iphigénie will be killed, yet at the end she is saved and Eriphile serves as the human sacrifice instead. There is no attempt to excite sympathy for Eriphile in the way that sympathy is excited for Taxile by Cléofile's tears. Clearly the final moments of *Iphigénie* are moments of intense relief at Iphigénie's deliverance. But Racine has prefaced them by a spectacular scene of visual torment. Iphigénie is led off to her death by the guards. Clytemnestre struggles to follow them but finally gives up: 'But all these people throw themselves in my path [. . .] I am wearing myself out with useless efforts' (*Iph.* V. iv. 1668–71). This struggle is glossed by Clytemnestre as a form of death: 'Shall I die so many times and yet not leave this life?' (*Iph.* 1673). She then delivers a series of apostrophes of exceptional vigour—to Eriphile, to the sea, to the sun. The sound of thunder signals the turning point. Clytemnestre interprets it as a sign that an avenging god is intervening (*Iph.* 1699). Arcas enters to announce that Achille is trying to save Iphigénie. Once again Clytemnestre tries to leave the stage, but she is stopped by the arrival of her enemy, Ulysse, whose entrance signals to Clytemnestre that her daughter must be dead: 'Do I not see Ulysse? It is he. My daughter is dead, Arcas, it is too late' (*Iph.* V. v. 1719). Clytemnestre's frustrated exit echoes her obstructed exit at the end of the previous scene, and echoes its significance: 'Shall I die so many times and yet not leave this life?' (*Iph.* 1673). Only then does Ulysse report that Iphigénie has in fact been saved. An atmosphere of foreboding and fatality is engendered before final deliverance. Clytemnestre's twice attempted exit and her visible anguish create a surrogate death on stage parallel to Iphigénie's threatened death off-stage.

'Bérénice lets herself collapse into a chair' (SD, *Bér.* Act V, Scene v). She remains in this position for the dénouement of the tragedy, and, significantly, this is the only case where Racine specifies both the moment of sitting and of rising. During the time Bérénice remains seated she listens to speeches by Titus and Antiochus amounting to about a hundred lines. She herself utters only one word 'Hélas!' The speeches of both men contain threats of suicide: Titus first, then Antiochus (ll. 1420–2, 1459–

68). Antiochus's suicide threat is the moment Racine chooses for Bérénice to rise.

BÉRÉNICE *se levant*
Arrêtez, arrêtez. Princes trop généreux,
En quelle extrémité me jetez-vous tous deux!
                                        (*Bér*. V. vii. 1469–70)

Sainte-Beuve perceived the significance of this moment when watching Rachel play Bérénice: 'During Titus's long speech, she rests on the arm of the chair, her head desolate with grief. When at the end she gets up slowly, while the two princes debate, [. . .] then tragic majesty comes into its own' (quoted by Chevalley, p. 108). Bérénice is like a phoenix rising from the ashes. A new woman has been born. When she sank down she wanted only Titus or death. Now she faces the situation: 'I thought your love had run its course; I recognize my error: you love me still' (*Bér*. V. vii. 1481). She stands in recognition of this truth. The act of standing is an affirmation that her life will continue, even if she is separated from Titus. The act of rising also emphasizes Bérénice's 'sudden clearness of vision' (Supple, pp. 161–2). But it is not a static recognition; it leads to further action. In the penultimate line Bérénice orders her two lovers not to follow her. On a literal level this implies that she makes her exit alone, whilst Titus and Antiochus remain on stage. In this way Racine's ending is strongly differentiated in visual terms from Corneille's *Tite et Bérénice*, which concludes with a joyful 'Let us go' voiced by both Tite (l. 1761) and Bérénice (l. 1769). The exit of Racine's Bérénice in tragic isolation carries connotations of death, since final exits are repeatedly glossed by Racine to signify death. 'Junie's retreat to the Vestals, Bérénice's departure [. . .] are also less violent and more feminine ways of simulating the abandonment of life' (Emelina, p. 175). Julia Bartet, acting the part of Bérénice, conveyed the notion of the heroine passing from her dead relationship with Titus to her own tomb (Chancerel, p. 18). At the same time, the triangle formed by the departing Bérénice and the two static men, represents the image of all three serving as a universal example 'of the most tender and ill-fated love' (*Bér*. V. vii. 1501). It is equivalent to an apotheosis (Pl. 9).

(d) Transcendence

French classical drama held no rigid doctrine of tragedy. It was a broad church, whose amiable latitudinarianism caused no anguish to the consciences of seventeenth-century French drama-tists or audiences. Twentieth-century France has been more exacting. The notion of the tragic has been subjected to modern metaphysical exploration nourished by knowledge of ancient Greek drama. As Truchet has put it: 'These metaphysical per-spectives marked a decisive turning point in ways of envisaging this literary genre' (p. 174). The emphasis is on tragedy as a literary genre, rather than a theatrical experience. Truchet goes on to sketch the intellectual landscape of the essence of tragedy, linking it with culpability, freedom, and fatality (pp. 174–85).

Tragedy and culpability relate easily to the seventeenth-century, through Aristotelian *hamartia* and moral ambiguity. Racine would have had little difficulty in understanding and perhaps applauding Hegel filtered through Camus:

> The forces which confront each other in tragedy are both legitimate, both clad in the armour of righteousness. But in melodrama or the *drame* only one side is legitimate. In other words, tragedy is ambiguous, the *drame* simplistic. In the first, each force is at the same time right and wrong. In the second, one is good, the other is evil [. . .] Antigone is right, but Créon is not wrong. (Camus, p. 1705.)

The other landmarks in the tragic landscape—freedom and fatality—can also be discerned in Racinian tragedy, where char-acters are trapped in impossible situations or are victims of overwhelming forces. Culpability, freedom, and fatality have a metaphysical dimension which can be usefully approached through Gouhier's formula: 'An event is not tragic in itself but by what it signifies, and this significance is tragic when it introduces the sign of a transcendence' (p. 34). What are the signs of transcendence in Racinian tragedy and how are they made visible in theatrical terms?

The gesture of raising eyes and hands heavenwards was well known to a Christian audience: 'Let us raise to the Lord both our hands and our eyes.' This occurs in a hymn from the Roman breviary which Racine translated (*Œuvres*, i. 1003). Rotrou showed it on stage when Adrian is seen to receive God's grace after 'looking at the sky and meditating for a while' (SD, *Saint*

Genest, Act IV, Scene v). Assuérus notices Esther's posture: 'I see your eyes look up to heaven as I speak' (*Est.* II. vii. 682). The chorus in *Esther* carries a similar exhortation: 'Let us raise our eyes towards the sacred mounts' (I. v. 295). This gesture, which signals belief in some higher power, is seen in *Britannicus*, provided that the implicit stage directions are followed. While Britannicus rejoices at the prospect of reconciliation with Néron, he is irritated by Junie's demeanour: 'Why, when you are listening to me, do your sad eyes keep looking heavenward? What are you afraid of?' Junie implies that she seeks protection against a vague menacing force: 'I do not know. But yet I fear' (*Bri.* V. i. 1501-4). This visible sign has been anticipated in Néron's description of Junie's abduction. He saw her 'sad, raising heavenward her tear-filled eyes' (*Bri.* II. ii. 387). This gesture distinguishes Junie's innocence from Néron's guilt. For Néron is ashamed to raise his eyes: 'He walks haphazardly; his wandering eyes dare not lift heavenward their demented gaze' (*Bri.* V. viii. 1758). In other plays where gods, heaven, or destiny are invoked verbally, conventional *actio* might well require a heavenward glance or gaze. Sorel writes of actors who spent most of their time 'looking up to heaven or to some other place whence they are inspired with passion'.[14] Only in *Britannicus* and *Esther* does Racine write this gesture into the text with an implicit stage direction.

Décor can provide visible signs of the transcendent. Titus's dilemma at the end of Act IV of *Bérénice*, torn between two doors behind which are the Roman senators and Bérénice respectively, signifies on one level a purely human choice between political reality and personal passion. Racine also invests the scene with a transcendental dimension. Rutile's words announcing the summons from the senators are interpreted by Titus as a call from the gods:

TITUS Je vous entends, grands Dieux. Vous voulez rassurer
    Ce cœur que vous voyez tout prêt à s'égarer.

                  (*Bér.* IV. viii. 1245-6)

So, on the other side of the door are signs of a divine power drawing Titus away from his dangerous passion. 'Titus is torn

---

[14] *La Maison des jeux*, i. 414.

apart [. . .] The voice of Rome, of its people, of its gods, remind him of their exigences' (Goldmann, p. 381). The emperor chooses the higher exigences, and Bérénice is left behind. This is only a fleeting evocation of the divine, for when Titus returns to Bérénice in Act V, he still does not know what to do: 'I came to you without knowing my design' (*Bér.* V. vi. 1382). In other plays the décor serves as a permanent sign of the transcendent. Racine does not use the sea merely as a picturesque change from the interior of a palace or of tents. In *Andromaque* it is evoked in the dialogue as a sign of the destiny which sent Greek ships sailing to Troy, the destiny which brought Oreste to Epirus, and the route by which Oreste will defy the gods when he abducts Hermione (*And.* Act I, Scene i, and Act III, Scene i). In *Iphigénie* the backdrop of sea and becalmed ships is even more clearly linked to the divine power which delays the Greek fleet at Aulis and which demands so terrible a sacrifice from Agamemnon, though by the end of the drama the gods have saved Iphigénie by the substitution of Eriphile. Mardochée's entrance into Esther's quarters is explicitly glossed by Racine as a sign of divine intervention; Esther exclaims that an angel must have guided him (*Est.* I. iii. 157). The scenic backdrop of whole episodes can be read for signs of transcendence. Athalie's cry: 'Pitiless God, thou alone hast wrought all this' (*Ath.* V. vi. 1774), rings out when Joad has given the signal for armed priests to emerge from hiding to ambush Athalie. It is the sign of God at work, reinforced by the opening of the interior of the temple which suggests the presence of God in the recesses of the tabernacle.

Hybris is a human challenge to the gods which takes the form of overweening pride. Racine noted *hybris* in the *Ajax* of Sophocles: 'Reason for the anger of the gods against Ajax: his pride and overweening self-confidence and his contempt for their assistance' (*Œuvres*, ii. 860).[15] The visible errors of judgement noted earlier in this chapter often have a strong element of *hybris*. Consequently, when such errors are seen on stage, the spectre of divine retribution is irresistibly evoked. Hermione's overweening confidence that she has finally won Pyrrhus leads her to spurn Andromaque's plea (*And.* Act III, Scene iv). Britannicus rashly refuses to recognize the danger of lingering

---

[15] Connotations of the Greek word *hybris* in Barnwell, pp. 240–2.

outside Néron's apartment (*Bri.* Act III, Scene vii). Bajazet, weapons in hand, exults in anticipated victory over his brother, blind to Atalide's distress (*Baj.* Act III, Scene iv). In Racine's last tragedy, Barnwell describes *hybris* at work: 'Athalie and Mathan fall into the same error. Their boasting expressed their unwarranted confidence in their ability to overcome right with might, [. . .] and it takes the spectacular form of their entry into the sacred and forbidden precinct, only to be faced with the terrifying, unsuspected truth' (p. 244; *Ath.* Act III, Scene i; Act V, Scene v). The choice of words—spectacular entry into a forbidden precinct—reveals the visual dimension of *hybris* in action, and the actions invite punishment from on high.

Coincidences can reveal the hand of the gods. By convention, entrances in seventeenth-century French tragedy needed some explanation, explicit or implicit. The most explicit references are not necessarily the most significant. The notion of lucky chance (*heureux destin*) bringing a character on stage is hardly more than a figure of speech (*And.* II. iii. 603; *Bér.* V. ii. 1259). It is the unlucky chance which can betray the hand of the gods. Some well-established views tend to stress the lack of surprise and the inevitability of the tragic action in Racine. 'The superior forces which destroy the tragic heroes wear no masks as far as we are concerned, nor is their strategy baffling [. . .] The entrance or exit of a character is not only fully justified, but its motivation is part of the mechanism' (Mourgues, pp. 39, 41). Mourgues's discussion is focused on the absolute nature of the characters' passions, and in this context there may be a logical mechanism at work. But it is not the whole story. Coincidence often brings characters on stage at crucial moments, and coincidences may conceal the strategy of the superior forces, unless the signs are read aright. Mere chance for Aristotle is neither artistic nor tragic, but, 'matters of chance seem most marvellous if there is an appearance of design as it were in them'. He gives an example: 'The statute of Mitys at Argos killed the author of Mitys's death by falling down on him [. . .]. Incidents like that we think to be not without meaning' (*Poetics*, ch. 9). Chance entrances in Racine rarely lack some plausible explanation; but plausibility is not the same as logical necessity. There is no logical reason why Andromaque should meet up with Hermione just before Pyrrhus arrives, thus giving Racine one minute in which to show Hermione spurning Andromaque's plea (*And.*

Act III, Scene iv). It is quite by chance that Junie happens to appear unexpectedly, just when Narcisse is telling Britannicus that she is with Néron (*Bri.* Act III, Scene vii). Certainly when Roxane breaks in upon Bajazet and Atalide at the precise moment that Bajazet is determined to disabuse Roxane, it is plausible, as Mourgues points out, that Roxane should not be far away: 'we knew she could not be elsewhere and had not stopped circling round Bajazet' (p. 43; *Baj.* Act III, Scene V). But there is no logical reason why she should not have arrived one minute sooner or one minute later, with quite different consequences for the development of the action. Racine's chance meetings, thanks to their plausible motivation, do give some impression of inevitability. However, that impression is evident to the leisurely reader rather than to the excited spectator, for whom the element of surprise obscures the hints of verisimilitude. And surprising coincidences can be read for deeper significance. Barnwell spells out the implications of Aristotle's views on coincidence: 'The fall of the statue was a chance event. The fact that it fell on the murderer of the man whom it commemorated may also be thought of as a chance event, but properly presented it can be seen as a representation of divine justice and retribution' (p. 220). Applied to the sequence of chance meetings in Act III of *Andromaque, Britannicus*, or *Bajazet*, the Mitys paradigm conjures up the workings of transcendent forces, in the shape of justifiable retribution from the gods on high.

The concept of a transcendent power watching over humans can be stimulated by the visual realities of theatrical performance—characters on stage eyeing each other, and the spectators themselves watching the performance. Hence a multivalent interpretation of watchful eyes in Racinian tragedy:

All Greece has its eyes on its ambassador Oreste and King Pyrrhus (in *Andromaque*); Rome watches the loves of Titus (*Bérénice*); Phèdre knows she is seen by the Sun; and the religious plays unfold under the eye of God. In every case the guilt of the characters piles up under the supreme glance of this transcendent witness—or, sometimes, Judge. Every glance exchanged by the human heroes is spied upon by this inexorable eye, which judges and condemns. (Starobinski, p. 99.)

This adds an extra dimension to the concept of error and guilt. When the curtain falls on Racine's tragedies the visible misery of madness or death—Créon, Oreste, Atalide—is often accompanied by an intellectual recognition of self-inflicted catastrophe and an admission of guilt before a higher tribunal. This recognition is a perception of the higher laws which govern human life or of the deeper truths which underlie it: 'A keenness of vision that, far from ending the tragic error, only increases it [. . .]. If illusion and blindness can be done away with, it will lead to the imposing of a truth that kills' (Starobinski, p. 98). In addition, madness is traditionally a sign of the transcendent: *Quem Jupiter vult perdere, prius dementat*. The Erinyes drive Orestes mad in Aeschylus' *Choephori* (ll. 1048–62). The storm that engulfs Lear has a divine origin. He refers to 'the great gods | That keep this dreadful pother o'er our heads'. Then Lear confesses 'My wits begin to turn' (*King Lear*, Act III, Scene ii). In Racine, Créon and Oreste go mad; Phèdre has her wits taken from her by the gods (*Phè*. I. iii. 181).

Thus, in all these ways, Racine offers visible signs of the transcendent. But attempts to systematize the metaphysical elements in Racinian tragedy run into formidable problems, involving the sacrifice of much of his theatre. Goldmann's analysis based on the triple relationship—god, humanity, and the world—produces only three and a half 'authentic' tragedies, leaving the remainder untragic. The three tragedies are *Britannicus, Bérénice,* and *Phèdre*, whilst Andromaque's 'innocent stratagem' makes her only half-tragic:

Andromaque is tragic in so far as she refuses the alternative. In opposition to the world she voluntarily refuses life, and freely accepts death. However, she is no longer tragic when having decided to accept marriage with Pyrrhus before killing herself, she employs deceit against the world in order to transform her moral victory into a material victory which will survive her. (Goldmann, p. 358.)

For Goldmann the hidden God, the Jansenist *deus absconditus*, comes in various configurations: Hector-Astyanax for Andromaque, the gods vainly invoked by Junie, Rome for Titus and Bérénice, the sun and Venus for Phèdre (pp. 354, 368, 378, 422). The tragedy of the protagonist lies in the lonely dilemma of irreconcilable imperatives imposed by the hidden god and in the rejection of the materialistic values of the world. In pursuit of this structure Goldmann dismisses *La Thébaïde* and *Alexandre* as 'obviously to be left aside' (p. 23); he classes the sequence of plays from *Bajazet* to *Iphigénie* as 'drames intramondains', through which Racine gropes his way towards the authentic tragedy of *Phèdre*. The final plays are no longer tragedies of the hidden God, because God is present and manifest in *Esther* and *Athalie* (p. 440). After the sacrifice of so much, the remaining plays confirm Goldmann's thesis.

Goldmann's thesis merits examination for it is implicitly a theatrical reading in some respects.[16] His interpretation of *Britannicus* refers to a number of theatrical effects. Junie's entrance implies a clash with Néron; Néron behind the curtain is the devil incarnate; Junie's exit after the spying encapsulates 'the insurmountable opposition' between her and the emperor: Néron's 'Madam . . . ' is cut short by Junie's 'No, my lord' (*Bri.* II. vii. 744); despite Junie's efforts to restrain Britannicus, he goes off joyfully to the banquet where he will be assassinated. Each of the examples adduced by Goldmann is an example of visual highlighting of Junie's predicament, and, though he does not mention Junie's heavenward glances discussed above, these would reinforce his argument and perhaps make an even stronger case for the 'hidden god'. But this reading throws too much that is central into the shade and highlights the peripheral. For Goldmann the tragic structure of *Britannicus* depends upon the opposition between the world and the tragic character. There are wild beasts (Néron and Agrippine), villains (Narcisse), self-deluders (Burrhus), and passive victims (Britannicus) (p. 363). These represent the world, and 'on the periphery Junie, the tragic character, standing against the World, rejecting even the thought of compromise' (ibid.). However, to interpret *Britannicus* as a tragedy solely in terms of Junie, is to miss the interlocking errors of judgement by Britannicus, Agrippine, and Néron in Act III, which illustrate Racine's claim that 'my tragedy is no less the disgrace of Agrippine than the death

---

[16] Goldmann notes the disorder of Bérénice's hair (p. 379; *Bér.* Act IV, Scene ii) and her collapse into a chair (pp. 381–2; *Bér.* Act V, scene v); Hippolyte's perpetual impatience to leave (pp. 423–7; *Phè.* Act I, Scene i); the stage directions for Phèdre's entrance, the 'solitary dialogue' between Phèdre and Œnone, the solemn raising of Œnone from her knees (pp. 429–32; *Phè.* Act I, Scene iii), and finally the retrospective stage directions in Act III, Scene i, relating to Hippolyte's sword (p. 435).

of Britannicus' (second preface, p. 409). Certainly one must accept Goldmann's caveat concerning the intentions expressed in Racine's prefaces: 'It does not necessarily follow that a writer should have understood the meaning and the objective structure of his writings' (p. 353). But where Racine's statements about his tragedy do conform to its identifiable structure, which in the case of *Britannicus* depends upon the errors committed on stage, then this combination of evidence should not be lightly discarded in favour of a schema which so confidently dismisses three-quarters of Racine's tragedies as untragic.

If there is metaphysical coherence in Racine's eleven tragedies it seems to lie in the ambiguous texture of the transcendental forces, which pervade rather than shape his theatrical and tragic vision. This ambiguity has analogies with the moral ambiguity of Racinian mortals. The forces signified by the sea in *Andromaque* are mysteriously benign and malign. In *Iphigénie* they are clearly malevolent yet dispense acceptable justice by the end of the play. Whatever supernatural force was invoked by Junie's uplifted eyes, it did not save Britannicus, any more than the gods, guardians of innocence, protected the credulous Hippolyte (*Phè.* V. i. 1351). Even the god of Jew and Christian in *Athalie*, whose sanctuary is evoked when the recesses of the temple are revealed, places on the throne as part of his plan for mankind's salvation a king who will one day commit murder. 'The powerful ambiguity between fair and foul assumes supernatural proportions in the constant and disturbing ambiguity of God' (Mourgues, p. 125). A transcendent element is undoubtedly implied in most of Racine's tragedies, but it is expressed polyphonically rather than univocally. The voices sing many melodies, from Jocaste's cry of despair at the gods who prompt crime (*Thé.* III. ii. 608) to Achille's defiant assertion of man's capacity to rival the gods by his own efforts (*Iph.* I. ii. 259). This polyphony culminates in the final chorus of *Athalie* with its anguished questions: 'Are you no longer the jealous god? Are you no longer the god of vengeance? Are you no longer the god of forgiveness?' (*Ath.* IV. vi. 1470 and 1475).[17] Perhaps the 'hidden god' is really the two-faced Janus.

[17] The crucial importance of this chorus and of Joad's prophecy is discussed in Forman, 'Lyrisme et tragique dans l'*Athalie* de Racine'.

A theatrical reading can demonstrate that Racine's tragedies offer the spectator the pleasure of *seeing* the key elements of tragedy according to the main theoretical criteria of the genre. Racine's prefaces, with their insistence on moral ambiguity and *hamartia*, steer the reader towards an Aristotelian interpretation on these lines. Even modern interpretations of the tragic, such as those offered by Starobinski or Goldmann, find some support from visual elements. But definitions of the tragic were not the dominant concern of the spectators who crowded into the Parisian theatres. They came for many other reasons. There was an alternative agenda.

(e) The Alternative Agenda

Dandin invites Isabelle to come and watch the excruciating pain inflicted by judicial torture. Isabelle gives the respectable reaction: 'Ah, how can one watch these wretches suffering?' to which Dandin replies cheerfully 'Well it always helps to pass an hour or two' (*Pla*. III. iv. 851). Tragedy offered just such a spectacle. Racine wrote into *Britannicus* suggestions for spectator response. Néron was delighted to see Britannicus suffer: 'The picture of his pain delights my mind' (*Bri*. II. viii. 751). Pictures of pain are the unifying theme of Chauveau's illustrations for Racine's theatre. They depict the visible signs of suffering. Many are taken from actual scenes in the play. For *Alexandre* and *Mithridate* it is the wounded Porus and Mithridate; Andromaque is shown on her knees to a remorseless Pyrrhus; Atalide collapses before Roxane (Pls. 5, 6, 10, and 11). Even the sedate illustration to *Bérénice* with the weeping heroine flanked by her two lovers mirrors the weeping figure of Pity in the frontispiece to Racine's tragedies and evokes the vision of a painful parting (Pls. 4 and 9). For the other plays, in order to depict agonized expressions, it was advantageous to base the illustration on scenes which were narrated. For *La Thébaïde*, King Etéocle is mortally wounded lying in his blood with his brother towering above him (*Album*, p. 119). Britannicus's head is grotesquely tilted back as he sprawls poisoned on the couch (Pl. 8). For *Iphigénie* a wide-eyed Eriphile points a dagger at her own heart; the horror of the situation is enhanced by the forbidding figure of Calchas who dominates the centre of the picture

(*Album*, p. 187). Naturally for *Phèdre* the most painful scene is the lacerated body of Hippolyte lying beside his shattered chariot. This was chosen by Le Brun (Pl. 12). These illustrations did not have to represent what was seen on stage, any more than the publicity poster for a modern film needs to be based on actual scenes from the film itself. They can stand in emblematic relationship to the plays. As images of pain and horror they unmistakably invite the reader or spectator to enjoy the spectacle of suffering, either directly when the agony is on stage or indirectly through the anguish of characters reacting to narrations of brutal deaths which have taken place off-stage.

Picard postulates a dichotomy between the aesthetics of Racine and Chauveau: 'How then could Racine fail to be shocked by illustrations which so completely misunderstood the spirit of his plays?' ('Racine and Chauveau', p. 268). It would be wrong to assume that Chauveau misunderstood Racine. Theatre-going was often turbulent and sometimes violent. In Molière's theatre in 1672 a man in the audience was beaten by several others 'and was badly injured'.[18] Real suffering was never far away. Public executions were a part of everyday life. The execution of the marquis de Courboyer was a rival 'spectacle' which lured many regular theatre-goers away from the first night of *Britannicus* (Boursault, p. 231). D'Aubignac applauded suffering as the essence of good theatre: 'Almost no character should appear on stage without an agitated mind, [. . .] without being compelled to suffer greatly (*souffrir beaucoup*); it is the place where reigns the Demon of disquiet, of disturbance, of disorder' (*Pratique*, iv. 4, p. 281). Tragedy on stage had a sadistic streak.

Another item on the alternative agenda was prominently advertised by high-minded churchmen. Those who had professional charge of the morals of society were strong in condemning the passions into which the theatre-goer was inveigled. Spectators came to scrutinize other spectators.[19] Actors were 'smooth and effeminate'; the ladies present 'idolized their bodies'.[20] The

[18] Lough, p. 87, quoting a document in E. Campardon, *Documents inédits sur J. B. Poquelin Molière* (Paris, 1871), 31–2; see also Yarrow, *Seventeenth Century*, pp. 124–7.

[19] Segrais, *Eugénie*, in *Les Nouvelles françaises* (Paris, 1657), i. 76; Capatti, p. 26 n.

[20] *Décision faite en Sorbonne touchant la comédie par M l'abbé L★ P★* (Paris, 1694), 31, 65; Capatti, p. 43 n.

actress on stage was the focus of hundreds of pairs of eyes: 'The nudity of her breasts, her face covered with make-up and *mouches*, her lascivious winks, her amorous words, her affected ornaments, all this apparatus of lust, is a snare in which the most respectable can be caught.'[21] This idea is echoed by Pradon writing of Racine: 'The particular quality of the theatre is that an excellent actor or actress often causes the success of a play [. . .] the thrilling performance of a handsome person excites our interest in it, and the sound of an admirable voice awakens in our hearts even the most dormant passions.'[22] Another writer may have had Racine specifically in mind when he wrote reproachfully: 'The intentions of the poet are always criminal [. . .]. He always wants his action to be full of passion, and that it should have a disturbing effect upon the spectator (*exciter du trouble dans le coeur*).'[23]

When characters made their declarations of love on stage, their desire could be written on their face. Racine gave directions for Phèdre to feast her eyes upon Hippolyte: 'Yes, I burn for Thésée [. . .] looking like a god, or as I see you now' (*Phè.* II. v. 634–40). Le Brun depicted the passion (Pl. 17) and described its visible signs: 'Eyebrows close knit and prominent above the eyes, which will be open wider than usual [. . .], the tongue may appear on the edge of the lips, more inflamed than in the portrayal of love; all these movements revealing the agitation of the soul' (p. 16). Every one of Racine's profane tragedies offers a scenario for such a spectacle. In *Phèdre* alone desire inspires horror, which Le Brun describes: 'The mouth will be half-open, but more tense in the middle than at the edges, which will be drawn backwards making lines in the cheeks' (p. 9; see Pl. 16). Horror and desire are the visual extremities of Phèdre's performance, which oscillates between them:

---

[21] J. de Voisin, *La Défense du traitté de Monseigneur le prince de Conti touchant la comédie* (Paris, 1671), 477; Phillips, *The Theatre and its Critics*, p. 188.

[22] *Nouvelles remarques sur tous les ouvrages du Sieur D**** (The Hague, Jean Strik, 1685), 77; Picard, *Carrière*, p. 256.

[23] Goibaud du Bois (?), *Réponse à l'auteur de la lettre contre les Hérésies imaginaires et les visionnaires* (Paris, 1666); NCR 36. This *Réponse* was a reply to Racine's *Lettre à l'auteur des hérésies imaginaires et des deux visionnaires*, which appeared anonymously in 1666; see Picard, *Carrière*, pp. 119–22.

J'ai pris la vie en haine, et ma flamme en horreur.

(Phè. I. iii. 307)

Racine also linked physical pain and sexual desire. Néron enjoyed the sight of Junie's arrest by his soldiers: 'Excited by some curious desire, I saw her come last night into this place, depressed and lifting up her tear-filled eyes, which glistened amidst the flames and weaponry [. . .] Perhaps the darkness and the flames, the shouts and silence, the fierce demeanour of her stern abductors, enhanced the sweetness of her fearful eyes' (*Bri.* II. ii. 385). Starobinski has analysed this sadism in detail: 'As love is inflamed, the monster is born and grows in this man' (p. 92).[24] Elsewhere the situation is presented from the female viewpoint, where women were subjected to savage men. Andromaque conjures up a vision of Pyrrhus's ferocious conduct when Troy fell to the Greeks, and imagines the man she may have to share her bed with: 'Think, think again, Céphise, of that cruel night [. . .] Remember Pyrrhus, with his eyes ablaze, invading the palace through the gleaming flames, leaving my brothers' corpses in his path. Covered with blood he cheered the carnage on [. . .] This is the man you want me now to wed' (*And.* III. viii. 999–1008). Eventually Andromaque consents to wed the brutal Pyrrhus. In *Iphigénie* Eriphile recalls analogous experiences with Achille in a reluctant confession to her confidant: 'I say this once to you and then will be silent forever.' She remembers the day they were both made captive by Achille. She dwells on Achille's cruel hands which seized her and caused her to faint. Finally she recovered consciousness and saw herself 'pressed with a bloodstained arm; I trembled, Doris, and feared to meet the fearful face of a savage conqueror'. But suddenly she found Achille pleasurable (*Iph.* II. i. 479–502). For Néron and Eriphile physical violence is a stimulus to sexual desire. For Andromaque the link is offered to the spectator's imagination rather than located explicitly in Andromaque herself, though some have seen Andromaque sexually attracted to Pyrrhus[25] or flirting with him.[26]

---

[24] Thibaudet explores the eroticism of tears in both *Andromaque* and *Britannicus* ('Les Larmes de Racine').

[25] An interpretation refuted by Picard in *Œuvres*, i. 1108 and 1111.

[26] Robinet's comment on Andromaque 'sous le visage d'une actrice [Du Parc] grande tentatrice des humains' (ii. 1091) may support this view (Capatti, p. 155).

The theatrical depiction of sexual desire culminates in *Phèdre*. The play can of course be read as tragedy in the Aristotelian mould in which a heroine who has some good qualities commits an error and brings catastrophe upon herself. That is how it is presented in Racine's preface and that was the thread which guided the analysis of significant visual effects in the sections above on moral ambiguity and errors of judgement. But a consideration of the way in which visual and verbal elements reflect each other in *Phèdre* suggests other structuring processes.

One of the ways in which the patterning of theatrical effects can become structural elements is through mirror scenes, that is when a later scene reflects an earlier one either verbally or visually.[27] The protagonists in *Phèdre* declare their love in two parallel scenes: Hippolyte to Aricie in Act II, Scene ii, and Phèdre to Hippolyte in Act II, Scene v. This pattern is evident even from a literary reading of the text, but a theatrical reading reveals the visual contrast between this pair of scenes. Hippolyte's declaration to Aricie is anxious and embarrassed: 'You see before you a most pitiable prince.' Hippolyte apologizes for his inept manner of talking of love: 'Remember that this language is foreign to me; do not reject my ill-expressed proposal' (*Phè.* II. ii. 530 and 558). Although the reference is to language, Hippolyte's declarations must also have a visual dimension; the spectator not only hears but also sees the awkward youth stammer his love to a female. This contrasts visually with Phèdre's declaration, which starts in trepidation and rises to a climax of fury: 'Know then Phèdre in all her passion . . . Here is my heart. There must your hand strike' (*Phè.* II. v. 673–704). The contrast between the clumsily tender scene between Aricie and Hippolyte and the appalling revelations of Phèdre to Hippolyte can be highlighted by the positioning of the two couples for their respective declarations, enabling the spectator to observe the pattern of similarities and note the differences. Barrault suggests that Hippolyte should be hemmed in by Phèdre in the same spot that Hippolyte himself immobilized Aricie (p. 111 n. 26).

The common element in these mirror scenes is sexual desire.

---

[27] Lapp examines some aspects of reflections and 'double vision' (pp. 53–5) and applies the notion to the *récit* of Théramène (pp. 168–70).

Hippolyte's for Aricie in Act II, Scene i, contrasted with
Phèdre's for Hippolyte in Act II, Scene v. This desire is the
monster in Phèdre herself, which assails Hippolyte, and a
monster within Hippolyte, which diverts him to the forbidden
love of Aricie. The link between monster and sexual urge is
established during Phèdre's struggle with Hippolyte: 'Deliver
the world of a monster who maddens you [. . .] This hideous
monster must not escape you' (II. v. 701 and 703). These are
Phèdre's words as she invites Hippolyte to stab her with his
sword. For Thésée, Hippolyte's sexual desire makes him a
monster: 'Monster, [. . .] after the fury of horrendous love has
borne you frenzied to your father's bed' (*Phè*, IV. ii. 1045). In
vain Hippolyte reminds Thésée that the horrors of incest and
adultery are in Phèdre's blood not his (*Phè*. IV. ii. 1150). These
words 'love' and 'monster' provide the links between what the
spectator sees in the scenes so far alluded to (Act II, Scenes ii and
v), and the final element in this reflecting structure, namely
Théramène's narration of Hippolyte's death (Act V, Scene vi).
Here Hippolyte's struggle with a monster is evoked in purely
verbal terms, but the words evoke visual effects which have
parallels with his encounter with Phèdre in Act II. In both cases
the monstrous enemy comes upon Hippolyte while he is preoccupied with Aricie. Phèdre interrupts Hippolyte's declaration
of love to Aricie (Act II, Scene v); Hippolyte is on his way to
'marry' Aricie when the sea-monster attacks (Act V, Scene vi).
In both cases Hippolyte's parentage is alluded to: in Act II
Phèdre invited Hippolyte to strike her, invoking him as the
'worthy son of the hero who gave you birth' (II. v. 700). The
phrase is echoed when Théramène describes Hippolyte facing
the sea-monster: 'Hippolyte, alone, worthy son of a hero' (V.
vi. 1527). The battle between Hippolyte and the sea-monster
takes a different course from his encounter with Phèdre, yet
both are fatal. Whereas the spectator saw Hippolyte incapable of
drawing his own sword to strike Phèdre,[28] in Théramène's
narration the hero's son does hurl his spear at the monster, a

---

[28] Subligny, who saw the play in 1677, was highly critical of Hippolyte's
immobility because a warrior would not have let his sword go: 'Hippolyte stands
like a log (*demeure comme une souche*) [. . .] but when dramatists are seeking theatrical
effects (*jeux de théâtre*), we mustn't be too critical' (*Dissertation*, p. 379).

detail which occurs neither in Euripides nor Seneca. But the courageous action brings about Hippolyte's downfall, for the monster's collapse causes his horses to bolt, and Hippolyte is dragged over rocks and brambles until his disfigured body comes to rest.

Could the audience listening to Théramène's narration have associated a sea-monster with sexual desire? Racine's text itself establishes the link between monster and love. In addition, the connection between sea-monster and sexuality is explicit in Desmarests's epic poem *Clovis*, which appeared in a number of editions between 1657 and 1673, where a sea-monster, believed to be Neptune in disguise, is described as having intercourse with Ildegonde (Book V). The episode is described by Chapelain as 'crude and filthy'. Desmarests's lines are an indication that the monster in Théramène's narration could have been seen by contemporary spectators as a symbol of aggressive, destructive sexuality (Maber, pp. 53–5). If this link is accepted, then Théramène's narration of the combat with the sea-monster reflects Phèdre's aggressive sexual encounter with Hippolyte in Act II, Scene v, which itself correlates with Hippolyte's declaration of love of Aricie. The verbo-visual pattern provides an alternative reading of the drama. It shows Hippolyte brought low in his struggle with the monster of sexuality, caught between Phèdre's desire for him and his own desire for Aricie. Jacques de Sève, the first artist to provide more than a single illustration for Racine's plays, brings out these visual cross-references. His illustrations are partly mimetic, partly allegorical. At the beginning of each volume are explanations of the allegories. There is a visual pattern linking Hippolyte's abandonment of his sword to Phèdre, represented allegorically (Pl. 21), and his courageous attack with his spear upon the monster (Pl. 22). The hero without his sword becomes the hero brandishing his spear. Prefacing the whole play is a vignette showing Hippolyte overcome by the sea-monster and by the god of love. The vignette is glossed as 'Hippolyte represented allegorically by the symbol of innocence [i.e. the sheep], victim of the frenzy of love' (Pl. 20). The final illustration is explained as 'the sea-monster wounded and dying' (Pl. 23). Sève exploits the potent symbolism of weapons and monster, confirming pictorially the theatrical implications of the text.[29] The tension between this theatrical reading, which gives equal prominence to Phèdre and Hippolyte, and the moral reading in Racine's preface, which stresses in such detail the moral ambiguity of Phèdre whilst omitting any reference to her declaration of love to Hippolyte, is reflected in Racine's hesitation over the title of the play. The final title—*Phèdre* alone—emphasizes the moral dimension: whereas the suppressed title *Phèdre et Hippolyte* encompasses the full theatrical reality.[30]

Recognition was also on the agenda. It may seem strange not to have considered recognition as a conventional ingredient of tragedy, alongside moral ambiguity or *hamartia*. After all *anagnorisis* has an equally respectable Aristotelian pedigree as an element of tragic action. The difficulty lies in what Aristotle meant by the term. For Aristotle *anagnorisis* is especially associated with material recognition of identity by means of visual signs (*Poetics*, chs. 11 and 16).[31] A theatrical reading confirms the centrality of the visual and the material in Racinian drama, but material recognition in Racine has been disparaged and devalued in favour of intellectual recognition. Racine has attracted commentaries emphasizing characters' recognition of their own delusions, errors, or tragic predicament. Such interpretations draw the reader into the self-discoveries of individual characters and thence into their own recognition of man's tragic predicament. Cave has convincingly argued for a reconsideration of this critical tradition with regard to Racine. Intellectual prejudice against the primitive simplicity of material discovery has caused critics to avert their eyes from the recognitions in plays like *Bajazet* or *Athalie*. This aversion can claim some support from neo-classical theory, which did prefer the abstract as opposed to the concrete, and indeed Racine's own statements

---

[29] Siguret compares Sève and Le Brun as illustrators of Hippolyte's encounter with the monster but does not comment on the visual links between Sève's several illustrations.

[30] According to Bayle the play started as *Hippolyte*; it was published in 1677 as *Phèdre et Hippolyte*; ten years later it was renamed *Phèdre* (Picard in *Œuvres*, i. 1168); Ubersfeld's application of a *modèle actantiel* to *Phèdre* highlights analogous shifts of perspective (pp. 97–101).

[31] See Cave's detailed discussion of recognition (pp. 27–54) and of signs and tokens (pp. 242–55).

contribute to this bias. But Racine's practice is at odds with this theory. Therefore, 'to accept the *doxa* at face value is to neglect the extent to which the outlawed properties still insinuate themselves into the higher tragic mimesis, denouncing its imposture' (Cave, pp. 341–9). The tension between theory and practice can be seen in the case of *Athalie* where a defensive preface provides respectable testimonials for a potentially disreputable melodrama or a disturbing subtext. Cave's reading stresses that *Athalie* is a horror story: 'It renews, of course, the nightmare of Oedipus groping his way through error towards a truth which will blind him.' It is a ghost story: 'Athalie's melodramatic dream haunts her before she sees Joas' (pp. 366–7). When the veils are lifted and Joas is recognized, Athalie's final *ekplexis* can leap across the stage to infect the spectator. *Athalie* is a theatrical 'tale of the unexpected' ending with a melodramatic recognition.

Other Racinian dénouements point to melodramatic scenarios which lay in future French drama. Where his sources offered the death of a wholly virtuous and innocent woman—Monime or Iphigénie—Racine changed the dénouement so that Injustice did not triumph over Innocence. Where a man was involved—Britannicus, Bajazet, Hippolyte—then Injustice was permitted to triumph because the man had been given the opportunity to fight back in scenes of violent confrontation with the adversary. The man was a defeated combatant rather than a sacrificial victim. Hence the importance of actors bringing out the stereotypical masculinity of these conquered heroes. Mounet-Sully's performance accentuated Hippolyte's virility especially in the scenes where he defends himself against his father's unjust accusations.[32] Britannicus must assert himself in manly fashion against Néron (*Bri.* Act III, Scene viii); Bajazet likewise must display the 'ferocity of his nation' which Racine emphasizes in his preface to this play (p. 549). In this way the vanquished males differ from the maltreated females. Junie and Aricie, both invented by Racine, survive their predicament. So too does Monime, virtually invented since she is metamorphosed out of all recognition from her depiction in the historical sources. In order to cast Iphigénie the same mould, Racine had to change

---

[32] Sarcey, iii. 225–6; Descotes, 'Dénouements', p. 236.

the traditional story to avoid, as he said, 'defiling the stage with the horrible murder of such a virtuous and amiable character as Iphigénie' (preface to *Iphigénie*, p. 688). Racine, according to Descotes, 'had a keen sense of this necessity for distributive justice [. . .] which inhabits the unconscious of the crowd: one of the fundamental rules of melodrama [. . .], a popular genre par excellence, is that after having suffered greatly, the innocent heroine should finally be saved' ('Dénouements', p. 235). Racine himself spells out the theatrical pleasure to be derived from getting involved with the fate of a character: 'One has only to have seen the play performed to realize what pleasure I gave the spectator by saving this virtuous princess at the last moment' (preface to *Iphigénie*, p. 688). Not surprisingly Diderot admired *Iphigénie* more than any other Racinian play: 'It begins to seem possible that Diderot's fondness for *Iphigénie* derived from the fact that he found in it elements of the genre which he himself was hoping to create' (Connon, p.249). Zimmermann has drawn attention to the way in which other persecuted characters—Astyanax, Esther, and Eliacin-Joas—are all finally delivered from peril ('L'Innocence', pp. 181–5).

This view of the dénouements shows Racine sliding away from Aristotelian orthodoxy, which recommended depicting the destruction of a tragic hero who is neither wholly good nor wholly bad. It draws attention to Racine's choice of plots in which the central figure *is* a wholly innocent woman or child threatened with death or an unpleasant fate. Racine respects the letter, though not the spirit, of Aristotle's precept, not by avoiding virtuous heroines altogether, but by providing the spectator with the theatrical pleasure of seeing the heroine in danger and then finally saved. Just as the melodramatic recognitions in *Bajazet* and *Athalie* are situated firmly in the visuality of the theatre, so the endings of *Mithridate* and *Iphigénie* provide theatrical satisfaction. Monime has poison dashed from her hand by order of Mithridate and her safety is finally guaranteed by Mithridate handing her over to Xipharès (*Mit.* Act V, Scenes iii–v). Clytemnestre's struggle with the soldiers is a visual substitute for her daughter's peril which is taking place off-stage, and Clytemnestre's 'peril' is abruptly terminated by the entrance of Ulysse with news of Iphigénie's deliverance (*Iph.* Act V, Scene iv).

Molière's apt phrase for comedy, 'Let us surrender in good faith to things which seize us by the entrails', can be applied to melodrama which, with its sensational and violent appeals to the emotions, also 'seizes by the entrails'.[33] Diderot, too, expressed theatrical pleasure with the image of entrails. It occurs many times in his writings on the theatre, for example: 'in an instant one's entrails are moved, one cries out, one's head swims, tears flow' (*Paradoxe sur le comédien*, p. 260). Although he is here describing the spectator's reaction to a 'tragic incident', his words suggest a melodramatic *frisson* rather than metaphysical anguish, and yet his words are consistent with Aristotelian *ekplexis*, which is a kind of panic fear, consternation, or emotional shock (Cave, pp. 44–5). Melodrama communicates with that which lies within, a communication with the immanent rather than the transcendent. Perhaps it was no accident that when writing *Athalie* for performance by children, Racine, with horror story, ghost story, and final recognition, should have played overtly with deeper means of communication than those normally used by adults contaminated with more prestigious forms of knowledge.

There was other business on the agenda. Tragedy had close links with comedy in the public theatres of Paris. The programme of entertainment was often a tragedy followed by a short farce. In 1664–5 *La Thébaïde* was followed at different performances by *Le Médecin volant*, by *Le Cocu imaginaire*, by *Gorgibus dans le sac*. In Lyons in 1672 Racinian tragedy was followed by Racinian farce when the programme advertised *Andromaque* followed by *Les Plaideurs*. The advertisement emphasized the entertainment that would be provided by this twin performance.[34] Indeed, an ignorant spectator thought the double bill of *Andromaque* and *Les Plaideurs* was all one play and complimented Racine afterwards: 'Monsieur, I am delighted with your *Andromaque*. It's a delightful play, but I'm a bit surprised that it finishes on such a happy note. At first I felt like shedding tears, but the sight of the puppies made me laugh.' Racine only

---

[33] 'Laissons-nous aller de bonne foi aux choses qui nous prennent par les entrailles'. Molière, *Critique de l'École des femmes*, Scene vi, p. 663.

[34] La Grange, *Registre* in NCR 24–9 (for *La Thébaïde*); J. Tricou, 'Une affiche théâtrale lyonnaise du xviiᵉ siècle', *Cahiers d'histoire* (1963), in NCR 68 (for *Andromaque*).

told this anecdote when he was in a good mood (Louis Racine, *Mémoires*, p. 81).

Laughter could of course erupt into the tragedy itself. In the *parterre* there were 'certain spectators who laugh at everything' (Chappuzeau, p. 146). There was merriment at Pyrrhus's inability to get Andromaque out of his mind (*And.* Act II, Scene v). Dubos said that the scene caused as much laughter as a scene from comedy (i. 125). At the first performance of *Bérénice*, the reading of Bérénice's letter to Titus gave rise to the witticism that this was 'Bérénice's last will and testament' or a 'funereal love-note'. For later performances Racine modified his text so that Titus read the letter to himself.[35] Sometimes actors have been tempted to exploit the ambivalence of the text. Jean Marchand as Acomat in *Bajazet* 'gave some of his lines a flavour of black humour which the audience did not fail to greet with discreet laughter'.[36] Some of the audience at Jonathan Miller's *Andromache* (London, 1988) saw only the funny side of Hermione's 'Who told you so? (*Qui te l'a dit?*)' (*And* V. iv. 1543) and burst into laughter.

None of this is surprising. Seventeenth-century tragedy and comedy had a symbiotic relationship and employed the same theatrical techniques. D'Aubignac's *Pratique du théâtre* is written on the assumption that comedy and tragedy have a common dramatic basis. Corneille claimed that Aristotle's *Poetics* were applicable to both genres, because 'although in treating of this matter [drama] he speaks only of tragedy, all that he says is equally applicable to comedy' (*Discours du poème dramatique*, p. 7). This common dramatic language meant that the writer of tragedy always risked causing laughter instead of tears. Racine took many risks. In his edition of Racine's theatre, Picard repeatedly draws attention to what he calls comic situations in Racinian tragedy (e.g. *Œuvres*, i. 1107 and 1108). Characters acting like puppets under the influence of obsessions they cannot control, situations involving acts and events which give the illusion of life but the feeling of mechanical contrivance— Bergson's criteria for the comic apply equally to the tragic. The blind obsessions of Oreste, Hermione, or Pyrrhus are like

---

[35] *Bér.* Act V, Scene v; Villars, p. 252; Louis Racine, *Remarques*, p. 534.
[36] Anon., '*Bajazet* à la Comédie Française', p. 139.

the *idées fixes* of an Arnolphe, an Alceste, or a Harpagon.[37]
Larthomas compares Bajazet's exit after Roxane's 'Sortez' (*Baj.*
Act V, Scene iii) to Varlin's exit in Feydeau's *La Dame de chez
Maxime* (i. 23); 'Everything seems to be different [. . .] and yet
these two theatrical moments are very close to each other' (p.
139). The theatrical resemblance between Mithridate's testing of
Monime (*Mit.* Act III, Scene v) and Harpagon's testing of
Cléante in Molière's comedy was noted by one of Racine's
contemporaries: 'The only difference between these two scenes
is that one is touching while the other excites laughter; but the
difference comes from that which distinguishes tragedy from
comedy.'[38]

But what did distinguish tragedy from comedy? It was not
moral ambiguity, errors of judgement, or recognitions which
created tragedy. These are found in comedy too. Molière stressed
the mixed character of Arnolphe, 'ridiculous in some respects
but a gentleman (*honnête homme*) in others' (*Critique de l'École des
femmes*, Scene vi, p. 666). Molière's Arnolphe and Tartuffe think
their actions will bring them success; but each commits errors
which bring them down. Each play has material recognition:
Tartuffe's arrest on the order of the king conclusively reveals
him for the imposter he is; Agnès acquires a new identity as
the daughter of Henrique and is recognized as betrothed to
Horace.[39] This common theatrical basis of tragedy and comedy
subverts any attempt to define tragedy in terms of tragic vision.
'It is not the tragic which defines tragedy but tragedy which
creates the tragic.'[40] The two genres are distinguished by the
contextualizing techniques employed. As theatrical entertainment, both genres hold up the same dramatic vision of the
world. Whether this vision qualifies as tragic or comic depends
not upon its conformity to any a priori definition of the tragic or
the comic but upon the response of the spectators. In the simplest terms 'Does the play make them laugh or weep?' There
are, of course, many other reactions: amusement, astonishment,
admiration, and so on. The response is never simple nor con-

[37] Picard, 'Racine: Comique ou tragique?', pp. 60–3, drawing on H. Bergson, *Le
Rire*, 1st edn. (Paris, 1900).
[38] Mouflette, *De la prévention de l'esprit et du cœur* (Paris, 1689), 71; *NCR* 228.
[39] *Le Tartuffe*, Act V, Scene vii; *L'École de femmes*, Act V, Scene ix.
[40] Picard, 'Racine: Comique ou tragique', p. 64.

tinuous. It varies all the time, unless it congeals into boredom. The debate about comic elements in Racine or tragic elements in Molière dissolves as their plays cross the footlights. They are at the mercy of the actors and the spectators who create the spectacle.

Of course, the challenge for the dramatist aiming to write within a particular genre was to provide the necessary context to ensure that the appropriate response was generated. To do this the dramatist had to wrestle with theatrical language until it produced the desired effect. It is a challenge because the visual component of theatrical language is never entirely neutral. Even the simple act of entering or leaving a room, even common actions like pointing or sitting down, carry connotations derived from their cultural context. Courtin's *Civilité* shows how, in the seventeenth century, behaviour at the door, entering a room, waiting in an antechamber are activities fraught with significance. The connotations of physical actions are usually ambiguous and cannot be readily classified as comic or tragic. For example, is the theatrical device of catching a kneeling man at a woman's feet tragic or comic? It certainly seems to be comic, and for a contemporary spectator it was 'an effect which has been around a long time in the most trivial farces and is too vulgar and commonplace to be tolerable even in inferior comedies'.[41] Racine obviously did not want people to laugh when he used this in *Britannicus* (Act III, Scene viii; Pl. 26) and *Esther* (Act III, Scene vi); yet there was a risk that they might do so.

The problem of appropriate contextualization was much discussed by Corneille. He starts from the principle that 'the difference between tragedy and comedy lies only in the dignity of the characters and in the actions imitated' (p. 7). By 'actions' he seems to mean both situations which provide the plot and physical actions performed on stage. Such actions or situations were problematical, because almost anything that gave theatrical pleasure was potentially undignified. Above all, love was the enemy of seriousness: 'Love is a characteristic designated for comedy because at bottom there is nothing so ridiculous as the

---

[41] Subligny, *Dissertation*, p. 412. He is criticizing the scene in Pradon's *Phèdre et Hippolyte* (1677) where Thésée catches Hippolyte kneeling to Phèdre (Act IV, Scene v).

character of a lover; this passion makes men fall into a kind of childishness.'[42] Although love was a virtually indispensable ingredient of seventeenth-century tragedy, Corneille finally sought to deny the name of *tragédie* to a play in which the love interest was predominant (*Discours du poème dramatique*, pp. 8–9). Beaumarchais took a more nuanced view and, even though writing in ebullient self-defence, gives valuable insight into the problem. Picking up the similarity of amorous intrigue in Racine's *Mithridate* and Molière's *L'Avare*, he argued that such a plot could be turned into a tragedy, a comedy, a *drame*, or an opera: 'The genre of a play, as of an action, depends less on the substance of the matter than on the character of those who are involved' (*Lettre modérée*, p. 27).

Following up the implications of Corneille's view of tragic dignity and Beaumarchais's concept of character casts light on the contextualizing process in Racinian tragedy and at the same time reveals its potential instability. Everyone agreed that dignity of character could be achieved by high social status. This status would be signalled on stage by their rich costume, but it had to be reinforced by giving them a historical or mythological identity. Hence the expositions which bristle with prestigious proper names, the most economical way of providing the appropriate contextualization. But as soon as one considers dignity in relation to situation it becomes clear how flimsy the contextualization is. In itself Oreste's projected abduction of Hermione in *Andromaque* would have all the excitement of comedy, were it not invested with the pomp and circumstance generated by the names of Menelaus and Hector, by the references to the Trojan war, and by the allusions to fate and destiny, all of which are so prominent in the exposition. Take away the high-sounding names and tragic dignity is lost. This is exactly how Boileau analysed the problem of the scene between Pyrrhus and Phoenix. According to Louis Racine, Boileau told him that he had admired this scene for a long time, but then changed his mind, 'having recognized that it did not accord with the dignity of tragedy. In fact, he told me, take away the name of Pyrrhus from this scene and stop thinking about the son of Achilles and

---

[42] *Bolaeana* (Amsterdam, 1742), 58–9 quoted in Picard, 'Racine: Comique ou tragique', p. 58.

what do you find but the depiction of foolish hesitations' (*Remarques*, p. 554). Boileau quoted a verse from Terence to show that the foolish hesitations in *Andromaque* were more appropriate to comedy.

Another way of giving dignity was through stylistic register. Spitzer in 'Racine's Classical *Piano*' has analysed a host of devices which aspire to solemnity: the distancing effects of impersonal speech, periphrasis, abstract nouns, and many others. But here too Racine took risks. The elevated register rubs shoulders with words or expressions which go as low as tragic dignity might permit: Antiochus ladder in hand, Agrippine bedded with the Emperor Claudius (*Bér.* I. iii. 110; *Bri.* IV. ii. 1137). Boursault, after the first performance of *Britannicus*, ironically excused Racine's colloquialisms: 'One can't deny that he has repeatedly used the phrases "What am I doing?", "What am I saying?" and "Be that as it may (*Quoi qu'il en soit*)", which are hardly fine poetry, but [. . .] it is a natural way of speaking into which even the most austere genius can lapse' (p. 233). Baron didn't approve of the second line of *Iphigénie*: 'Viens, reconnais la voix qui frappe ton oreille'; the inventive actor substituted his 'more poetic' version: 'Viens, et prête à ma voix ton cœur et ton oreille' (Allainval, p. 226). Pommier has warned against considering Racine's language as exclusively abstract, insisting on the many colloquial expressions and on the rich appeal to the senses in his vocabulary (pp. 241–65).

Another potential pitfall was the use of material objects. Dignity was associated with intellectual side of man not his physical behaviour. Excursions into the physical could be construed as lapses from tragic dignity. The snatching of the sword in *Phèdre*, Act II, Scene v, is one example. Subligny criticized it (*Dissertation*, p. 379). Pradon disparaged the use of the sword by Racine as being on the same low level as the royal ring in Quinault's *Astrate*.[43] Picard seems to share Pradon's view: 'as early as the seventeenth century, people criticized this artifice which, like the letter in *Bajazet*, assuredly belongs to the outmoded dramatic repertoire (*vieil arsenal dramatique*)' (*Œuvres*, i.

---

[43] *Le Triomphe de Pradon sur les satires du sieur D**** (Lyons, 1684), 84; *NCR* 166. Boileau made an oblique criticism of Quinault's use of the ring in *Astrate* (*Satire*, iii. 194–6).

1171). Racine, however, worked hard to invest visual effects with dignity and to integrate them into the thematic symbolism of his plays. Hippolyte's sword, which Phèdre snatches from him, is more than just a sword. It is the sword with which Thésée armed his son 'for a more noble use' (*Phè*. IV. i. 1010). Thésée is the successor of Hercules as a slayer of monsters, and Hippolyte is acutely conscious of his duty to emulate his father in this heroic respect (I. i. 75). So the sword which is seen on stage is intended to carry a weighty mythological charge. The same technique is at work in the poisoning of Phèdre. Although the poison is not seen on stage, like Monime's in *Mithridate*, Act V, Scene iii, its effects are visible when Phèdre appears in her death throes. The poison which she has drunk is not just any poison. It is 'a poison which Medea brought to Athens' (*Phè*. V. vii. 1638). Here again the mythological dimension is an aid to tragic dignity, since the name of Medea conjures up a prestigious myth (Branan, pp. 30–2). Another example is Mathan's potentially comic exit in *Athalie*, Act III, Scene v. Mathan tries to exit by the wrong door. Instead of leaving the temple, he makes for the inner sanctum, and has to be guided by Nabal in the right direction. Racine sought to avoid ridicule by appropriate contextualization. Mathan is a renegade priest (III. iii. 923). Perhaps he is drawn by old habits towards the holy spot, perhaps the hand of God is at work.[44] Just as Molière scandalized his contemporaries by contaminating their concepts of high comedy with farce, so Racine delighted some and scandalized others by offering the pleasures often associated with comedy under the label of tragedy. The criticisms which Racine attracted in his own time are an indication that his audacity was not always admired, nor was his every attempt at appropriate contextualization necessarily successful. But the nature of Racinian tragedy is better understood by exploring the elevated aspirations of the contextualizing process than by disparaging the visual dimension with deprecatory glosses.

It is here that parodies are helpful, for parody subverts the serious by decontextualizing it. Whilst Subligny's *La Folle Querelle* (1668) is not strictly a parody of *Andromaque*, it amusingly highlighted the ways in which Racine could be accused of

---

[44] Scherer, *Racine et/ou la cérémonie*, pp. 47–8.

failing to achieve tragic dignity. Racine's *Bérénice* was parodied in Fatouville's *Arlequin Protée* (1683). In a few lightning strokes the parody exposes the theatricality of *Bérénice*, and gives a far more accurate impression of the dramatic nature of the play than the commentaries which label it a mere elegy. Act IV, Scene v, of *Bérénice* provides most of the material which is exploited in Scene iv of the parody. Colombine/Bérénice erupts on stage, tearing herself from restraining hands. With anxious interrogations she begs Arlequin/Titus for a reply. Arlequin remains silent. The stage direction specifies 'She pulls his sleeve and tears it.' Arlequin laments 'Alas, how you tear me apart! (*Que vous me déchirez*)' using Titus's very words, which in the tragedy should be uttered with anguish after a dramatic pause. The emperor's incongruous weeping is offered as a derisive spectacle for the whole universe:

> Il faut que l'univers reconnaisse sans peine
> Les pleurs d'un empereur, et les pleurs d'une reine.
>   (*Arlequin Protée*, Scene iv, p. 142)

Fatouville's unerring eye picks out the visual effects in *Bérénice*: the significant entrance, the persuasive interrogation, the dramatic pause, and the incongruous tears, all of which are manifest in a theatrical reading of Racine's text.[45] For good measure Fatouville throws in humorous references to lovers being caught by rivals at their mistress's feet (Scene i; cf. *Bri.* Act III, Scene viii). He insists too on Bérénice's *actio*—languorous tone, sighs, weeping, and shouting (pp. 140, 144). Perhaps this is parody of La Champmeslé's actual performance.

Parody subverts the dignity which Corneille described as indispensable to tragedy. Coarse gestures and ribald remarks dislocate the pretensions of the tragic universe, especially when Fatouville proffers his notorious rhyme. 'Que fait la reine Bérénice?' asks Arlequin/Titus: 'Elle est là-haut qui pisse', replies Scaramouche/Paulin (Scene iii, p. 141). This rhyme particularly upset Racine, when he watched a performance of the parody. 'He seemed to laugh like everyone else, but he admitted to his friends that he was only laughing on the surface. [. . .] At such moments he felt disillusioned with his career as a poet' (Louis

---

[45] *Bér.* IV. v. 1041 (entrance), 1153 (*déchirez*), 1154 (*vous pleurez*).

Racine, *Mémoires*, p. 52). The parody ends with anagnorisis. A second-hand clothes dealer recognizes Arlequin playing the role of the emperor and strips him of his jerkin to pay his debts. The high-class packaging of tragedy is torn away and its scandalous content exposed.

In the parody the actors do not identify with the characters they represent, they emphasize detachment and even incompatibility.[46] Colombine explains:

> Pour moi, je vais jouer en style magnifique
> Avec mon cher Titus un sérieux comique [. . .]
> Tantôt devant Titus il faut que je soupire,
> Mais quoi? mon sérieux fera mourir de rire.

> (*Arlequin Protée*, Scene ii, p. 140)

Tragedy depends upon the emotional involvement of the spectator, whilst comedy excludes such a sympathetic response: 'Life is a comedy to those that think, a tragedy to those that feel' as Horace Walpole put it.

Racine's own parodic skills are evident in one of his most successful plays. A measure of the centrality of *Les Plaideurs* in Racine's dramatic output is its statistical popularity at the Comédie-Française, where, during the seventeenth, eighteenth, and nineteenth centuries, it was by far the most frequently performed of all Racine's plays. In the twentieth century *Phèdre* alone caught up and by 1964 had outstripped it—by one performance: *Phèdre* 1350 performances, *Les Plaideurs* 1349 (Abraham, p. 8). Some of the entertainment in *Les Plaideurs* derives from Racine's parody of *Le Cid*, the most celebrated tragedy of his rival Corneille: there is verbal parody when a couple of lines are put to comic use, and visual parody when Racine transposes the sword, symbol of Don Diègue's life, into a bag of lawyer's briefs, symbol of Dandin's life.[47] But Racine's *Les Plaideurs* does not just poke fun at his rival. Retrospectively we can read it as a comic commentary on the theatrical language

---

[46] See Picard, 'Racine: Comique ou tragique', pp. 64–6, on this point in relation to Fatouville's parody. Michaut is indulgent enough to print the 'clean' parody, *Tite et Titus* (1673), but he draws the line at *Arlequin Protée*, consigning it to metaphorical death: 'The absolute nullity of this play decided me to leave it buried where it was' (p. 354).

[47] See Picard's comments in *Œuvres*, i. 1114–15.

of his own tragedies. The whole range of his theatrical techniques appear in humorous form in *Les Plaideurs*. The décor,
with the doors of Dandin and Chicanneau, is seen again in the
doors of *Britannicus* and *Bérénice*. The comedy starts with Petit
Jean's sleepy and rambling narration, a comic reversal of the
animated and cogent *récits* of the tragedies (Ekstein, p. 123).
Petit Jean's bizarre behaviour at the crack of dawn prefigures
Agrippine's matutinal vigil with which *Britannicus* opens. When
Petit Jean laments the fatal day when Dandin engaged him (I. i.
3) and the irreversible decapitation of the cock for the crime of
oversleeping (I. i. 35), he employs the past historic tense, which
evokes the dead past in the tragedies. Ratermanis comments on
the use of this tense by Petit Jean: 'It is hardly necessary to point
out that here we have a sort of parody where the tragic falls to
the level of the trivial' (p. 408). The parodic links are much
more obvious in the visual effects. Arrests and other forms of
bodily contact are supposed to be a serious matter in the
tragedies but are recast in comic vein in *Les Plaideurs*. The
persuasive skills of the orator are mocked through the conventional and incongruous *actio* of L'Intimé and Petit Jean in the
trial of the dog. The device of the incriminating letter of
Léandre to Isabelle (Act II, Scene iii) reappears in *Bajazet* and
Iphigénie. Dandin's sinister comment about enjoying the spectacle of suffering raises the central issue of tragedy in comic
context. Two key words of tragic drama—tears and compassion—are transposed into comic register when the puppies
urinate and their mishap is turned to advantage by the defence
counsel who, seeking to avert the danger to the accused, puts
into their mouth the plea: 'Sir, see our tears' (III. iii. 826; Pl. 7).
The judge confesses to being moved to compassion. Fear and
Pity descend from tragic heights to the lower bodily functions.
This joke of Racine's aptly illustrates the maxim, 'Humour is
about real behaviour—tragedy with its trousers down.'

Seeing the tragedy is no simple affair. Certainly Racine highlighted by visual means some of the conventional mechanisms
of tragedy, and by following these visual clues one can gain a
clearer understanding of these mechanisms. But this theatrical
underpinning reminds us that the theatre has a life of its own,
which fights hard against the straightjacket of literary categories.

That Racine had a real talent for visual comedy is obvious from *Les Plaideurs*, and he did not hesitate to exploit strongly visual situations in his tragedies as well. He devoted all his theatrical talent to making his tragedies dramatic and to getting his drama accepted as tragedy. Moreover, he raised the stakes considerably by introducing a transcendent element. Whilst his immediate predecessors were contracting the frontiers of tragedy, Racine was extending them. Such theatrical brinkmanship called forth warnings. Pradon, admittedly a jealous rival, suggested with regard to Racine's *Phèdre* that 'the finest and most serious passages are sometimes susceptible of the greatest comic effect'.[48] The higher the pinnacle the more precarious the foothold. Yet the very laughter which turns the sublime into the ridiculous is instructive. It is a reminder that the sublime and the grotesque do coexist in Racinian tragedy, in spite of Victor Hugo's clever manipulation of half-truths to misrepresent French classical tragedy as wholly based on verbal narrations and devoid of visual effects (*Preface de Cromwell*, p. 233). Hugo's blueprint for a new type of theatre was a combination of the physical and the spiritual: 'The body must play its part like the soul [. . .] In his triumphal chariot Caesar will be anxious not to overturn' (p. 227). But Racine had trodden the path evoked by this image. His situations balance on the knife-edge between elevated aspirations and bodily weakness. Bérénice's solicitude for Titus was a theatrical gamble: 'You are emperor, my lord, and yet you weep' (*Bér.* IV. v. 1154). This worked for some of Racine's spectators but not for others: 'This always makes the spectator laugh and always will', claimed Villars (p. 257); 'This line has such power to excite pity', claimed Racine's defender (Saint-Ussans, p. 289). This is valuable contemporary evidence that the duality located in Racine's text inspired contradictory responses in his audience. Because tragedy on stage has to obey theatrical imperatives, it is inevitably an impure genre. In Racine's case sadism and sexuality, mystery, suspense, and surprise go hand in hand with the transcendent and the sublime. This has been held up as a matter for regret: 'Racine is undoubtedly a very impure author, baroque one might say, in

---

[48] (Pradon), *Nouvelles remarques sur tous les ouvrages du Sieur* *** (The Hague, 1685), 77; *NCR* 183.

whom elements of true tragedy are mixed discordantly with the seeds of the bourgeois theatre of the future' (Barthes, p. 143). Such a mixture may indeed frustrate the desire for metaphysical consistency, but this is to be applauded rather than deplored. It is the calculated discords that are characteristic of Racine's theatre: they create tension and attention. Pure tragedy is a solitary and intellectual pursuit, whilst the communal and the physical are the essential conditions of the theatre. Racine triumphantly embraced theatricality at the expense of tragic purity.

Conclusion

Diderot startled fellow theatre-goers by blocking his ears at a performance to see if he could follow the action simply by watching the actors (*Lettre sur les sourds et muets*, pp. 52–3). How would Racine stand such a test? The traditional answer is that all would be lost if the words could not be heard: 'Language reigns supreme in Racine [. . .] Language is everything' (Mourgues, p. 139). But at the start of *Phèdre*, provided Racine's stage directions were followed, the deaf spectator would see Théramène trying to restrain a restive Hippolyte; then, in successive scenes, Phèdre in a state of collapse, Hippolyte awkwardly offering his love to Aricie, Hippolyte fidgeting to be away from Phèdre, Phèdre lustfully gazing upon Hippolyte then suddenly snatching his sword from him. Almost every scene in the play can be characterized by some visual effect. Of course, the spectator with blocked ears would not hear the guilty secrets which are communicated by one character to another nor the dynamic arguments in scenes of persuasion, accusation, or defence. Racine's poetry would pulsate unheard. However, Racine's linguistic virtuosity should not blind the reader to his theatrical expertise. His theatrical language is active on both the visual and the verbal fronts. This can be seen when Racine is stripped of his theatricality.

Handel's oratorio *Athalia* (1733) is closely based upon Racine's *Athalie* (1691). If language were everything, little would be lost in transforming the tragedy into an oratorio. In fact, a comparison between the two shows how much was sacrificed by the librettist, sometimes in order to be more faithful to the Bible, which Racine embellished for theatrical effect. In Racine's version Athalie's dream is narrated in response to urgent attempts to make her leave the temple where she has planted herself in a chair. The librettist discards the physical setting and Athalia simply recounts her dream to Mathan after awakening from sleep. Racine's vivid picture of the young Joas leaping into the high priest's arms followed by the child's astonishment at seeing the high priest prostrate himself upon the ground under-

1. Spectators on stage
(see pp. 9, 37, 51)

2. The *parterre*
(see p. 10)

3. Good seats at the Palais Cardinal
(see pp. 11, 37)

4. Fear and Pity
(see pp. 81, 196, 211, 222)

5. A wounded king, *Ale.* V, iii
(see pp. 49, 211, 222)

6. Kneeling, *And.* III, vi
(see pp. 71, 175, 222)

7. Costume, urine, and tears,
Pla. III, iii (see pp. 53, 84, 241)

8. Death by poison, *Bri.* V, v
(see p. 222)

9. Painful parting, *Bér.* V, vii
(see pp. 213, 222)

10. Fainting, *Baj.* IV, iii
(see pp. 53, 72, 222)

11. The last embrace, *Mit.* V, v
(see pp. 49, 77, 222)

12. Death by laceration, *Phè.* V, vi
(see p. 223)

13. Significant entrance, *Est.* II, vii
(see pp. 33, 47, 52, 73)

14. Recognition, *Ath.* V, v
(see pp. 35, 69, 90, 196)

15. Fear
(see pp. 115, 196)

16. Horror
(see pp. 115, 224)

17. Desire
(see pp. 115, 224)

18. Static focus, *Bri.* V, vi
(see p. 163)

19. Snatching the sword, *Phè.* II, v
(see p. 76)

20. Love and the monster
(see p. 228)

21. Hero without sword, *Phè*. II, v
(see pp. 76, 228)

22. Hero with spear, *Phè*. V, vi
(see p. 228)

23. The monster vanquished
(see p. 228)

24. Significant entrance, *Thé.* I, iii
(see pp. 46, 53, 73)

25. Restraining, *Thé.* V, vi
(see p. 75)

26. Caught in the act, *Bri.* III, viii
(see p. 235)

27. Focus on leaving, *Mit.,* III, v
(see pp. 160, 167)

28. Headband and poison, *Mit.* V, ii
(see p. 86)

29. Bodily contact, *Phè.* II, v
(see p. 76)

30. Interrogation, *Ath.* II, vii
(see pp. 69, 162)

31. Book, sword, and diadem, *Ath.* IV, iii
(see p. 87)

goes similar dilution. The librettist omits the child's embrace and attenuates the high priest's prostration into a sedate genuflection: 'Oh, Joas! Oh, my king! thus low to thee, I pay my homage on my bended knee' (Act III, Scene i). Racine's theatrical hiding of Joas behind a curtain and then revealing him to Athalie is transformed into Joad's pale command: 'Ye priests, the youth before her bring! Proud woman, there behold our king!' And when Racine's Abner kneels to Joas to signify his transfer of allegiance from Athalie to the new king, the librettist omits the eloquent gesture and expands Abner's single spoken line in Racine into a vindictive tirade against his former sovereign. All this provides Handel with an opportunity for musical delight, but the comparison highlights Racine's uncompromising theatricality.

The main argument of this study has been that Racine's theatrical language has a more important visual component than is usually conceded. A considerable body of evidence has been offered to support this view. The décor of Racine's plays varies considerably from one play to the next. Each set represents a single precise place which is important to the action of the play. Often an element of the scenery will be highlighted by references to it in the dialogue between the characters. Within this setting characters are constantly coming and going. Racine invests their entrances and exits with meaning, showing great versatility in handling these key articulations. Physical actions such as sitting, kneeling, or embracing recur from play to play, attracting attention by their relative rarity and acquiring significance from differing contexts. The same is true of costume and stage properties. Visually, Racine achieves maximum effect with minimum means. He exploits visual language throughout his career. It is not confined to *Esther* and *Athalie*.

It has also been argued that Racine's words have theatrical power. Racine creates verbal action by endowing his characters with all the skills of the orator in the construction of a speech, in the display of passion, in the use of facial expression, gesture, and tone of voice. Racine contrives scenes in which persuasive powers are brought into conflict and in which utterances can have momentous consequences. So, even when language predominates, Racine is theatrical because the words are both active and acted. The many-faceted relationship between action and speech can also be seen in the way Racine's text not only gives guidance for the actor's delivery but also for the listener's performance. This interaction between speaker and listener has a particular impact when persuasion and interrogation are combined. Also characteristic of Racine's theatrical language is the technique of visual focus when speech focuses on action, or action gives shape to speech. Yet Racine the director is not busy all the time planting stage directions in his written text. Speech and action usually perform jointly in Racinian drama, but sometimes one will step back and the other take the limelight.

Some elements of the tragic action such as moral ambiguity and *hamartia* are highlighted in visual terms. Racine contrives that the spectators actually see characters committing errors of judgement. He thus satisfies the normative requirements of his chosen genre. The persuasive power of his prefaces causes his drama to be explored primarily as tragedy. This is a legitimate concern, but it can obscure precisely those dramatic and theatrical qualities which link Racine with men of the theatre before and after him. Racine's theatrical language is too powerful to be constrained within the narrow bounds of genre definition. There was an alternative agenda subverting the decorous precepts of Aristotle. Racine wrote subtle and magnificent poetry, but he did not shrink from exploiting erotic cruelty and the spectacle of suffering in theatrical situations often associated with melodrama or comedy. Once the straightjacket of tragedy is loosened, Racine's theatrical language is unleashed.

Bibliography

This bibliography contains only those works which are actually referred to in the text.

ABRAHAM, PIERRE, 'Racine à la scène', *Europe*, 45/453 (1967), 3–9.

Album théâtre classique: La Vie théâtrale sous Louis XIII et Louis XIV, ed. S. Chevalley (Paris, 1970).

ALLAINVAL, LÉONOR-CHRISTOPHE DE SOULAS, ABBÉ D' (George Wink), *Lettre à Mylord ★ ★ ★ sur Baron et la Demoiselle Lecouvreur*, in *Mémoires de Molière* (Paris, 1822), 215–44.

ANAXIMENES, *see* Aristotle.

ANON., '*Bajazet* à la Comédie Française', *Cahiers raciniens*, 3 (1958), 139–40.

—— *Lettre sur les remarques qu'on a faites sur la 'Sophonisbe' de Monsieur Corneille* (1663), in Granet, *Recueil*, i.

—— *Tite et Titus ou les Bérénices* (1673), in Michaut, *Bérénice*.

ARAGON, C., 'Étude de quelques actes de langage dans *Bajazet*', *Cahiers de littérature du XVIIᵉ siècle*, 5 (1983), 75–106.

ARISTOTLE, *The Poetics*, ed. W. Hamilton Fyfe (London, 1927; Loeb edn.).

—— *The Works of Aristotle*, ed. J. Smith and W. Ross, 12 vols. (Oxford, 1908–52: xi contains Anaximenes' *Rhetorica ad Alexandrum*).

—— *The Art of Rhetoric*, ed. J. Freese (London, 1926; Loeb edn.).

AUBIGNAC, FRANÇOIS HÉDELIN, ABBÉ D', *La Pratique du théâtre*, ed. H.-J. Neuschafer (Geneva, 1971: facsimile of the 1715 Amsterdam edn.).

—— *Dissertations* on Corneille's *Sophonisbe, Sertorius* (i), and *Œdipe* (ii). Texts in Granet, *Recueil*.

—— *Projet pour le rétablissement du théâtre français*, in *La Pratique du théâtre*, ed. H.-J. Neuschafer.

BACKÈS, JEAN-LOUIS, *Racine* (Paris, 1981).

BARKO, IVAN, 'La Symbolique de Racine: Essai d'interprétation des images de lumière et de ténèbres dans la vision tragique de Racine', *Revue des sciences humaines*, 115 (1964), 353–77.

BARLOW, GRAHAM, 'The Hôtel de Bourgogne according to Sir James Thornhill', *Theatre Research International*, 1/2 (1976), 86–98.

BARNETT, DENE, 'The Performance Practice of Acting: The Eighteenth Century, Part I. Ensemble Acting', *Theatre Research International*, 2/3 (1977), 157–86; 'Part II. The Hand', 3/1 (1977), 1–19; 'Part III. The

Arms', 3/2 (1978), 79–93; 'Part IV. The Eyes, the Face and the Head', 5/1 (1979/80), 1–36; 'Part V. Postures and Attitudes', 6/1 (1980/1), 1–32.

BARNETT, RICHARD L., 'The Non-Ocularity of Racine's "Vision"', *Orbis Litterarum*, 35 (1980), 115–31.

BARNWELL, HARRY T., *The Tragic Drama of Corneille and Racine: An Old Parallel Revisited* (Oxford, 1982).

—— '"They Have Their Exits and Their Entrances": Stage and Speech in Corneille's Drama', *Modern Language Review*, 81 (1986), 51–63.

BARRAULT, JEAN-LOUIS, see Racine, *Phèdre*.

BARTHES, ROLAND, *Sur Racine* (Paris, 1960).

BEAUMARCHAIS, PIERRE-AUGUSTIN CARON DE, *Lettre modérée sur la chute et la critique du 'Barbier de Séville'* (1775), in *Théâtre*, ed. J.-P. de Beaumarchais (Paris, 1980).

BERNARD, MICHEL, 'Esquisse d'une théorie de la théâtralité d'un texte en vers à partir de l'exemple racinien', in *Mélanges pour Jacques Scherer: Dramaturgies, langages dramatiques* (Paris, 1986), 279–86.

BIBLE, *La Sainte Bible*, tr. by Samuel Le Maistre de Saci (Paris, 1714).

BLANC, A., 'L'Action à la Comédie Française au XVIIIᵉ siècle', *Dix-septième siècle*, 132 (1981), 319–327.

BOILEAU-DESPRÉAUX, NICOLAS, *Œuvres*, 2 vols. (Amsterdam, 1718).

BOURSAULT, EDMÉ, *Artémise et Poliante: Nouvelle* (1670), in Racine, *Œuvres*, ed. P. Mesnard (Paris, 1866), ii. 229–39.

BOYER, CLAUDE, *Porus* (Paris, 1648).

BRANAN, A. G., '*Dramatis Res* and *Couleur Mythologique* in Racine's *Phèdre*', *Romance Notes*, 23 (1982), 29–33.

BRAY, RENÉ, *Molière, homme de théâtre* (Paris, 1954).

BRODY, JULES, '*Bajazet*, or the Tragedy of Roxane', *The Romanic Review*, 60 (1969), 273–90.

BROSSETTE, CLAUDE, *Mémoires sur Boileau*, in *Correspondance entre Boileau-Despréaux et Brossette*, ed. A. Laverdet (Paris, 1858).

BUTLER, PHILIP F. *Classicisme et baroque dans l'œuvre de Racine* (Paris, 1959).

CAMUS, ALBERT, 'Conférence prononcée à Athènes sur l'avenir de la tragédie', in J. Grenier and R. Quilliot (eds.), *Théâtre, récits, nouvelles* (Pléiade; Paris, 1963).

CAPATTI, ALBERTO, *Teatro e 'imaginaire': Pubblico e attori in Racine* (Rome, 1975).

CAVE, TERENCE, *Recognitions: A Study in Poetics* (Oxford, 1988).

CHANCEREL, LÉON, 'De quelques interprètes de *Bérénice*', *Cahiers de la compagnie Madeleine Renaud Jean-Louis Barrault*, 8 (1955), 17–22.

CHAPPUZEAU, SAMUEL, *Le Théâtre français*, ed. G. Monval (Paris, 1876).

CHEVALLEY, SYLVIE, 'Les deux Bérénice', *Revue d'histoire du théâtre*, 22 (1970), 91–124.

CLAIRON, HIPPOLYTE, *Mémoires et réflexions sur l'art dramatique* (Paris, An VII).

CONNON, DEREK, 'Diderot and Racine', in A. Howe and R. Waller (eds.), *En marge du classicisme: Essays on the French Theatre from the Renaissance to the Enlightenment* (Liverpool, 1987), 243–62.

CORNEILLE, PIERRE, *Œuvres complètes*, ed. G. Couton, 3 vols. (Pléiade; Paris, 1980–7).

——*Discours de l'utilité et des parties du poème dramatique, Discours de la tragédie, Discours des trois unités,* and *Examens,* in P. Corneille, *Writings on the Theatre,* ed. H. T. Barnwell (Oxford, 1965). This edn. is cited for Corneille's theoretical writings.

CORNEILLE, THOMAS, *Théâtre complet,* ed. E. Thierry (Paris, 1881).

COURTIN, ANTOINE DE, *Nouveau traité de la civilité qui se pratique en France parmi les honnêtes gens* (Paris, 1677).

COURVILLE, XAVIER DE, *see* Racine, *Bajazet.*

DESCOTES, MAURICE, *Les Grands Rôles du théâtre de Jean Racine* (Paris, 1957).

——'Le Dosage du tragique dans les dénouements de Racine', *Revue d'histoire du théâtre,* 25 (1973), 229–38.

DESMARESTS DE SAINT-SORLIN, JEAN, *Clovis ou la France chrétienne, poème héroïque* (Paris, 1657).

DIDEROT, DENIS, *Lettre sur les sourds et les muets,* ed. P. H. Meyer, in *Diderot Studies,* 7 (1965), 37–121.

——*Paradoxe sur le comédien, De la poésie dramatique,* in *Writing on the Theatre,* ed. F. C. Green (Cambridge, 1936).

DONNEAU DE VISÉ, JEAN, *Critique de la 'Sophonisbe'* (1663) in Granet, *Recueil,* i (first publ. in *Nouvelles nouvelles,* part iii).

——*La Défense de la 'Sophonisbe' de Monsieur Corneille* (1663), in Granet, *Recueil,* i.

DU RYER, PIERRE, *Esther,* ed. P. Gethner and E. J. Campion (Exeter, 1982).

DUBECH, LUCIEN, *Jean Racine politique* (Paris, 1926).

DUBOS, JEAN-BAPTISTE, ABBÉ, *Réflexions critiques sur la poésie et la peinture,* 2 vols. (Paris, 1719).

DUSSANE, BEATRICE, 'Du Nouveau sur Racine', *Le Divan,* 238 (1941), 49–63.

EDMUNDS, JOHN, 'Rehearsing *Phèdre:* Act I, scene 1', *Romance Studies,* 4 (1984), 44–50.

EDWARDS, MICHAEL, 'Créon: Homme de théâtre', *Jeunesse de Racine* (1963), 67–81.

EKSTEIN, NINA, *Dramatic Narrative: Racine's 'Récits'* (New York, 1986).

ELAM, KEIR, *The Semiotics of Theatre and Drama* (London, 1980).

ELISABETH-CHARLOTTE, DUCHESS OF ORLÉANS (Princess Palatine), *Correspondance,* ed. E. Jaeglé, 2nd edn., 3 vols. (Paris, 1890).

EMELINA, JEAN, 'Les Morts dans les tragédies de Racine', in *Mélanges pour Jacques Scherer: Dramaturgies, langages dramatiques* (Paris, 1986), 173–84.

ESSLIN, MARTIN, *The Field of Drama: How the Signs of Drama Create Meaning on Stage and Screen* (London, 1987).

EURIPIDES, *Works*, ed. A. S. Way, 4 vols. (Loeb edn.; London, 1912).

FATOUVILLE, ANNE MAUDUIT, SIEUR DE, *Arlequin Protée: Parodie de Bérénice* (1683), in Gherardi, *Théâtre italien* (Paris, 1695).

FELMAN, SHOSHANA, *Le Scandale du corps parlant* (Austin, Tex., 1980).

FLAUBERT, GUSTAVE, *Le Théâtre de Voltaire*, ed. T. Besterman, 2 vols. (Geneva, 1967).

FLOWERS, MARY LYNNE, *Sentence Structure and Characterization in the Tragedies of Jean Racine* (Rutherford, NJ, 1979).

FORMAN, EDWARD, 'Lyrisme et tragique dans l'*Athalie* de Racine', in *Mélanges pour Jacques Scherer: Dramaturgies, langages dramatiques* (Paris, 1986), 307–14.

FOURNIER, NATHALIE, 'L'Aparté dans la tragédie racinienne', in *Mélanges de langue et de littérature française offerts à Pierre Larthomas* (Paris, 1985), 175–94.

FRANCE, PETER, *Racine's Rhetoric* (Oxford, 1965).

—— and MCGOWAN, MARGARET, 'Autour du *Traité du récitatif* de Grimarest', *Dix-septième siècle*, 132 (1981), 303–17.

FUMAROLI, MARC, 'Rhétorique et dramaturgie: Le Statut du personnage dans la tragédie classique', *Revue d'histoire du théâtre*, 24 (1972), 223–50.

FURETIÈRE, ANTOINE, *Dictionnaire universel*, 3 vols. (The Hague, 1690).

GARAUD, CHRISTIAN, 'La Déclaration d'amour au 17ᵉ siècle: Remarques sur la rhétorique galante dans *L'Histoire amoureuse des Gaules*', *Degré second*, 1 (1977), 13–35.

GETHNER, PERRY J., 'The Staging of Prayer in French Theatre of the Seventeenth Century', *Papers in French Seventeenth-Century Literature*, 9/16 (1982), 21–36.

GHERARDI, ÉVARISTE, *Le Théâtre italien ou recueil de toutes les comédies et scènes françaises qui ont été jouées sur l'Hôtel de Bourgogne*, 3rd edn. (Paris, 1695).

GOLDMANN, LUCIEN, *Le Dieu caché: Étude sur la vision tragique dans les 'Pensées' de Pascal et dans le théâtre de Racine* (Paris, 1959).

GOODDEN, ANGELICA, *'Actio' and Persuasion: Dramatic Performance in Eighteenth-Century France* (Oxford, 1986).

GOSSIP, CHRISTOPHER J., *An Introduction to French Classical Tragedy* (London, 1981).

GOUHIER, HENRI, *Le Théâtre et l'existence* (Paris, 1952).

GRANET, F., *Recueil de Dissertations sur plusieurs tragédies de Corneille et de Racine*, 2 vols. (Paris, 1739).

GREAR, ALLISON, 'Rhetoric and the Art of the French Tragic Actor 1620–1750: The Place of 'Pronuntiatio' in the Stage Tradition' (Ph.D. thesis, Univ. of St Andrews, 1982).

GRIMAREST, JEAN-LOUIS LE GALLOIS, SIEUR DE, *Traité du récitatif* (Rotterdam, 1740; 1st edn. 1707).

——*La Vie de M. de Molière*, ed. G. Mongrédien ([Paris], 1955: contains *Addition à la vie de Monsieur de Molière, contenant une réponse à la critique que l'on en a faite*).

GUIBERT, NOËLLE, 'L'Iconographie de Racine à la bibliothèque de l'Arsenal', *Cahiers raciniens*, 27 (1970), 9–151.

HAFFTER, PIERRE. 'Le Narrateur chez Racine', in J. Robertson (ed.), *Mélanges de littérature française offerts à M. Shackleton et C. J. Greshof* (Cape Town, 1985), 13–25.

HAWCROFT, MICHAEL, 'Verbal Action and Rhetoric in the Tragedies of Jean Racine' (D.Phil. thesis, Univ. of Oxford, 1988).

——'Racine, Rhetoric and the Death *Récit*', *Modern Language Review*, 84 (1989), 26–36.

HERZEL, ROGER, 'The Décor of Molière's Stage: The Testimony of Brissart and Chauveau', *Publications of the Modern Language Association of America*, 93 (1978), 925–54.

HEUZEY, JACQUES, 'Du costume et de la décoration tragique au XVIIᵉ siècle: À propos d'une gravure du XVIIᵉ représentant une scène de la tragédie de *Cinna*', *Revue d'histoire du théâtre*, 12 (1960), 20–33.

HOURCADE, PHILIPPE, 'Racine et le goût du spectacle dans *Bérénice* et *Bajazet*', *Jeunesse de Racine* (1968) 66–82.

HOWARTH, WILLIAM D., *Molière: A Playwright and His Audience* (Cambridge, 1982).

——'L'Alexandrin classique comme instrument du dialogue théâtral', in *Mélanges pour Jacques Scherer: Dramaturgies, langages dramatiques* (Paris, 1986), 341–54.

——'Some Thoughts on the Function of Rhyme in French Classical Tragedy', in P. Bayley and D. Coleman (eds.), *The Equilibrium of Wit: Essays for Odette de Mourgues* (Lexington, Ky., 1982), 150–65.

HUBERT, JUDD, 'Les Ecarts de Trézène', in R. L. Barnett (ed.), *Relectures raciniennes* (Paris, 1986), 81–97.

HUGO, VICTOR, *La Préface de Cromwell*, ed. M. Souriau (Paris, n.d.).

ISSACHAROFF, MICHAEL, *Le Spectacle du discours* (Paris, 1985).

KIBÉDI-VARGA, ARON, 'Analyse d'une tragédie', *Het franse boek*, 40 (1970), 55–63 (on Corneille's *Sertorius*).

KNIGHT, ROY C., *Racine et la Grèce* (Paris, 1951).

——'Sophocle et Euripide ont-ils "formé" Racine?' *French Studies*, 5 (1951), 126–39.

——'A Minimal Definition of Seventeenth-Century Tragedy', *French Studies*, 10 (1956), 297–308.

KOWZAN, TADEUSZ, *Littérature et spectacle* (The Hague, 1975).

LA ROCHEFOUCAULD, FRANÇOIS, DUC DE, *Maximes*, ed. J. Truchet (Paris, 1967).

LANCASTER, HENRY CARRINGTON, *A History of French Dramatic Literature in the Seventeeth Century*, 9 vols. (Baltimore, 1929–42).

LAPP, JOHN C., *Aspects of Racinian Tragedy* (Toronto, 1955).

LARTHOMAS, PIERRE, *Le Langage dramatique: Sa nature, ses procédés* (Paris, 1972).

LAURENT, MICHEL, see *Mémoire de Mahelot*.

LAWRENSON, THOMAS E., *The French Stage and Playhouse in the XVIIth Century: A Study in the Advent of the Italian Order*, 2nd edn. (New York, 1987).

LE BIDOIS, GEORGES, *De l'action dans la tragédie de Racine* (Paris, 1900: the 2nd and subsequent edns. are entitled *La Vie dans la tragédie de Racine* with same pagination).

LE BOULANGER DE CHALUSSAY, *Elomire hypocondre* in Molière, *Œuvres complètes*, ed. G. Couton, ii.

LE BRUN, CHARLES, *Méthode pour apprendre à dessiner les passions* (Amsterdam, 1702).

LE CLERC, MICHEL, *Iphigénie* (Paris, 1676).

LE COAT, GÉRARD, 'Mimique de l'acteur et du musicien: Réflexion sur la théorie classique de l'expression corporelle en France', *Papers in French Seventeenth-Century Literature*, 9/16 (1982), 179–211.

[LE FAUCHEUR, MICHEL], *Traité de l'action de l'orateur ou de la prononciation et du geste* (Paris, 1676: 1st edn. 1657; sometimes attributed to Valentin Conrart).

LE ROY, GEORGES, see Jean Racine, *Athalie*.

LOUGH, JOHN, *Seventeenth-Century French Drama: The Background* (Oxford, 1979).

LYONNET, HENRY, *Les 'Premières' de Jean Racine* (Paris, 1924).

MABER, RICHARD G., 'Monsters in Seventeenth-Century French Epic Poetry', *Durham French Colloquies*, 1 (1987), 43–58.

McAULEY, GAY, 'The Spatial Dynamics of *Britannicus*: Text and Performance', *Australian Journal of French Studies*, 20 (1983), 340–60.

McGOWAN, MARGARET, 'Racine, Menestrier and Sublime Effects', *Theatre Research International*, 1/2 (1975), 1–13.

—— 'Racine's "lieu théâtral"', in W. D. Howarth, Ian McFarlane, and M. McGowan (eds.), *Form and Meaning: Aesthetic Coherence in Seventeenth-Century French Drama: Studies Presented to Harry Barnwell* (Avebury, 1982), 166–86.

MAGENDIE, MAURICE, *La Politesse mondaine et les théories de l'honnêteté en France au XVIIᵉ siècle de 1600 à 1660*, 2 vols. (Paris, 1925).

MAHELOT, see *Mémoire de Mahelot*.

MARMONTEL, JEAN-FRANÇOIS, *Éléments de littérature*, 3 vols. (Paris, 1879).

MASKELL, DAVID, 'La Précision du lieu dans les tragédies de Racine', in *Actes du troisième Colloque Vinaver, Manchester 1987*, ed. C. M. Hill (Vinaver Studies in French 5), Manchester, 1991, pp. 151–71.

Mémoire (Le) de Mahelot, Laurent et d'autres décorateurs de l'Hôtel de Bourgogne et de la Comédie Française au XVIIe siècle, ed. H. C. Lancaster (Paris, 1920).

MICHAUT, GUSTAVE, *La 'Bérénice' de Racine* (Paris, 1907).

MITTMAN, BARBARA G., *Spectators on the Paris Stage in the Seventeenth and Eighteenth Centuries* (Ann Arbor, Mich., 1984).

MOLIÈRE, *Œuvres complètes*, ed. G. Couton, 2 vols. (Pléiade; Paris, 1971).

MORAVCEVICH, JUNE, 'Racine and Rotrou', *French Review: Special Issue*, 45 (1972), 49–60.

MOREL, JACQUES, *Jean Rotrou: Dramaturge de l'ambiguïté* (Paris, 1968).

Morgan (Lady) in France, ed. P. J. Yarrow and E. Suddaby (Newcastle upon Tyne, 1971: extracts from Lady Morgan, *France* and *France in 1829–30*).

MOUREAU, FRANÇOIS, 'Du côté cour: La Princesse Palatine et le théâtre', *Revue d'histoire du théâtre*, 35 (1983), 275–86.

MOURGUES, ODETTE DE, *Racine or the Triumph of Relevance* (Cambridge, 1967).

MURATORE, M. J., 'Racinian Stasis', in R. L. Barnett (ed.), *Re-lectures raciniennes* (Paris, 1986), 113–25.

MURRAY, TIMOTHY, 'Non-Representation in *La Pratique du théâtre*', *Papers in French Seventeenth-Century Literature*, 9 (1982), 57–74.

NIDERST, ALAIN, *Les Tragédies de Racine: Diversité et unité* (Paris, 1975).

OSBORNE, CAROL MARGOT, 'Pierre Didot the Elder and French Book Illustration 1789–1822' (Stanford Univ. thesis, University Microfilms, 1984).

PARISH, RICHARD, '"Un calme si funeste": Some Types of Silence in Racine', *French Studies*, 34 (1980), 385–400.

PFOHL, RUSSELL, *Racine's 'Iphigénie': Literary Rehearsal and Tragic Recognition* (Geneva, 1974).

PHILLIPS, HENRY, *The Theatre and its Critics in Seventeenth-Century France* (Oxford, 1980).

——'The Theatricality of Discourse in Racinian Tragedy', *Modern Language Review*, 84 (1989), 37–50.

PICARD, RAYMOND, 'Racine and Chauveau', *Journal of the Warburg and Courtauld Institutes*, 14 (1951), 259–74.

——*La Carrière de Jean Racine* (Paris 1956).

PICARD, RAYMOND, *Nouveau corpus racinianum: Recueil-inventaire des textes et documents du XVIIe siècle concernant Jean Racine* (Paris, 1976).
——'Les Tragédies de Racine: Comique ou Tragique?' in R. Picard, *De Racine au Parthénon* (Paris, 1977), 57–70 (1st publ. in *Revue d'histoire littéraire de la France*, 1969).
——see also Jean Racine, *Œuvres complètes*.
POISSON, RAYMOND, *Le Poète Basque* (1669), in *Aspects de théâtre dans le théâtre au XVIIe siècle: Recueil de pièces*, ed. G. Forestier (Toulouse, 1986).
POMMIER, JEAN, *Aspects de Racine* (Paris, 1954).
POWELL, JOCELYN, 'Making Faces: Character and Physiognomy in *L'École des femmes* and *L'Avare*', *Seventeenth-Century French Studies*, 9 (1987), 94–112.
PROPHÈTE, JEAN. *Les Para-personnages dans les tragédies de Racine* (Paris, 1981).
QUINAULT, PHILIPPE, *Stratonice*, ed. E. T. Dubois (Exeter, 1987).
QUINTILIAN, *Institutio oratoria*, ed. H. E. Butler, 4 vols. (Loeb edn.; London 1920).
RACINE, JEAN, *Œuvres*, 2 vols. (Paris, 1687: contains the illustrations by Chauveau, 1st publ. in Racine's *Œuvres*, 1676, and by Le Brun, 1st publ. in *Phèdre*, 1677).
——*Œuvres*, 3 vols. (Paris, 1760: illustrations by Jacques de Sève).
——*Œuvres*, ed. Luneau de Boisjermain, 7 vols. (Paris, 1768: illustrations by Gravelot).
——*Théâtre orné de 57 estampes* (Paris, Pierre Didot, 1813: illustrations by Prud'hon, Gérard, Girodet, Chaudet, Serangeli, and Peyron which were 1st publ. 1801–5). Bodleian Library: Broxbourne 67.3.
——*Œuvres*, ed. P. Mesnard, 2nd edn., 8 vols. (Paris, 1865–73).
——*Œuvres complètes*, ed. R. Picard, 2 vols. (Paris, 1951–2; pagination in later edns. differs slightly).
——*Théâtre complet*, ed. J. Morel and A. Viala (Paris, 1980).
——*Andromaque: Texte de l'édition originale* (1668), ed. R. C. Knight and H. T. Barnwell (Geneva, 1977).
——*Athalie, tragédie tirée de l'Ecriture sainte* (Paris, 1691: frontispiece by Jean-Baptiste Corneille).
——*Athalie*, ed. G. Le Roy (Paris, 1952).
——*Athalie*, ed. H. Maugis (Paris, 1959).
——*Athalie*, ed. H. P. Salomon (Paris, 1969).
——*Bajazet*. ed. X. de Courville (Paris, 1947).
——*Bajazet*, ed. L. Lejealle (Paris, 1963).
——*Esther, tragédie tirée de l'Ecriture sainte* (Paris, 1689: frontispiece by Le Brun).
——*Iphigénie*, ed. D. Achach (Paris, 1970).

——*Phèdre*, ed. J.-L. Barrault (Paris, 1972: 1st publ. 1946).

——*Phedra: English Stage Version*, tr. by Robert David MacDonald (Oxford, 1985).

——*Phèdre*, ed. C. Geray, C. Vandel-Isaakidis, and R. Temkine (Paris, 1986: Collection théâtre et mises en scène; productions by Antoine Vitez and Jean Gillibert).

——*Les Plaideurs*, ed. J. Fabre (Paris, 1981).

——*La Thébaïde*, ed. M. Edwards (Paris, 1965).

RACINE, JEAN-BAPTISTE, *see* Vaunois.

RACINE, LOUIS, *Œuvres*, 6 vols. (Paris, 1808).

——*Mémoires sur la vie et les ouvrages de Jean Racine*, in Jean Racine, *Œuvres complètes*, ed. R. Picard, vol. i.

——*Remarques sur les tragédies de Jean Racine*, in *Œuvres*, 1808 (*La Thébaïde, Alexandre, Andromaque, Les Plaideurs, Britannicus, Bérénice, Bajazet*, in v; *Mithridate, Iphigénie, Phèdre, Esther, Athalie*, in vi).

——*Traité de la poésie dramatique*, in *Œuvres* (1808), vi.

RATERMANIS, J. B., *Essai sur les formes verbales dans les tragédies de Racine* (Paris, 1972).

ROBINET, CHARLES, *Lettres en vers à Madame* (1665–1667), in *Les Continuateurs de Loret*, ed. J. Rothschild (i and ii), J. Rothschild and E. Picot (iii), 3 vols. (Paris, 1881–9).

ROMANOWSKI, SYLVIE, 'The Circuits of Power and Discourse in Racine's *Bajazet*', *Papers in French Seventeenth-Century Literature*, 10 (1983), 849–67.

ROTROU, JEAN, *Œuvres*, ed. Viollet-le-Duc, 5 vols. (Paris, 1820).

ROY, DONALD H., 'La Mise en scène des pièces de Racine', *Jeunesse de Racine* (1959), 15–23.

——'Acteurs et spectateurs à l'Hôtel de Bourgogne: Vers une notation de la communication théâtrale', in J. Jacquot (ed.), *Dramaturgie et société: Rapports entre l'oeuvre théâtrale, son interprétation et son public aux XVIe et XVIIe siècles*, 2 vols. (Paris, 1967), ii. 287–96.

SAINT-ÉVREMOND, CHARLES DE MARGUETEL DE SAINT-DENIS, SIEUR DE, *Œuvres en prose*, ed. R. Ternois, 4 vols. (Paris, 1962–9: *Dissertation sur le grand Alexandre*, vol. ii; *L'Amitié sans amitié*, vol. iii).

——*Lettres*, ed. R. Ternois, 2 vols. (Paris, 1967–8).

[SAINT-USSANS, PIERRE DE SAINT-GLAS, ABBÉ DE], *Réponse à la critique de la Bérénice de Racine* (1671), in Michaut, *Bérénice*.

SARCEY, FRANCISQUE, *Quarante ans de théâtre*, 8 vols. (Paris, 1900–2).

SARTRE, JEAN-PAUL, *Les Séquestrés d'Altona*, ed. P. Thody (London, 1965).

——*Un théâtre de situations*, ed. M. Contat and M. Rybalka (Paris, 1973).

SAYCE, RICHARD, 'Racine's Style: Periphrasis and Direct Statement', in

R. C. Knight (ed.), *Racine: Modern Judgements* (London, 1969), 132–46.

SCARRON, PAUL, *Le Roman comique (1651–63)*, in *Romanciers du XVIIe siècle*, ed. A. Adam (Pléiade; Paris, 1958).

SCHERER, JACQUES, *La Dramaturgie classique en France* (Paris, 1950).

—— 'Aspects de la mise en scène de *Bajazet* et de *Tartuffe*', in J. Jacquot and A. Veinstein (eds.), *La mise en scène des œuvres du passé* (Paris, 1957), 211–16.

—— *Racine: Bajazet* (Paris, 1971; Cours de Sorbonne).

—— *Racine et/ou la cérémonie* (Paris, 1982).

SCOTT, CLIVE, *The Riches of Rhyme: Studies in French Verse* (Oxford, 1988).

SCUDÉRY, GEORGES DE, *La Comédie des comédiens* (1635), ed. Joan Crow (Exeter, 1975).

SEALE, DAVID, *Vision and Stagecraft in Sophocles* (London, 1982).

SÉVIGNÉ, MARIE DE RABUTIN-CHANTAL, MARQUISE DE, *Correspondance*, ed. R. Duchêne, 3 vols. (Pléiade; Paris, 1972–8).

SIGURET, FRANÇOISE, '"Le Ciel avec horreur voit ce monstre sauvage": Genèse de textes et d'images', *Papers in French Seventeenth-Century Literature*, 14 (1987), 83–102 (on Racine, Le Brun, and Sève).

SLATER, ANN PASTERNAK, *Shakespeare the Director* (New Jersey, 1982).

SOPHOCLES, *Works*, ed. F. Storr, 4 vols. (Loeb edn.; London, 1917).

SOREL, CHARLES, *La Maison des jeux*, 2 vols. (Paris, 1657).

—— *De la connaissance des bons livres* (Paris, 1671).

SPITZER, LEO, *Essays on Seventeenth-Century French Literature*, tr. and ed. David Bellos (Cambridge, 1983).

—— 'Racine's Classical *Piano*' (1928–31), in *Essays* (1983), 1–113.

STAROBINSKI, JEAN, 'The Poetics of the Glance', in R. C. Knight (ed.), *Racine: Modern Judgements* (London, 1969), 88–100.

STEWART, WILLIAM M., 'Mise en scène d'*Athalie*', in J. Jacquot and A. Veinstein (eds.), *La Mise en scène des œuvres du passé* (Paris, 1957), 241–53.

—— 'Racine's Response to the Stagecraft of Attic Tragedy as Seen in His Annotations', in M. J. Anderson (ed.), *Classical Drama and its Influence: Essays Presented to H. D. F. Kitto* (London, 1965), 177–90.

SUBLIGNY, ADRIAN-THOMAS PERDOUX DE, *La Folle Querelle* (1668), ed. Jacob (Paris, 1881).

—— *Dissertation sur Phèdre et Hippolyte* (1677) in Granet, *Recueil*, ii.

SUPPLE, JAMES J., 'The Role of Antiochus in *Bérénice*', *Seventeenth-Century French Studies*, 11 (1989), 151–62.

TALLEMANT DES RÉAUX, GÉDÉON, *Historiettes*, ed. A. Adam and G. Delessault, 2 vols. (Paris, 1960).

TAPLIN, OLIVER, *Greek Tragedy in Action* (London, 1985).

THIBAUDET, ALBERT, 'Réflexions: Les Larmes de Racine', *Nouvelle revue française*, 38 (1932), 890–900.

THODY, PHILIP, *see* Sartre, *Les Séquestrés d'Altona*.

TRUCHET, JACQUES, *La Tragédie classique en France* (Paris, 1975).

UBERSFELD, ANNE, *Lire le théâtre* (Paris, 1977; Les Classiques du peuple).

——*L'École du spectateur: Lire le théâtre II* (Paris, 1981).

VAN DELFT, L., 'Language and Power: Eyes and Words in *Britannicus*', *Yale French Studies*, 45 (1970), 102–12.

VANUXEM, J., 'Racine, les machines et les fêtes', *Revue d'histoire littéraire de la France*, 54 (1954), 295–319.

VAUNOIS, LOUIS, *L'Enfance et la jeunesse de Jean Racine* (Paris, 1964: text of reminiscences of Jean-Baptiste Racine).

VAUVENARGUES, LUC DE CLAPIERS, MARQUIS DE, *Réflexions critiques sur quelques poètes: Corneille et Racine (1746)*, in *Œuvres complètes*, ed. H. Bonnier, 2 vols. (Paris, 1968), i.

VENESOEN, C., 'Le Néron de Racine: Un cas curieux d'impuissance verbale', *Information littéraire*, 33 (1981), 130–6.

VILLARS, NICOLAS-PIERRE-HENRI DE MONTFAUCON, ABBÉ DE, *Critique de Bérénice* (1671), in Michaut, *Bérénice*.

VILLIERS, PIERRE DE, *Entretien sur les tragédies de ce temps* (1675), in Granet, *Recueil*, i.

VINAVER, EUGENE, 'Action and Poetry in Racine's Tragedies', in R. C. Knight (ed.), *Racine: Modern Judgements* (London, 1969), 147–60.

VOLTAIRE, *Discours sur la tragédie à Milord Bolingbroke*, in *Théâtre de Voltaire* (Paris, 1874).

VOLTZ, PIERRE, '*Bérénice, Bajazet, Athalie*: Réflexions dramaturgiques à partir de la notion d'espace dans la tragédie racinienne', in P. Ronzeaud (ed.), *Racine: La Romaine, la turque, et la juive (regards sur Bérénice, Bajazet, Athalie): Rencontre de Marseille* (Marseilles, 1986), 51–65.

WOSHINSKY, BARBARA, '*Esther*: No Continuing Place', in R. L. Barnett (ed.), *Re-lectures raciniennes* (Paris, 1986), 253–68.

YARROW, PHILIP J., *Racine* (Oxford, 1978).

——*A Literary History of France: The Seventeenth Century* (London, 1967).

YASHINSKY, J., '"Pourquoi ce livre saint, ce glaive, ce bandeau?": commentaires textuels sur *Athalie*', *Lettres romanes*, 38 (1984), 65–75.

ZIMMERMANN, ÉLÉONORE M., *La Liberté et le destin dans le théâtre de Jean Racine* (Stanford, Calif. 1982).

——'La Lumière et la voix: Étude sur l'unité de *Britannicus*', in *La Liberté et le destin*, pp. 163–78.

——'L'Innocence et la tragédie chez Racine: Le Problème de *Bérénice*', in *La Liberté et le destin*, pp. 179–91.

Index of Racine's Works

Index of Names

Index of Topics